D0560931

Milton and the Sense of Tradition

Christopher Grose

Milton and the
Sense of Tradition

Yale University Press   New Haven and London

Designed by Nancy Ovedovitz and set in Garamond No. 3 by
Eastern Graphics. Printed in the United States of America by
BookCrafters, Inc., Chelsea, Michigan.

Library of Congress Cataloging-in-Publications Data
Grose, Christopher.
Milton and the sense of tradition / Christopher Grose.
p.   cm.
Bibliography: p.
Includes index.
ISBN 0-300-04171-3 (alk. paper)
1. Milton, John, 1608–1674—Criticism and interpretation.
2. Christian poetry, English—History and criticism.   3. Milton,
John, 1608–1674. Paradise regained.   4. Milton, John, 1608–1674.
Samson Agonistes.   5. Samson (Biblical judge) in literature.
I. Title.
PR3588.G76   1988
821'.4—dc19   88-1707
                                                                 CIP

The paper in this book meets the guidelines for permanence and
durability of the Committee on Production Guidelines for Book
Longevity of the Council on Library Resources.

10 9 8 7 6 5 4 3 2 1

For Julie, Douglas, and Alan

Contents

Contents

꧅

Preface

Most of this book deals with Milton's volume of 1671, *Paradise Regained . . . to which is added Samson Agonistes*. My study began as an investigation of *Samson Agonistes*. Looking at Milton's career from the vantage-point of the tragedy, however, one can easily suppose (to adapt Satan's riposte to Abdiel) that there was virtually no time when this author was not as now, in 1671. Long before he published the major poems, Milton himself had suggested the method for the way his modern readers still understand him, when he sought to divide his own canon into the separate jurisdictions of his right and left hands. There is a direct connection, I believe, between this auto-biographical mission and the long-standing question of Milton's Independent brand of Puritanism, a central issue in Milton studies ever since the earliest editors sought to discover an authentic poet beneath the surly Republican exterior. The result of those quests, a congenial soul that dwelt apart, has a considerable twentieth-century progeny, including the important and influential investigations into Milton's humanism undertaken by Arthur Barker, A. S. P. Woodhouse, and Douglas Bush. All of them agree (perhaps like most readers of Milton) that this poet more than many others has a special connection with our own time. And with certain remarkable exceptions like the work of Georgia Christopher, the critical deference continues; it is not easy to find a new book or article on Milton (often avowedly historicist) that *does not* in some way describe a transcendental aspect of a particular poem or a prophetic status for the poet himself.

It was the prose side of Milton's canon, of course, that largely constituted the gruff Puritan exterior which bore such a suspicious resemblance to the Faithorne engraving; and a word of explanation may be in order for what may seem to be the inordinate space it occupies in a book on the brief epic and "added" Euripidean tragedy. In 1637, in the privacy of a letter to

Charles Diodati, Milton had used Euripides (and virtually the same final chorus of *Samson Agonistes*) to announce a literary career, virtually at the moment two publications (the *Masque at Ludlow Castle* and *Justa Edouardo King*) inaugurated that career in the eyes of the nation at large. But there are significant differences between the sense of "literary" matters intimated in these texts and the invidious formulations Milton offered in the very influential *Reason of Church Government* and *Second Defence*. And the *Apology against a Pamphlet*, published only three months later than the *Reason* and on the very eve of the "great event" to which my last chapter title refers, explains these differences and suggests the relevance of the early prose in any attempt to reconstruct a mature, integral, two-handed Miltonic engine. The relatively neglected *Apology* provides a far fuller and more candid memory of the crucial later 1630s than either of the more commonly cited autobiographical sources. Together with *Areopagitica* and *Of Education*, this final pamphlet in the antiprelatical series makes clear the way in which Milton thought those years had in some fundamental ways verified his early musings—not only "Lycidas," but *Comus*, *Ad Patrem*, and even the academic prolusions. At the same time, the *Apology* provides us with a neglected link to Milton's mature (and distinctly postmillennialist) thought in the form of a sketch of how a prophetic scenario could break down, in what various ways a prophet's voice or acts could be met with the considerable power of "human traditions." I submit that we need to adjust the dating of Milton's "Independent" phase and to think of it more clearly as a postlude to that ambiguously conceived "great event" to which I have referred above. Both works in the great volume of 1671 reexamine this kind of aftermath. Within two quite different fictional frames, the brief epic and the Euripidean tragedy review the momentous recognition that an author writes not always "to the world" but often beyond it, "to aftertimes." For Milton himself, this was a truth entertained unexpectedly early, we may suppose, and not necessarily with the kind of bitterness commonly attributed to the poet's later years. In April 1642, Milton thought of himself, without a sense of paradox, as a writer of *literary prose*, someone whose major works were not necessarily future projects in prose or rhyme. When he finally turned to the long poems, what were the effects of this early decision that he had discovered something like the autonomous life of a New Critic's sort of poem, the presence of an "uncontrollable intent" within his own youthful compositions?

Preface

ACKNOWLEDGMENTS

It is a pleasure to acknowledge the encouragement and assistance of students, friends and colleagues during the preparation of this book. I am grateful to Thomas Wright and the staff of the William Andrews Clark Library, and to the staff and directors of the Henry E. Huntington Library; to the Research Committee of the UCLA Academic Senate for their generous support; to my colleagues in the Department of English, and to the Chancellor of the University of California at Los Angeles, who provided time free from teaching and other academic duties. In the past several years of teaching graduate and undergraduate students at UCLA, I have learned much about Milton's recall of his own "knowledge in the making" from conversations with Steven Buhler, Gary Hall, Janet Halley, David Joslin, Mike Patton, Karl Precoda, James Ransom, Victoria Silver, Jeff Svoboda, and Constance Woo. At various times I have discussed parts of this book with Charles Gullans, James Holstun, Paul Sheats, Paul Stevens, and Shari Zimmerman. At different stages, the manuscript benefited from the generous and learned scrutiny of Thomas Kranidas, Jonathan F. S. Post, Stanley Stewart, and Joseph H. Summers. I am also indebted to the editorial acumen of Alexander Metro of the Yale University Press, to the industry and dedication of my research assistants Jennifer Andersen and Nina McLaughlin, and to Esther Gilman, who made the index.

In different forms, parts of chapters 3–5 and 11 have appeared in *English Language Notes*, *Hartford Studies*, *Journal of English and Germanic Philology*, and *Milton Studies*; I am grateful to the editors for permission to reprint. Versions of chapters 7 and 8 were read at the UCLA Seventeenth-Century Discussion Group, the Modern Language Association, the Southern California Renaissance Conference, and the LeMoyne Conference on Religion and Literature held in October 1983. Some material in chapter 8, on Luther's notion of the "White Devil," will appear in a forthcoming festschrift for Joseph H. Summers. With exceptions as indicated, quotations from Milton's poetry follow the text of Merritt Y. Hughes, *John Milton: Complete Poems and Major Prose* (Odyssey Press, 1957).

Abbreviations

AP	*Apology against a Pamphlet.* In Vol. 1 of *CPW*
AR	*Areopagitica.* In Vol. 2 of *CPW*
AV	Authorized Version, *Holy Bible*
Carey	*The Poems of John Milton*, ed. John Carey and Alastair Fowler. London and Harlow: Longmans, 1968
CPB	*Commonplace Book.* In Vol. 1 of *CPW*
CE	Columbia edition of *The Works of John Milton.* Edited by F. A. Patterson et al. 18 vols. New York: Columbia University Press, 1931–38
CPW	*Complete Prose Works of John Milton.* gen. ed. Don M. Wolfe. 8 vols. New Haven: Yale University Press, 1953–82
Defence	*Pro Populo Anglicano Defensio Secunda.* In Vol. 4 of *CPW*
Doctrine	*De Doctrina Christiana.* In Vol. 6 of *CPW*
ELN	*English Language Notes*
ELR	*English Literary Renaissance*
Hughes	*John Milton: Complete Poems and Major Prose.* Edited by Merritt Y. Hughes. New York: Odyssey, 1957
JEGP	*Journal of English and Germanic Philology*
LR	*The Life Records of John Milton.* Ed. J. Milton French. 5 vols. New Brunswick: Rutgers State University Press, 1949–58
LW	*Luther's Works.* St. Louis: Concordia
MLN	*Modern Language Notes*
MP	*Modern Philology*
Parker	*Milton: A Biography.* Oxford: Clarendon, 1968
Patrides	*John Milton: Selected Prose*, ed. C. A. Patrides. Rev. ed. Columbia: University of Missouri Press, 1985
Reason	*The Reason of Church Government.* In Vol. 1 of *CPW*

REW	*The Ready and Easy Way to Establish a Free Commonwealth.* In Vol. 7 of *CPW*
Science	Georgia Christopher, *Milton and the Science of the Saints.* Princeton University Press, 1984
TKM	*The Tenure of Kings and Magistrates.* In Vol. 3 of *CPW*
Trinity	*John Milton: Poems Reproduced in Facsimile from the Manuscript in Trinity College, Cambridge.* Menston: Scolar Press, 1970
UTQ	*University of Toronto Quarterly*

Milton and the Sense of Tradition

Chapter One

Prologue:
Paradise Regain'd . . .
To which is added
Samson Agonistes

Everyone knows the story of Thomas Ellwood's part in the production of Milton's final volume and the way this story centers on Ellwood's remedy for the deficiencies of *Paradise Lost*. Here is the passage from Ellwood's *Life* which offers the nearest access to the project as Ellwood presented it:

> I pleasantly said to him, Thou hast said much here of *Paradise Lost*; but what hast thou to say of Paradise Found? He made me no answer, but sate some time in a Muse: then brake of that Discourse, and fell upon another subject. [*LR* 4:417]

We do not know the subject to which Milton turned the conversation, of course. To Ellwood, for all we know, the brief epic formed the contents of that "muse." Whatever Milton handed him when they next returned to the subject, Ellwood eventually decided that he had touched off the completion of a historic literary design—very likely on the basis of what Milton now said to him, once again "in a pleasant tone":

> "This is owing to you, for you put it into my head by the question you put to me at Chalfont, which before I had not thought of." [*LR* 4:417, 419–20]

Prologue

The whole episode is one of the more curious in Milton's later years. We know what Milton thought of readings premised upon the "frontispiece" of a book or "a word on / A title page"; we know how seldom Milton made admissions of the kind he says Ellwood provoked "by the question you put to me at Chalfont."[1] Certainly, there are those who wonder how easily the poet of *Paradise Regained* could manage a "pleasant tone" under any circumstances. But if Ellwood has remembered what Milton said with any accuracy at all—and one doubts this—Milton's generosity is hard to explain. Certainly it is not because Ellwood found it wanting that the notion of a "Paradise found" within *Paradise Lost* has been discussed so extensively. It is itself, in fact, the poem's great Argument—something quite distinct, as I have suggested elsewhere, from the "sad task" of narration.[2] As a whole, *Paradise Lost* seeks to unfold the oracle believed to reside in Gen. 3:15; it strives to read the *protevangelium* as comedic myth. And this intent is given special prominence in the final two and one-half books, which finally deliver not only the oracular text for which the entire work is an essay in explication but also Michael's highly attenuated, prophetic account of the Church's final teachers in the world's history, and in general the doom's "verification" in human history to the end. And *strives* is the word here because a prime function of the poem's invocations is to spell out the many contingencies which might well prevent the successful communication of that argument, including old age, "cold Climate," an "age too late," and (perhaps closely related) an unfit audience. In effect, then, the project Ellwood seems to have thought he touched off was one which Milton had diligently pursued throughout the poem. Ellwood seems to have been the kind of reader who might have asserted that Milton had indeed justified the ways of God to men, at least in the two works taken together, and had thus kept his promise to the "knowing reader" (1642). Here was a genius with staying power!

"Thomas Ellwood," as Milton's modern biographer reminds us, "says nothing anywhere about *Samson Agonistes*."[3] The purpose of the following study is not so much to alter Ellwood's account of Milton's final volume as to augment it: to fill in the contents of that extensive "muse," to present a fuller account of *all* that was owing to Ellwood at Chalfont. In simplest terms, I propose to do this by adding some heft to whatever else Milton handed to the young Quaker so pleasantly. Readers have followed Ellwood (and the bookseller too) in thinking of the 1671 volume as containing separate works, whether or not they consider the brief epic to be the completion of an earlier project. But I will argue that Milton's title for this book, (*Paradise Regain'd . . . to which is added Samson Agonistes*) conceals a unity of outlook and literary purpose which is firmly rooted in Milton's lifelong preoccupation with the ambiguities of the poet's calling and the very idea of literature. The entire volume is strongly affected, in particular, by a widespread feeling of cultural belatedness, the recognition of England's historical distance from the early Reformers and what Donne called "the maine battell"[4]; for Milton long before 1671, the Reformation itself had become history, with its own traditionality. Considered as a significant pairing and also a sequence, the final volume of poetry presents two protagonists looking back at (and considerably revising) the early and vulnerable phases of a literary career which Milton is often thought to have projected along the lines of Shelley's ideal "legislator of mankind."

Ellwood may or may not have noticed that a central purpose of *Paradise Regained* is to unpack once *again* the same crucial text (3:15) of Genesis, the *protevangelium* that had provided the "great Argument" of *Paradise Lost.* In other words the brief epic expatiates the final two books of the first epic and brings into somewhat bolder relief their emphasis on a victory "by wisdom," not "of arms"—a distinction worked out in the invocation to Book 9 and elsewhere, usually not without dust and heat. But it is fair to say that in the process of doing this, the brief epic exacerbates the privateness of an inner paradise by locating Christ's triumph *as God* prior to the public ministry. For the Son's triumphant wisdom is defined partly as the private mastery of texts. The brief epic's abundance of quotation, including the various renditions of the Holy Spirit's appearance at Jordan, makes it clear that the Son's self-conscious relation to the texts which both precede and follow him are central issues here. His function as the displacer of fable and philosophy (Book 4), as the "recapitulator" which seventeenth-century mythographers found intimated in Ovid and more ancient poets like Euripides, is thus central to Milton's conception of his protagonist. Milton shows that the Son *can* be imaginative, in good Pindaric fashion; though he chooses not to indulge his imaginative, "humane" side, he is presented as a discursively flexible character, even as he appears to originate some crucial Gospel pronouncements—to fulfill the fundamental promise of Scripture (in Gen. 3:15). But Milton's young recapitulator is confronted with the very model of an unfit onstage audience in the person of the brief epic's adversary, a different Miltonic Satan who is conceived as the ultimate *traditor*, in the fashion of Luther's "white devil." The expert in the false authority of human traditions and the more immediate powers of aesthetic fascination, this new Satan has extensive influence over his human counterparts in the poem (like the "new-baptiz'd"), the narrator, and perhaps (beyond the poem's confines) the author himself.

A central critical concern in readings of *Paradise Regained* has been the presumed affiliation between the later Milton and the divine Son of the poem, and consequently the embarrassments of the attack by "Milton" on learning and literature in the final book of the brief epic. But as he had done in the fourth book of *Paradise Lost*, Milton makes his narrator conspicuously susceptible to the very minutiae the Son can so easily do without —so much so that we may well have difficulty distinguishing him from the author, or at least from the Milton repeatedly described in the autobiographical materials which Milton summed up in the early 1640s: enamored, if anyone ever was, with the idea of beauty and everywhere pursuing its "shapes and forms," possessed of a vehement nature like Luther's, but also possessed of the infallible sign of the poet, a "soft and delicious temper." *Paradise Regained* concludes ambiguously, leaving the divine Son within the private sphere, not quite entered upon the public ministry that was to become the Christian Church; the portrayal and the eventual "escape" of Satan too suggest that the Son's victory has its limitations. And the brief epic's insistent thought that the Son's deeds are "unrecorded" would give the Ellwood story extra bite by suggesting a bit of ironic depth for Milton's professed gratitude to his young friend Ellwood in presenting him with *Paradise Regained*.

Or did Milton hand him the volume as a whole? Both *Paradise Regained* and *Samson Agonistes*, of course, record the memories, private thoughts, and conversation which precede the definitive speeches/acts of the biblical character we thought we knew. Like other Miltonic characters—the uncouth swain of "Lycidas" or the young Milton himself—both protagonists must inhabit the narrow verge between the encroaching worlds of myth and traditional text. The tragedy too involves the reader in all that precedes and explains its protagonist's definitive actions, as well as in an aftermath which considerably qualifies our sense of his historical impact. Like Milton conversing with Ellwood at Chalfont, Samson looks back from a quite different kind of retirement upon "godlike" triumphs and a career which specifically denies its private status (1211). If *Paradise Regained* brings us once again to the verge of that long delayed moment when God shall be "All in All," as it seems to do, the tragedy provides in effect that most disturbing next request in *PL* 3:341–42: "But all ye Gods, Adore him." It puts squarely before us a counterpart to that long stretch of historical space traversed by Michael as part of Adam's reeducation in Book 12.

4

Like the final phase of Michael's instruction, Milton's tragedy denies us the visual spectacle of the temple's destruction. Its place is taken by Samson's "great act," seen here as the decision to move offstage, following the memories, thoughts, and hypotheses which take up most of the work. Milton points to much that his hero shares with the eventual Philistine victims, and he also underlines the ironies of the climactic destruction of the Philistine temple. Viewed with the appropriate literalism, the tragic catastrophe is at first an ambiguous noise and then a literary construction; presented in two versions, it is initially the confused memory of a breathless eyewitness, the "Messenger," then the uncomprehending and passive collective celebration of the work's final choruses. The surviving Danites seem genuinely incapable of understanding or exploiting an event or a dispensation fundamentally alien to their ways. And this incomprehension, together with the shrines and legends they proceed to construct, provides the entire 1671 volume, not just *Samson Agonistes*, with an ending which strikingly qualifies the brief epic's triumph over Satan; in the place of the Son's public ministry is the entirety of this Euripidean tragedy: a history of the church in the guise of an Old Testament world seemingly beyond time itself, the abyss beyond the "world's great period" (*PL* 12:555).

Let us say, then, that in a supreme gesture of answerability to the greater epic's final vision, Milton added to the volume, if not to Ellwood's own next assignment, a work which comments brilliantly on the Ellwood incident in the very way it offers a kind of surrogate ecclesiastical history. For the tragedy makes Samson's public—the counterparts to the "new-baptiz'd" of *Paradise Regained*—a far more conspicuous character. That Euripidean "close" is a marvelous thing and echoes clearly the great dictum which had first attracted Milton to Pauline humanism (quoted in 1637 in Milton's last letter to Diodati). But it is a mocking echo. Behind its appealing rhythms are the characteristically fatigued and spectatorly observations of the Danite chorus, whose literary masterpiece could easily be taken for an early draft of Pope's "Essay on Man." Thus does Milton suggest an almost instantaneously legendary status for his Nazarite; like the shrine Manoa proposes to erect ("With all his Trophies hung, and Acts enroll'd / In copious Legend, or sweet Lyric Song"), the work's own conclusion represents the growth of a tradition that seemingly includes Judges itself. In a sense, the whole tragedy is aftermath, and Milton's tragic conclusion provides the entire volume (once again, not just the story of Samson) with what is seemingly withheld in the brief epic. The portion of Scripture which gave Milton his material is projected within the work as this public's own creation, far more remote and legendary in its nature than the Gospel which provides such an immediate issue (though by no means the exclusive source) for *Paradise Regained*. The self-consciously ethnic choral sonnet provides a final comment—in the vein of the Wisdom books, but also in the divinely authorized, manifold idiom of the ancient poets—on both works in this volume. It is a most ironic situation indeed for this bit of Wisdom literature: a Danite provenience for the Euripidean echo, and the coincidence Milton noticed so early in his career between that portion of Scripture and the primeval burden of the ancient poets: "Many are the shapes of things divine."

In their behavior and reception, both protagonists in 1671 are the immediate successors of the latter-day evangelical teachers described by Michael in the final book of *Paradise Lost*; in a sense, they continue the work begun in the first epic by Abdiel (5–6) and perhaps the narrator himself, in the more censorious passages of 1–3. But *1671* continues a reminiscence of longer standing. Taken as a whole, Milton's final volume reconsiders the primary literary and polemical issues that concerned Milton from 1632 to 1645, including the theological idea of *recapitulation* itself. The brief epic and the tragedy alike depend upon the prophetic vocabulary which Milton developed in his own behalf during the 1630s, and which he exploited (sometimes brilliantly) in the 1640s. Both works in the 1671 volume revisit Milton's critical early years—the focus of all Miltonic autobiography—in striking detail; both sons in the last volume are recognizably the heirs of the ideal poet as Milton had once described him. The most critical junctures of the tragedy (Samson's recollections of knowing God through "intimate impulse," his pretense of feeling "some rousing motions") employ the special terminology to be found first in the familiar correspondence, the antiprelatical pamphlets of 1641–42 (especially the *Apology against a Pamphlet*) and also the *Areopagitica* and *Of Education* (both of 1644); the true prototypes for both conscientious sons of *1671* are the speakers of the *Apology against a Pamphlet* and the *Areopagitica*.

If both sons of the final volume engage in extensive review, Milton himself had done so surprisingly early, in the retrospective prose of 1641–42 and again (from a different vantage point) in the *Second Defence* of 1654. Both autobiographical endeavors are necessarily revisionist; but it is remarkable to what extent even the 1642 prose recasts the intentions of the poet's earliest work, including the academic Prolusions. In the study or in performance, these texts may have originated as the rhetorical or conventionally playful exercises so well described by Leishman, Tuve, and others.[5] But the *Apology* in particular shows that in 1642 Milton remembered them differently. He now spoke of an "instinct and presage of nature" in connection with his own earlier writings. To adapt the phrase from *Samson*, they had become instances of "uncontrollable intent," words engaged with external events. Indeed, the *Apology* presents its anonymous speaker as a literal and historical embodiment of the earlier, playful speeches and poems, from the academic ideals of the prolusions (or "Il Penseroso," for that matter) to the more evidently sectarian visions and prayers of the current antiprelatical pamphlets. And even more important, that speaker is (or has been) representative, a "member incorporate" of the nation at large and as such an author (or collaborator) in its heroic deeds. Milton looks back upon Strafford's execution, the fall of the bishops, and the defeat of rebellion in Ireland as the heroic acts of what he calls wisdom's "majesty," as the deeds of a Parliament whose collective zeal expressed and somehow projected Milton's own ardent personality. These events are clearly enough among the necessary conditions for Milton's inaugural volume of poems, with its headnote for "Lycidas" claiming that the author had foretold "the ruin of our corrupted Clergy then in their height." But the period 1637–42 (and especially the developments of that critical year 1637) furnishes the paradigmatic incidents for the final volume as well. "A universal insight into things," perhaps the most striking phrase in *Of Education*, reprinted two years after *Paradise Regained/Samson Agonistes*, refers to what Milton proposed to furnish, ultimately, to his young scholars. But this new name for the wisdom of Milton's uncouth swain is also the special talent of Samson.[6]

Between them, the *Apology* and the *Areopagitica* provide us with the moment when Milton most clearly revised his optimistic early view of the poet's influence in the state and world at large. The subtle modulations of these pamphlets afford us an early glimpse of much that explains the power of Milton's later poetry. In ways fundamentally unlike the preceding efforts in Milton's prose, the *Apology* and the *Areopagitica* anticipate the way in which *Paradise Regained* and *Samson Agonistes* offset the earlier prophetic claims by incorporating the perspective of the individual prophet's biography and reception (his "story") within the fictional setting. It is hardly unusual to mention the *Areopagitica* in connection with *Paradise Regained*; for the brief epic is embarrassing chiefly for the way its hero (and some would say its author) disparages the authentic vehicle of Reformation in

1644, that humanistic instrument for polishing Truth's armory. I would put the emphasis rather differently; it is in the oration that Milton completed the scenario for 1671 by filling in the historical dilemma—the discursive predicament in the widest sense—of his later protagonists. The performance of such characters, as Milton appears to have discovered shortly before he wrote his oration, may well be dismissed "ere we well understand them." This is one reason the *Areopagitica* seeks to avoid the status of a mere text and aspires to the condition of living speech. Potentially, it could be the catalyst for the "perfection" of Reformation (as Milton called it, in late Neoplatonic fashion)—one of the dragon's teeth sown by Cadmus. But too often, as Milton sees it, even the most conscientious efforts congeal into a false formalism, a text or (worse) a "system." The famous remark that "Books are not absolutely dead things" shows Milton's full awareness of both possibilities: books are contingently dead things.

But if the great document of Milton's humanism completed the scenaro for the final volume of poetry, that scene had been fully furnished about two years earlier in a relatively neglected work almost always considered separately and as belonging to a different, presumably single-minded group. In fact, as we shall see, the *Apology against a Pamphlet* clearly involves a number of interesting and previously unrecognized departures from the earlier antiprelatical pamphlets and some intriguing innovations in the developing body of Milton's thought—political, philosophical, and literary. Even as he indulges in some fairly straightforward bishop-baiting, Milton argues from a standpoint which virtually contradicts an important element in the autobiography of the *Reason of Church Government*, published just a few months earlier. The Apologist's position matches up (much better than Milton's in the *Reason*) with the relevant documents of the period treated in both autobiographies; and it looks ahead to some of the most individual elements in Milton's later thought. Among other things, the *Apology* is an exploratory text in the kind of philosophic materialism that has been commonly believed to have originated in the *Areopagitica* of two years later. Most striking of all, perhaps, is the way in which the Apologist, the first really interesting theoretician in Milton's prose, domesticates a whole range of volatile terms—the ones remembered, as I have suggested, in *Samson*. The most disturbing and violent proposals are offered up in comfortable and historically misleading terms, vague and conflicted thoughts which we often now pack into the word *literature*. These meanings would shortly be recommended to Samuel Hartlib in the guise of "insight" (itself an aspect of poetry), and the *Poems* of 1645/1646 enshrines them once again in its deceptively casual headnote to "Lycidas." Thus does the *Apology* help us recover the full intentions of the Miltonic poet and define the question of how he might exercise literary influence. The pamphlet thus enables us to see how youthful efforts like "L'Allegro" / "Il Penseroso" (1631) and "Lycidas" (1637) became part of the paradigmatic itinerary Milton was to offer in *Of Education* of 1644. We may now turn to the question of what is at stake and explore further the significance of these two groups within the prose and within the literary canon.

Chapter Two

Prose and the "Literary" Milton:
The *Second Defence*

In a period of protracted reflection and review in the mid-1650s, Milton looked back on his early career and found it neatly divided into private and public segments, poetry and prose (the work of his "left hand"). Back from the Italian journey, he had turned again "with no delight to my interrupted studies" (Patrides 70; *CPW* 4[1]:621) and to the goal his father had planned from childhood days, a professional life "in humane letters" or (as Merritt Hughes translates the Latin) dedicated "to the pursuits of literature."[1] But the prose career itself had a conspicuously patterned quality; it had progressed in an orderly fashion and in direct response to the needs and the events of the time, needs and events themselves straightforwardly ordained, as it seemed. Milton wrote that he had worked to promote "the three species of liberty . . . ecclesiastical, domestic, and civil." And such was the sense of an efficient collaborative process that he remembers something at first glimpse most un-Miltonic—a willing submission to all that now seems so well taken care of: "leaving without difficulty, the issue of things more especially to God, and to those to whom the people had assigned that department of duty" (70; 621).

The *Second Defence* is not the first of Milton's attempts to argue in this fashion for the severe discrimination of prose and verse. In the very first of the antiprelatical pamphlets (*Of Reformation*, 1641) Milton had looked forward to a special kind of vocal conjunction that could be called "literary": "Amidst the Hymns, and Hallelujahs of Saints some one may perhaps bee heard offering at high strains in new and loftly *Measures* to sing and celebrate thy divine Mercies, and marvelous Judgements in this Land throughout all Ages" (*CPW* 1:616; italics deleted). In conventional Miltonic biography, this passage became that "contract with the knowing reader" which Milton himself did not propose as such until the *Reason of Church Government* (January 1642); and the biographers were understandably inclined to identify the vocal conjunction in question with a specific literary production, the future *Paradise Lost*. There was certainly no lack of precedent, then, for the distortions of the *Second Defence*; the poet himself had provided the impetus for conventional Miltonic biography. Written in the heat of the antiprelatical skirmish, the first of his several self-portraits pictured Milton as being unpleasantly but inescapably interrupted in studies which he had specifically (and rather leadingly) called "delightful"; indeed, he claims to have been "put from beholding the bright countenance of Truth" in that cool and uncluttered environment that was long known as Milton's "Horton period." And the perpetrators were the same prelates who had "Church-outed" him (*CPW* 1:823). Understandably enough, he looked forward to the resumption of those studies—and of course, to their literary fruits—as a likely consequence of eventual leisure, something he associated with the silencing of these "hoarse disputes."

Understandably enough, observers and students of Milton's life and work have associated his achievement with periods of studious leisure, and they have filled these silences with various motives. Following the Restoration (as Marvell describes it in an intriguing passage of *The Rehearsal Transpros'd*), Milton "expiated himself in a retired silence."[2] This would have been a very different kind of revery, to be sure, from the one Thomas Ellwood thought he had dispelled some time later—a "private and retired life," and, more immediately, the prolonged "muse" of that famous conversation (*LR* 4:367; 5:57). At least one of the earliest observers evidently found it difficult not to think of this period of retirement in Milton's own way, as the kind of creative leisure that played such an important part both in *1671*'s pair of fictions and in those early discussions of literature which this volume recollects. This is the kind of Miltonic single-mindedness, at any rate, which Ellwood seems to have found in the incident, and there have been many more like him, the biographical and critical wayfarers from Edward Phillips down to our own time. Even the most scrupulous of Milton's modern champions (I will call them "the scholars") have been happy enough to follow the poet in the way he came to partition his career, filling in the relations of the texts in the second group and rationalizing the grouping he envisioned in 1654. The vantage point of the *Second Defence* became the basis for a long-standing consensus on the development of Milton's writing; as A. S. P. Woodhouse summed up the consensus, "we cannot do better in our survey than to adopt his scheme" (103). Indeed, the most valuable study of *Samson Agonistes* and its place in the Milton canon is organized on the basis of Milton's indexes in the *Commonplace Book* and the way in which these divisions match up with "the groupings under which he wrote the prose of his productive middle years." In the *Defence*, it is argued, Milton "described a consistent and systematic application of his gifts to specific intellectual ends."[3]

Following Masson, Milton's biographers went much further, amplifying Milton's retrospections of 1654 in another way by focusing on the private studies of the 1630s. In his landmark study *Milton and the Puritan Dilemma*, Arthur Barker retells the story as follows:

> He retired to his father's house . . . setting aside the thought of a career in the church and the inclinations which might make marriage desirable, to pursue a thorough course of study designed as a preparation for the writing of great poetry and as the fulfilment of the ideal of knowledge set forth in his last prolusion. [p. 9][4]

This is a scrupulous account of Milton's intentions after the days at Cambridge. We should notice that Milton's dismissal of an ecclesiastical career is implicitly dated early; Barker accepts the contents of the 1632 letter ("To a Friend") almost to the extent of quoting it. (As we shall see in chapter 3, this letter is by no means a very clear guide to Milton's literary plans.) Barker presents Milton's "designs": the retirement is to prepare "for the writing of great poetry" and to "fulfill the ideal of knowledge" proposed (very recently indeed) in the Seventh Prolusion. From this standpoint, the Milton of 1632 becomes a precociously conscientious Protestant, carrying a "humanist" or literary sensibility into the wars of truth. Barker goes on to imply, furthermore, that a prime attraction of the Puritan side in this conflict was an anticipated literary fulfillment; humanist that he was, Milton entered the antiprelatical battle in "the enthusiastic belief that the completion of England's reformation would bring with it the long-sought release of his poetical powers" (p. 17).[5] Barker's discussion incorporates qualifications which concern the high view Milton took of his poetic calling, and they go a long way toward mitigating the impression one could easily form here, that Milton took literature to be an essentially private matter. (Samson's sarcastic anticipation of Harapha's similar point is one of a number of signs that Milton was stung by the charge of being a mere "private.") The qualifications are necessary precisely because the conventional account is so clearly based on two very problematic sources, undeniably Miltonic: the *Second Defence* of 1654 and its true original, the *Reason* of January/February 1642.

The danger in all this, of course, is to take the poet's own belated word for it, to read the *Second Defence* and the *Reason of Church Government* into the retirement at Hammersmith, with a consequent misreading of both periods. The key here is the accuracy of Barker's word "designed," in the way our sense of a system or scheme affects our notions of Milton's development. If we consider Milton's canon to be "prophetic," in particular, a great deal in our final assessment of Milton will depend upon the way we think about the "ripening" he kept saying he needed—especially if we regard the earlier polemics as involving "the convictions of a largely unfocused idealism."[6] We need to look more carefully at the relation of his experience in 1643–44 and the place in Milton's poetry of "opinion," what he considered to be incipient or emergent doctrine. In the way the *Second Defence* alleges a time of "reflection" presumably antedating his own eventual work in the divorce tracts, *Of Education* and *Areopagitica*, we have a recollection that does not fit at all easily with the sense of the times we get, say, in the work of the 1640s—a period of Miltonic tranquillity recollected in a moment of some passion. Indeed, Milton's Isocratic orator had sharply distinguished the mansion house of liberty from its systematic antithesis (figured as the Temple in Jerusalem) by its "brotherly *dis*similitudes"; as Milton had presented it in 1644, a truly reformed culture is not so much a venue for encyclopedic learning as a nation of authors situated in a kind of prototypical Grub Street, full of "pens and heads there, sitting by their studious lamps, musing, searching, revolving new notions and ideas . . . others as fast reading, trying all things, assenting to the force of reason and convincement."[7] And he had gone on to make eloquent claims for the unsystematic or irregular procedures on the part of the ingenious Truth herself (*CPW* 2:554). In the way it seems to collapse distinctions between public and private, authorial genius and reception—between writing and reading, both at once active and contemplative—the passage presents a very different world from the *Defence*'s particular manner of denying influence or ulterior motives: a more circumscribed ethical situation, in which "the deeds themselves rendered this freedom of speech honourable to me" (73; *CPW* 4[1]: 627).[8] In the *Areopagitica* Milton had said that "writing is more publick then preaching" (*CPW* 2:548). The more privately oriented *Defence* consistently points to the threshold separating a commemorative function for poetry from heroic action itself, something he had earlier proposed as the locus of true poetry. It had seemed to him from his youth (as Milton often said) that the next best thing to heroic action itself was to record "great actions."

Milton's history of the early triumphs of his side makes fascinating reading, especially if we keep in mind the millennialism of the early 1640s. As in the sonnet to Cyriack Skinner, the chief purpose of the *Second Defence of the English People* is to recollect this heady time and his own early career in the wars of truth—to reconsider what he might have contributed "to the progress of real and substantial liberty" (71; *CPW* 4[1]: 624). For the political and cultural reformer of the day, the aftermath provided a time of virtually contemplative leisure as he recalls it, a chance to recognize from a prospect like Pisgah's the obvious categories (like the three species of liberty) and to take care of certain points of neglect. As he represents it in the *Defence*, indeed, the period has a great deal in common with those earlier studies for which he had shown such an "instinctive ardor"; it is in the idiom of one indulging "the sweetness of philosophy" that Milton remembers that he now "became perfectly awake" to all this (70; *CPW* 4[1]: 622). As he remembers the period of the mid-1640s, there was a considerable clarity of outline, a sense of order, and even sequence if only for a time. The steps to Reformation were now lined up into a "right way," a "direct line" in the fashion he associated with historical narrative as it ought to be. One could almost visualize the progression from "discipline originating in religion" directly to the morals and institutions of the commonwealth," and beyond that, indeed, "to the deliverance of the whole life of mortal man from slavery" (70; *CPW* 4[1]: 622). His account of the parliamentary victory makes a period of civil war and state executions even more mysterious than it seemed when (as the Apologist of 1642) Milton had referred to the Commons' wisdom as a verbal power issuing in majestic "virtue." Now we hear of a Parliamentary exertion of "vigor," as the Columbia translation puts it (*rem strenue gerente*, CE 8:128; *CPW* 4[1]: 621). An emphatically intentionalist syntax disjoins the Long Parliament's actions from any idea of effect or consequence: "Meanwhile, as the parliament acted with great vigour, the pride of the bishops began to lose its swell." That subsiding "swell" just *happens* (the Latin is *detumuit*); it is no more the effect of good or lucky physic than the eventual calm upon a stormy sea.

As for his own work at the time ("vehement" to the point of scurrility, thought one opponent), Milton rather modestly remembers nothing indecorous, no extraordinary or heroic decisions. The low-key prose is full of terms such as "accordingly" and "as was said"; in keeping with this manifestness of subject and the clarity of categories and topics, he remembers writing on divorce, next education, last—and "after the model of a regular speech" (*ad justae orationis modem*, CE 8:134)—a book on freedom of opinion. And all this was part of a collective effort in which Milton joined his own voice with "the opinions of others," including men irrefutably famous, like "our celebrated Selden" (72; *CPW* 4[1]: 625). The "our" here is conspicuously unqualified. So settled were the times Milton recalls that major topics could be handled with utmost brevity; in such circumstances, after all, a truly fit audience is not so much an audience as collaborator, virtually contributing to the real text in question and in this way answerable to its subject. At a time like this—and the very fullness of the *Defence*'s exposition is eloquent testimony to the period's differences from 1654—a "little" work like *Of Education* might be sufficient for "a subject than which there can be none of greater moment to imbue the minds of men with virtue, from which springs that true liberty which is felt within; none for the wise administration of a commonwealth, and for giving it its utmost possible duration" (72; *CPW* 4[1]: 625). Altogether, as Mary Ann Radzinowicz observes, there is relatively little defense in the *Second Defence*; "the remainder is a diagnosis of the political crisis in the state" (*Toward Samson Agonistes*, pp. 138–39). Thus does Milton underline once again the substantial difference between the period he now reviews and the present time—in need of stronger stuff, evidently, than the decorous brevity of that earlier occasion.

If the *Second Defence* reveals a Milton acutely aware of the poet's cultural isolation, it also testifies to the emergence of a "systematic" canon. In retrospect, the prose period seems neatly partitioned by subject and generic/stylistic purity, and also by a straightforward, almost programmatic, sequentiality. But for several of the scholars who accepted the grouping Milton suggested for his work in the early and mid-1640s, however, something else was happening. In their account, the *Areopagitica* became the object of a quest for prophetic humanism. An expression of Milton's early classical training, the oration also embodied the poet's supposed openness, including a new attitude toward reformation itself (74). As Ernest Sirluck has demonstrated, much in Milton's new outlook depended upon a revision in his views on *adiaphora*; the idea of "indifferent things" was an essential element in the high drama of the hermeneutic predicament Milton addressed in the divorce pamphlets. But there was a more fundamental point involved in the well-intentioned appreciation of the *Areopagitica*. What was emerging for these scholars was the controlling Miltonic idea of Christian liberty; and this was happening very much in the manner of the oration's own conception of "knowledge in the making." As Barker put it, "the divorce pamphlets, the *Areopagitica*, and the *Of Education* form a group not only in time but because each contributes to Milton's definition of Christian liberty, 'domestic or private'" (Barker, p. 118). Looking ahead though it does to the poet's later solutions to vexed problems of doctrine or ideology in poems (intimately connected though it may be to the toleration controversy of later days), the oration was also essentially reactive to Milton's own experience, domestic and literary alike. A kind of novelty in the developing canon, it was an effect of his own marital difficulties, of the divorce argument, and especially of the "painful exegetical labours of the first divorce tract" (Barker, p. 72), and finally the condemnation of his views on divorce. And it did not stop here; for "events between 1641 and 1660 forced him continually to reconsider, to readjust, to develop, to enlarge his opinions." It is almost as though time itself had retrieved Milton from the errors of the "sects" by revealing the implications of those principles which he had perhaps thoughtlessly accepted and expressed in the antiprelatical series (p. XIX).[9] The oration had become a watershed within the context of a career viewed in its entirety as responsive and adaptive in nature. As Barker put it, "Milton's zeal for the purity of Christian religion has been somewhat modified by the events of the three years since the publication of the last anti-episcopal pamplet. He has come to recognize that the reformation cannot be sudden; more than that, he has had proof of his own infirmity and imperfection" (p. 115). One can all too easily form the somewhat confusing impression that Milton's humanism was somehow a double thing at least: if it had been derived originally from reading the classics, it was also a product of mere maturity—of his experience as husband and author to the world.

As the scholars saw it, the new Reformation had clear links with the "paradise within" to be recommended in Milton's later poetry; the document forming the crucial connection with the toleration controversy embodied nothing less than the next, Independent phase of Milton's Puritanism, the first major break with what Woodhouse called Protestant "rigorism" (p. 114). There are some interesting problems inherent in this view. If Milton was turning away from the Presbyterians, his new position was also sharply distinguished from the sectarians; as Barker put it carefully, the *Areopagitica* was "less a defence of the sects than of learning and learned men" (p. 50). But the antithesis between learning and the sects was one which Milton had conspicuously abandoned as he revised the *Doctrine and Discipline of Divorce*; in the *Areopagitica* he had reintroduced it in strategically realigned form to anticipate the common rejection of those special authors whom "we commonly misjudge ere we understand them."[10] Far too much in the scholars' case for Milton's humanist revolution came at the sectaries' expense; and it depended too heavily on the sudden appearance of an open or adaptable Milton, something he opposed with considerable passion from his early, prescriptive phase to the final attacks on the opportunists and "hirelings" who had formerly been his allies. In fact, there were earlier signs of an emergent Independent Milton, signs which the scholars largely neglected. As we have seen, the *Second Defence* nowhere refers to antecedents for the second series of prose writings; it focuses instead on their schematic relationship. To the scholars Milton's earlier position had involved a belief in a divine pattern or prescript for reformation, as against the second group's advocacy of liberty, free reasoning, and the idea of a progressive search for truth. But when they sought to document that position, significantly their point of origin for the shift turned out to be 1641, the year of Milton's *entry* into the antiprelatical skirmishing:

> In 1641 he had thought of history as the record of the church's progressive degeneracy, and of the downfall of episcopacy as the effect of a sudden divine intervention, the prelude perhaps to the second coming. He now thinks of the future as a progression from truth to truth which will terminate only when the divine pattern is at length completely imparted to man at Christ's return. . . . To that extent he becomes less the reformer than the revolutionary. [Barker, p. 76]

Indeed, it seems clear that the scholars' idea of a relatively sudden development in Milton's canon depended on their finding an essentially uniform position lasting throughout the volatile period of the antiprelatical series, a more or less single viewpoint from which a "second group" substantially departed.

As it happens, much of what has long been considered unique to the second group—and primarily to the *Areopagitica*—can readily be found in the remarkable *Apology against a Pamphlet* of July 1642. There is no especially poignant autobiographical background for the final pamphlet in the first series of 1641–42; certainly what we can glimpse of the public references behind its sometimes overheated rhetoric has nothing of the personal appeal of the story behind the *Areopagitica*. But in many important respects, it differs sharply from the rest of the antiprelatical pamphlets and, most strikingly, from the *Reason of Church Government*, its immediate predecessor. We hear almost nothing of the great antitheses ("prosing or versing") which the *Reason* provided Milton two months earlier—and then again in 1654 (*CPW* 1:809). There is little here of the *Reason*'s unwelcome interruption of those congenial literary studies (getting "put from" the actual contemplation of Truth's bright countenance) by the present controversies. Whereas the Milton of the *Reason* had virtually claimed the prompting of divine command, the Apologist is here by choice as well as natural talent; he is the man for this particular job. In light of the *Reason*'s influence on the biographers, though, it is most important to add that the job at hand is unquestionably "literary." The Apologist's lecture to the Bishop on the pastoral duty of reprimand is the *same thing* as filling in Hall, the would-be satyrist, on the nature and Great Tradition of the mode. Whether acting as the earthbound historian and critic or soaring "as the Poets use," moreover, the Apologist clearly enjoys the expertise and discursive spontaneity he recommends in conversation or liturgy. When he ventures a passage of theory—and this is Milton's most interesting essay at poetics—he does so adding, very much in the impressive fashion of the Isocratic orator, that he *knows* whereof he speaks. Milton makes a conspicuous point of dramatizing as well as urging the theoretic value of "liberty and free reasoning." The Apologist not only *can* soar like the poets; occasionally, he seems to be a man almost driven by a "vehement" temper. Again, however, there is the *nature* of the occasion; Milton situates the Apologist in an ideal milieu for the very "free and unimposed expressions" which he had previously entertained only as a hypothetical end point to the Reformation itself. As a historian to the nation, finally, he finds that the Long Parliament has similarly experienced such verbal empowerment recently: the feeling, or rather the actual power, of being "begirt" with wisdom.

As we have seen, a prime feature responsible for the thought and rhetorical power of the second group of pamphlets was its author's presumed responsiveness to changing circumstances. The shifts these works were supposed to reveal (a modification of his zeal) were explained variously as a response to the events of the three years since the *Apology*. As Woodhouse put it somewhat more specifically, this change was "dictated by the course of the Revolution," including the condemnation of his divorce tracts (pp.

100–01). An intellectual alertness or adaptability had become a significant element in his humanism; but there was an ill-concealed uneasiness in these explanations, to be found (for example, again in Woodhouse's words) in the concession that "nothing is easier than to dismiss this shift of ground as mere opportunism" (ibid.). This uneasiness is perhaps unnecessary because the shift (and with it the modification in Milton's idea of reformation) had occurred already, in the *Apology* itself. Perhaps the pamphlet's most striking difference from the *Reason* of just a few months earlier is its candor about the argumentative value of recent events, indeed its flamboyant opportunism. In the place of a Milton who had taken such pains to suggest a divine command to "blow the trumpet" (and who seems eager, at the same time, to have entered the controversy "before the necessity and constraint appeared"!) we have an Apologist well suited by nature to the times. Milton alludes to such events as the Irish rebellion and the execution of Strafford; it is these developments above all which enable him to argue his case "perhaps with more success" than heretofore. Times like this *call* for a man naturally "vehement"; it is not a matter for inspiration or special instructions. Michael Fixler has reminded us that Milton more than once indicated that "the authority of men God sometimes designated to rule was not conferred by some ceremony from without, or transferred by blood or the laying on of hands, but rather emerged in just and pious men as triumphant wisdom and commanding virtue" (p. 161). The *Apology against a Pamphlet* is the first of Milton's works to indicate that all this has happened in fact.[11]

Apart from scholarly custom and convenience, it is not much of a distortion to think of the *Apology* as the first pamphlet of the second group, the true beginning of the rather brief period in which Milton's active mind flourished. Among the Apologist's various obiter dicta there is an item with the closest of ties to the writings on divorce and also to the *Masque at Ludlow*, the "incongruous afterthought" (as Sirluck called it) that "mariage must not be call'd a defilement."[12] And there are implications for long-term developments. It is in fact the *Apology* which initiates that striking development of "things indifferent" and the very basis of the Isocratic orator's arguments from principle that take us so clearly to the philosophical materialism declared by Raphael and *De Doctrina Christiana*.[13] Milton's argumentative appeals throughout the pamphlet are to a vestigial "groundwork of nature" which could be made the "proper mould and foundation of every mans peculiar guifts and vertues" (*CPW* 1:899–900). On this new basis the Apologist presents what amounts to a prototypical *Christian*

Doctrine: an essay by no means reduced or digested into a "system" but full of those doctrinal and historical clarifications that could only be called expert or authoritative. Among other things, we are told of the nature of Christ, and precisely how the Church has differed since the departure of its uniquely omnicompetent teacher.

As we have seen, this is the way Milton encourages us to read the canon generally. The *Apology* is best viewed, however, neither as an anticipatory document nor as a kind of timeless model, to be read back (as sometimes has happened) into the fictional world of such earlier works as the *Masque*. It is not so much in this sense a prophetic work in itself as an essentially historical one, a retrospective instrument for the author's own *formation* of a prophetic canon. The armed warrior Zeal has thwarted the "scarlet prelates" and taken Strafford to the "fatal block." It was the force of Parliament's single words—a wisdom begirt with "majesty"—that has confounded the hireling rebels. Milton's literary theory rests on the basis of thoughts like these. This is how a true poet's words can be said to move about him "like nimble and aery servitors" and "fall aptly into their own places"; it seems clear enough that the "places" in question are not so much locations in a sentence as the various sites of public affairs, out there on the battlefield (*CPW* 1:949). The *Apology*'s convergence of literary professionalism with a kind of divine history involves noticing the kind of conjunction of word and event that Milton frequently deployed in the name of "prevenient grace." Again, one thinks of later works in this context: the moans of those slaughtered saints; the wholesome preventive arrival of Patience, under certain conditions, to "prevent that murmur"; the muse of *Paradise Lost* herself.[14] But for readers interested in the development of Milton's canon, it is essential to recognize the early and demonstrably fictional precedents (or origins) of the situation: the meticulous interlacing of the rhetorical "honor due" and actual demonic arrival in the twin poems of 1631; the aspiration of the Bridgewater family (by "due steps," as in the desired choreography for the pensive nun), an aspiration exercised especially by the two brothers even as it is "prevented" by the Attendant Spirit. In the public version of this work, the Lady briefly indulged the "sacred vehemence" which had been unnecessary in the more nearly ideal world of Milton's Ludlow—and displayed in the Pilot's speech ("Lycidas") of the same year. This is the style discussed and justified at such length in the antiprelatical pamphlets, on the grounds of vocational (pastorly) decorum if not commanded by immediate revelation. In the *Apology*, though, it is recognized as a personal and emphatically literary style, shared by the

Apologist with Martin Luther and other authors of both prose and verse, sacred or "humane." Like the Apologist himself, "vehemence" is here given a history and a natural setting. We are sometimes told that Comus enacts the ideal discursive world of the *Apology*'s "nimble and airy servitors." In fact, the final antiprelatical pamphlet historifies the fictional worlds of the 1630s, and particularly the writings of 1637. It mystifies an essential ingredient of Milton's "humanism," his responsiveness to event, the way in which he had talked about a radically changing world. And it does so in a manner itself rooted in the humanistic thought and fictions he had indulged "in the quiet and still air of delightful studies."

Without doubt, the most important of all these precedents is the Seventh Prolusion, commonly considered the very basis of lifelong, fixed Miltonic convictions. And it is easy to see why the casual reader could mistake the Seventh Prolusion for the curriculum it had become, in effect, by 1644. Milton associates his youthful studies with Endymion's "trysts" (Latin *congressus*) with the moon and the "prophetic sleep" of Hesiod. He describes solitary contemplation as a means of copying "the eternal life of the gods with an extraordinary delight" (*voluptate*), the very word that would play such a critical role in the poet's recommendations for supplanting the endemic abstraction of the usual curriculum; and the arts are proposed it seems as a kind of methodical ladder to that eventual state. Very much in the manner of Bacon's compliments to James, this knowledge would displace the mere will in a kind of allegorical revolt, assuming "preeminence, renown, and majesty almost divine" (CE 12:261). It involves meteorology, anatomy, the knowledge of spirits (including geniuses and daemons). Having made the rounds (*orbes*), the sage will enjoy a peculiar relation to the world of eventuality (*casus atque eventus*) and time. Nothing will come as a surprise to one who has taken wisdom's "stronghold" (*arx*). Indeed, he will be a kind of god, virtually controlling land, sea, and stars. A virtual contemporary of "every age," he will "extort from an unwilling fate" a sense of immortality in his own time.

But far from presenting humanistic ideals as a program to be fulfilled, as the embodiment of principles of a "system" of divinity, of course, the Seventh Prolusion itself is presented as a playful interruption of its young speaker's "learned and abundant leisure." All its ideals are offered here with the kind of skeptical fun that we should expect of an evening dedicated to the witty proposition that all corporeal life, not alone the academy, is necessarily situated in "this gloomy house of correction" (CE 12:267;

ergastulo). If the prodigies of nature terrify "dull minds" (*inertes animas*), the Prolusion by no means guarantees that one may fulfill the perfect artist's endeavor of understanding the "nature and feelings of each living creature" or gain any knowledge whatever about the genii and demons. At every turn, Milton hedges on the sage's powers with the usual advertisements of qualification: "L'Allegro"'s "perhaps" and the would-be enforcer ("Surely") revert to their Latin counterparts: *Videbitur sane is esse, cuius . . .; plane ac si quis Deus . . . hoc est, Auditores, omni aetati quasi vivus interesse.* In the reading, the Seventh Prolusion seems clearly enough to be the kind of discourse Sir Thomas Browne called "soft and flexible"; it cannot easily be identified with the very kind of precocious high seriousness it so studiously disavows.

Moreover, the fun of this and the other prolusions (as in "L'Allegro" and "Il Penseroso") consists in measuring these very hypothetic ideals against the well-scripted performance of the speaker himself, another element so easily confused with the ethos Milton later adopted for his own. Like the brothers of the 1634 *Masque*, this speaker is young, underprepared for the mysteries of which he speaks; and he *sounds* interrupted in his studies, not to say awakened from one of those heavy Hesiodic "sleeps." Possessed of the Bridgewater children's (or the pensive man's) kind of earnest conscience, he is reluctant to snatch a false reputation by a hurried and premature mode of expression (*properato & praecoci stylo falsam praeripere* [CE 12: 248]). He does mention a certain ardor for his plans and purpose of mind. And it is true that his entertainment of the sage's ultimate powers, for all the qualifications I have mentioned, brings him to the point of forgetting his overarching antithesis between public and private:

> And shall I ignore a satisfaction to which no parallel can be found? To be the oracle of many peoples, to have one's home become a shrine, to be the object of invitations from kings and commonwealths and of visits from neighbors and distant foreigners, and of pride for still others who will boast it an honorable distinction merely to have had a single glimpse of one. These are the rewards of study and the profits that learning can and often does bring to those who cultivate her in private life.
>
> What then about public life? [Hughes 625]

But here, the abrupt awakening of "But what about public life" is a wonderfully theatrical coming to earth. It reminds us of the speaker's more ordinary, mundane procedures, his usual even step. Bound to "the pace and method of discourse" after all, he is promising but still a little young, as yet a creature of prose. He is almost woodenly methodical, like Prospero a little forgetful—or at least appealingly mindful that this sympathetic audience might think him so. In something like this manner, the Second Prolusion's consideration of the spheres' harmony had broken off just as it had approached a similarly enrapt contemplation of the golden age, leaving us with a speaker similarly "rude and quite lacking in rhythm" (CE 12: 157; *incondito minimeque numeroso stylo*, 156).

As we have seen, Woodhouse found in one passage of the Seventh Prolusion an instance of settled principle which he considered essential to Milton's humanism; and Barker thought it a text whose ideals Milton deliberately set out to fulfill in retiring to Hammersmith (p. 9). A careful reading of the *Apology* suggests that something rather different occurred. Speaking as he does so confidently of naturally "unsinning predominances" and "liquid things," the Apologist employs the idiom of Milton's last letter to Diodati, with its mention of a vehemence mysteriously "instilled" into the young correspondent. This is the language we find elsewhere in the national version of the *Masque*, published during the same critical year; and it is the basis of Samson's appeals to what Manoa calls "divine impulsion." In a most disturbing fashion, the final antiprelatical tract pretends to record the historical fulfillment—the literal embodiment—of the ideal speaker he had described with such playful irony only two years before he tested the young Bridgewaters' mettle. Even the Apologist's expert portrayal of the Church's ultimate teacher seems derived from the Second Prolusion's discussion of Pythagoras. That sagelike figure was characterized by a peculiar relation to the realm of events, an efficacy Milton strains to find displayed in the Long Parliament's words. And it seems clear from his concluding promise (of a prophetic vision for all who adopt his own earlier techniques in the wars of truth) that he has found another instance of this generalized discursive efficacy in that other vehement work of 1637, the prophetic monody called "Lycidas." In effect, the problem at hand is not so much whether the Seventh Prolusion embodies principles or a program of studies as what *became* of this text when it was reread in the light of 1637 and that year's "uncontrollable intent"; what happened to the undoubted fun of the prolusions when Milton reconsidered them in the light of events (in 1642, 1644, 1654, and so on). I suggest, then, that the *Apology* marks and celebrates what Milton considered to be the near completion, however temporary, of what had *turned out to be* an ambitious and finally impersonal project: the suggestive, perhaps deliberately nebulous, portrayal of talent and intent sketched in the 1637 letter to Diodati, and very likely altered in status by the way two crucial deaths made it a kind of testament.

If the *Apology* recalls and celebrates a triumph of this sort, however, it seems evident that it is a very different story from the one told in the *Second Defence*. The very nature and purposes of Miltonic autobiography seem bound to vitiate all but the most scrupulous efforts at biography. In their own way the *Second Defence* and the *Reason* (in many ways its early source) misrepresent the origin and development, and hence perhaps the very nature, of this "prophetic" canon. Again, in different ways (and for quite different reasons) both accounts can be taken to narrow the range and power of literary learning or "humanism" as other sources (primarily the *Apology*) do not.[15] Because we have too agreeably followed Milton in combining these two sources and then reading them back into the critical 1630s, it is useful to consider more closely some of the intriguing differences between them, including the very different ways in which each document makes sense of private, literary behavior. "Church-outed" he may have been in the sardonic wit of 1642, but in the *Reason*, it was to the Church that his father had "destined [him] of a child," not quite to the pursuits of litera-ture, as the *Defence* declares. In looking back upon the fall of the bishops and its aftermath from the vantage point of 1654, moreover, Milton views the leisure as having been the occasion, not at all for the resumption of that early indulgence, the "polite learning" (or "literature") for which he says his father had "destined [him] from a child" (66), but for a kind of sociopoliti-cal consolidation. And in his efforts to portray himself as the conscientious soldier of truth, Milton insists that his part in this consolidation occurred "within private walls," that his services were "gratuitously bestowed . . . upon the church, . . . [and] upon the commonwealth" (73)—a claim very different from both Milton's earlier self-presentation and Samson's claim (in answer to Harapha) that he was "no private but a person rais'd" and yet not acknowledged (*SA* 1211). Quite understandably (given the circumstances of the later 1640s), Milton downplays his influence, domesticates his own deeds almost to the self-sufficiency indicated in Samson's "conscience and internal peace": "The deeds themselves rendered this freedom of speech honourable to me" (73; *CPW* 4(1):627). Whereas the *Reason* presents the prose career as an interruption of private studies, the leisure of the *Second Defence* involves the experience of political or "real" clarification. Here, as we have seen, prose activity (the busyness of those writers and readers described in the *Areopagitica*) has modulated into a kind of contemplation-based curriculum, an ordered program of prose works. This is one of Milton's ways of saying he was no hireling; the conscientious man never sought the greatness thrust upon him by an unexpected turn of events. For among other things, the *Second Defence* is a chronicle of yet another intrusion in the would-be poet's early career. As a determinant of the shape and texture of his later poetry, indeed, the vestige of vocational disruption recorded here is almost as important as Milton's return from the Italian journey.[16]

To the extent that the *Second Defence* is autobiographical, the incident it centralizes is in fact neither the fulfilled promise of the 1630s nor the deliberation of the 1640s but something like what Dalila calls a "perverse event": the second phase in Milton's career to that point (1654), culminating with his appointment to the Council of State. After the fall of the bishops, Milton's leisurely prospect had taken in what we might well be tempted to call the self-evident scheme of things, including "the three species of liberty." There is a small note of surprise in Milton's consequent discovery of a threefold nature for domestic liberty alone, a minor flourishing which may well strike us as little more than rhetorical embellishment. We then encounter the following passage, which renders the circumstance of Milton's unanticipated reentry into the cool world of prose:

> But, when certain presbyterian ministers, at first the bitterest foes to Charles, unable to endure that the Independent party should now be preferred to them, and that it should have greater influence in the senate, began to clamour against the sentence which the parliament had pronounced upon the king (though in no wise angry at the deed, but only that themselves had not the execution of it) and tried to their utmost to raise a tumult, having the assurance to affirm that the doctrine of protestants, that all the reformed churches shrunk with horror from the atrocity of such a sentence against kings—then indeed, I thought it behoved me openly to oppose so barefaced a falsehood. [73]

In the midst of our tour, we are met with a renewal of the "tumult" we thought was over, a setback promulgated by "certain presbyterian ministers" and originating in the very quarter we thought was getting handled by the magistrate. The passage offers the core of Milton's many witticisms about the fate of the Solemn League and Covenant of 1643, for the men he now opposed had "promised better things" (*insignem hominum meliora profitentium*, CE 8:134). Given the radical nature of the reference, it should not surprise us that his appointment, or even the need for it, was something "which had never entered my thoughts!"[17] (Patrides 74). For once, Milton actually *professes* to have been taken by surprise.

The Columbia translation for Milton's description of his manner in opposing "the egregious ignorance or impudence of those men" is "almost with the zeal of a preacher," as though the *Defence* merely recalled the resumption of a Luther-style "vehemence," and we were listening once again to the "pastorly" Milton of *Comus*, "Lycidas," and the antiprelatical tracts—all of them written, of course, in the vernacular of "these British I[s]lands" (CE 8: 135, 137). But the Latin of this passage is unusually clear as to its allusive intent and testifies to a quite different outlook. The rare *contionabundus* suggests not so much an ardent or "eager" style as the more ambiguous "harangue" directed by a military officer at a reluctant and partly hostile audience. (Helen North translates the phrase "almost as if I were haranguing an assembly," *CPW* 4[1]:626.) Milton took it from Livy's account of Appius and Verginia, a story linked to the suicide of Lucretia and similarly tied to a critical transition in political history, to questions of monarchy (or the decemviral tyranny) and tribunician power. As Livy had used this word, it had referred to something like the precarious opposition of Abdiel and the kind of reception accorded to Enoch and Noah, the fervent angel's successors in *Paradise Lost*.[18]

In noticing the extraordinary neatness of Milton's career as viewed from the vantage point of 1654, Arthur Barker was rightly inclined to downgrade its accuracy. What seemed to be a kind of curriculum was not (as Barker saw it) so much a matter of "clumsy misrepresentation" on Milton's part as a tendency "to foreshorten and to see an ordered pattern where perhaps none existed" (p. XVI). "As Milton reviewed his career from the eminence of his *Pro Populo Anglicano Defensio Secunda*, it seemed to possess a striking inevitability; but it was an inevitability which followed the course of events rather than a preconceived pattern. . . . One must be wary of assuming that the impressive pattern he recognized was the result of conscious planning. Fate had designed it so" (p. XVII). We were not really dealing, in other words, with what Tillyard had called a "coherent body of thought which could only have been formed in the meditative period before the Civil War"[19] Instead we were to imagine a Puritan and especially a Miltonic "dilemma": the need, in Barker's view, to sort out "the relative effect on Milton's thinking of the humanistic defence and the Puritan condemnation of human nature" (p. XXIII). And Barker's very useful innovation was to view the relations among the texts of this canon—and even individual texts themselves—as dynamic, as parts of a process: the prose was "less the expression of ordered ideas than a record of the painful attempt of a sincere but not markedly precise mind to achieve coherence of thought in the midst of social disintegration" (p. XVIII). For Barker, this virtually lifelong effort centered on the developing idea of Christian liberty and Milton's presumed part in the toleration controversy. To my mind, this comes close to replacing one privileged moment in the canon with another: Tillyard's "coherent body of thought" with an eventual position (ibid.). And others have made similar attempts to locate more visionary kinds of sponsorship in Milton and other writers of the later Renaissance. But the great value of Barker's book is the way it allows us, first, to trace Milton's "painful attempts" within as well as among the prose texts and—more important—to see the prose and verse alike as part of the same literary struggle. Inevitably, this involves looking at Milton's canon in the manner recommended by the *Apology against a Pamphlet* and without the invidious distinctions to which Milton is so inclined in the *Second Defence* (and even the *Reason*). We continue to think of Milton's literary life virtually without reference to the full implications of that publicly embodied heroism which for Milton constituted the truest poetry. With Masson and his followers, that is, we fail to notice the partiality of the *Second Defence*, miss this "noble" speech's fully developed sense of a cultural heroism radically deflected and frustrated in reception. This is to subscribe to a view adopted by the poet himself only belatedly, during a period of vexation if not quite "defeat."[20] Much that we value in Milton's poetry (and I would include the pathos attending the epic poet as well as his Apostate rival) derived from the erstwhile allies who came to provide for Milton the very epitome of an antagonist orthodoxy. Those "new presbyters" had much to do with the way Milton's career (in 1654) seemed to have turned out; but they also affected the way in which the poet (and after him the biographers) came to suppose he had designed his life.

Chapter Three

Vestiges of Autobiography:
The Familiar Letters and
The Reason of Church Government

As we saw in chapter 2, biographies of Milton have commonly begun with the *Second Defence of the English People* and in effect worked backward, filling in their pictures primarily with the help of *The Reason of Church Government*; and the methodological deficiency is nowhere more damaging than in the resulting account of the turbulent and crucial 1630s. Neither Masson nor Parker does justice to the two documents dating from the crucial period itself, in particular the final surviving letter to Charles Diodati (1637), which suggests with relative clarity a resolution to Milton's vocational moratorium. Both the *Reason* and the *Second Defence* argue for a clear-cut relation between ideology and "literature"—and even document the emergence of this relation—in a way that is plainly misleading, at least to judge from the documents of the crucial period of 1631–37. They suggest, that is, that Milton thought of his literary career as a development necessarily and unfortunately forestalled by the antiprelatical controversy, as something to be resumed in all its purity once the interim, the prose period of his "left hand," was done with. They further imply that the prose period came about as a consequence of Milton's being "Church-outed by the prelates," and that his present circumstances have "put" him from "beholding the bright countenance of Truth" in the pleasant surroundings of his study, a fate roughly translatable, it is sometimes assumed, to being kept from writing poetry. Milton's biographers have sometimes insisted that these contradictions are the fictions of post-Romantic readers, something we presumably cannot blame the poet for inventing, though there is an increasing body of scholarship aimed at refining the way in which we consider this complex question. But it is clear that Milton himself shaped the pattern of these biographies and that he began to do so rather early in the autobiographical preface to the Second Book of the *Reason of Church Government*, published twelve years earlier than the *Defence*'s account of those literary parental intentions and the straightforward public career of the great poet.

Read with care, the familiar letters can help correct this impression, in part by offering a view of Milton's "humanism" that is fundamentally consistent with his own early endeavors and intentions in churchly matters. They suggest, indeed, a politically engaged Protestant humanism and even, perhaps, a formal acquiescence to the central mandate of Reformation polemic. But other texts of the period can also provide some much needed correctives. Almost from the moment of their composition, for example, "L'Allegro" and "Il Penseroso" were regarded as the work of a poet and no puritan; this was the preideological Milton, later to be ideologically kidnapped by the Sectarians, without quite letting down the cause of Poetry. (Empson was to tell a similar story, substituting Christianity itself for Sectarianism.) But both these poems, probably written in 1631, seriously question the possibility of the kind of sustained encounter with the divine suggested in the *Reason*. They do so by incorporating the speakers' susceptibility to distraction and a kind of forgetfulness—something we also encounter in the Seventh Prolusion (usually dated about a year later). And this rather different picture of Milton's crucial near-decade, suggested by these poems and the letters themselves, is completed by another source seldom cited by Milton's biographers, the *Apology against a Pamphlet*, published anonymously only two months after the *Reason* and known chiefly for its celebrated claim that at a certain point the Apologist was "confirm'd in this opinion, that he who would not be frustrate of his hope to write well hereafter in laudable things, ought himselfe to bee a true Poem" (*CPW* 1:890).

Sometime in 1633, Milton responded to a friends's charge that he was perhaps irresponsibly delaying his ecclesiastical career. The friend has found Milton still engaged in study and presumably headed (in the words of the sonnet for which this letter served as original setting) toward "that same lot . . . / Toward which Time leads me, and the will of Heav'n"; and the letter

29

is almost a list of reasons to keep himself "as I am." Woodhouse calls this letter "a somewhat disingenuous document" (p. 51). And indeed, it displays a good deal of gratuitous rationalization, if not moral complacency—of personal apology not very well *managed*. But there is also real strength and scruple here, in the way, for example, that resounding "Time leads me" jumps out of its muddled syntactic surroundings, or the way in which Milton further antedates his display of conscience by claiming that the sonnet itself (the operative and most impressive part of his response to the friend) was made up "some while since," as though he were an old hand at this sort of thing. In the letter and sonnet alike Milton everywhere seeks to give the impression that he is "something suspicious of [him]self" and endeavors "tymely obedience" to a command from above.

Nothing about this remarkable letter is more revealing in this last regard than its revisions—and in some cases the decision *not* to revise —which survive in the Trinity manuscript. Milton's work on these two pages, it seems to me, points to a "self-suspicion" that is impressively precise in its theological allusion; I suggest that these pages form part of an ongoing meditation, perhaps continuing from the private recesses of texts like the Seventh Prolusion, upon the theme of a special or an "extraordinary" calling. To judge from the texture of Milton's prose here as in the prolusions, this was a meditation no less intense for the seeming playfulness with which he wields the classical, but by no means purely humanist, learning.

In both versions of the letter, Milton refers to his life as thus far "obscure, & unserviceable to mankind." If his studies really involved nothing more than "an affected & fruitlesse curiosity of knowing," he writes —and here we are close to the core of the friend's charge—the young Milton would gladly throw off "this Pluto's helmet, as Homer calls it, of obscurity." The writer was evidently dissatisfied with this disclaimer-by-open-attribution; he removes the allusion in the second draft to suggest, with a striking paradox, that if he were to heed the friend's advice now, he would cut himself off from all significant action and become "the most helplesse pusillanimous, & unweapon'd creature in the word." It is a phrase which remained untouched in the revised version of the letter; a version, it may be added, that is by no means a fair copy (*CPW* 1:319).

The letter of 1633 shows a remarkably acute sensitivity to this matter of attribution. The crucial paragraph begins with an emphatically operative "if": "But if you thinke, as you said, that too much love of Learning is in fault, & that I have given up my selfe to dreame away my yeares in the armes of studious retirement like Endymion w[i]th the Moone as the tale of Latmus goes." In our attempt to retrieve Milton's position from the letter to his friend, it helps to notice that once Pluto's helmet has been withdrawn by way of revision, the only remaining bit of mythography (the reference above to "Endymion with the Moone") seems to be attributed in both versions of the letter to the friend himself. Milton has thus removed the last bit of mythological language from his own voice, so to speak, seeming to incorporate the reference to Endymion with the friend's charge that the young Milton was dreaming away his years at a time when "Christ commands all to labour while there is light" (draft 2, Trinity 7; CE 12:323). Milton has already commented on the text in the Seventh Prulusion of a year or so earlier, venturing to group Endymion with Prometheus and Hesiod as examples of those who profited from "intelligent and liberal leisure," if not divine illumination (Hughes 622, from the Latin *erudito & liberali otio,* CE 12:248). Now, having established that his correspondent brought up the allusion in the first place, Milton concentrates his own attention on the texts which can best serve to accommodate studious "dreaming," including the study of classical authors, to the issue clearly shared by both correspondents, public service perhaps divinely mandated.[1]

By introducing *his own* "unweaponed creature in the word," then, Milton had replaced the helmet which at once fortified and concealed its wearer with an unspecified potential "weapon." In the fables, Milton's substituted weapon was almost always considered in conjunction with the helmet. Together with a sword and other equipment from Mercury and Pallas, Pluto's helmet had helped furnish Perseus for his encounters with Medusa and the dragon menacing Andromeda. The whole story of Perseus was a prime example of why Ovid, like some other "Ethnick" poets who overlapped the pagan and Christian eras, was revered for the way he collected fables "far more ancient then any extant Author, or perhaps then Letters themselves," as George Sandys put it in the 1632 commentary which so profoundly influenced Milton. Sandys, whose early travels in the Mediterranean were partly instigated by the Ovidian poems he eventually translated and sought to expound, found in Perseus' armament "all the necessary accomplishments of a Souldier."[2]

For the commentators, furthermore, there were important affinities between the encyclopedic tendencies of poets like Vergil or Ovid and the methods of Paul himself, whatever his other advantages. In the case of Ephesians, the learned Apostle had set forth his material darkly "for that he would speak all things at once."[3] More specifically, wrote John

Chrysostom, this epistle "containeth profound and deep matter, and doth open the great and hid mystery of the calling of the Gentiles" (To the Reader, Sig. ii, verso). And for later reforming commentators, that "profound and deep matter" pertained specifically to the definition and function of the evangelists and more specifically to the question of "extraordinary" calling. Calvin agreed with most writers in explaining that "Apostles, Evangelists, and Prophets were bestowed on the church for a limited time only."[4] For John, the evangelists are simply "those that writ the Gospel" (p. 145). But for others, there were also "those cases where religion has fallen into decay, and evangelists are raised up in an extraordinary manner, to restore the pure doctrine which had been lost" (p. 280)—an argument which carried weight even with Calvin. And although Chrysostom for the most part accepted the traditional assignment of special duties to the various groups of prophets, evangelists, apostles, and the like, he further noted that the all-important exceptional case was a specific function of the last days, of that time when "we all believe alike." As he argued, the period of specialization itself is in effect for a limited time only, until "we all meet together into the unity of faith and knowledge of the son of God, unto a perfect man, unto the measure of the age, of the fullness of Christ" (pp. 145–46). After all, he went on, the divine teachers had "taken one work in hand"; and Paul's phrase "a perfect man" is the learned Apostle's way of pointing to the consummation of that work—to the unity to be experienced when God is, in this sense, all in all. In the context of the "extraordinary calling" (later commentators were inclined to mention Wycliff, Huss, and Luther by name) "Pluto's helmet, as Homer calls it, of obscurity" could indeed become part of the whole armor of God. But as Milton undoubtedly knew, his revision considerably deepens the power of an organizing allusion to that central *subject* in the pagan mysteries, as the reforming commentaries saw it: Paul's admonition to "put on the whole armor of God, that ye may be able to stand against the wiles of the devil" (Ephesians 6:11). Paul himself had explained that the "word of God" is figured in both the helmet and sword of the spirit; St. John Chrysostom added that the shield of faith signified "that faith whereby miracles are wrought" (p. 326). With this word / sword, John went on, "We cutte off even the Dragon's head, this crooked serpent" (p. 332). It is in this context, then, that Milton—speaking perhaps to the very man who had earlier introduced him to the classics—invokes the unmistakable allusion to a weaponed "creature in the word." And by mentioning such divine punishments as the "terrible seising of him that hid the talent," Milton shows himself aware of consequences perhaps unsuspected or forgotten by his esteemed critic: the necessity, given the public circumstances, of refusing to preach the Gospel in that ordinary or "visible" way to which the controversial literature (or even the friend himself, if we are right in thinking it was Thomas Young) might well have alerted Milton's well-schooled conscience (CE 12:324). Here again, he may well have followed Chrysostom, who had similarly cited the parable of the talents in a like context: applying it to "the gifte of Christ" in the manner of Milton's letter, and very much, too, in the way Milton would look *back* upon his entrance into the pamphlet controversy. "Therupon it commeth that he said: *wo unto me, if I preach not the Gospell*, in respect that he had received the gift of Apostle-shippe" (p. 141).

Because the letter's subject brings us so close to the nineteenth sonnet's consideration of the "one talent which is death to hide," it may be useful at this point to look more closely at the biographers' chosen materials for the momentous vocational decision. In the *Reason*'s autobiographical preface, Milton publicly and explicitly embraces literary study as his "portion in this life," even as he makes his first extended declarations about poetry. The decision, he goes on, is one to which he has been led by the approval of friends in Italy and at home, together with something seemingly more *datable*, an "inward prompting which now grew daily upon me" (*CPW* 1:810). In view of such an impressive array of motives, how does the *Reason* account for these early works of his left hand, as Milton was to describe them, almost regretfully, in the *Second Defence*? How does one resist, in particular, an "inward prompting" so delicately timed and urging him, it seems, in such a different direction? Literary art, as Milton views it in the *Reason*, is "the inspired gift of God"; at the same time, the "genial power of nature" has encouraged him in the indulgence, and he ventures the thought that literature is full of that secular (indeed almost physical) appeal for which he was now beginning to reserve words like "delicious" and "solid." As for prose controversy, Milton protests specifically that he made his appearance as a pamphleteer "before the necessity and constraint appeared"; he seems almost anxious to have acted spontaneously. But as most of the biographers have noticed, Milton hints broadly that some kind of coercion has made a free choice virtually impossible, and indeed now keeps him from the practice of literature and hence from his own more natural setting—the province too, it happens, of that "knowing reader" with whom Milton now makes his famous covenant. "Those sharp, but saving words," Milton writes (speaking of what he considers the obligatory manner of pastoral teaching under the present public circumstances), "would be a terror, and a torment in him to keep back"; he reports anticipating divine reproaches condemning him henceforth to a "brutish silence" (*CPW* 1:804). Milton appears to be claiming a divine prompting for his contemplative and also delightful pursuits—not to mention those encounters with truth's countenance. But there is every sign of an even stricter sanction for the prose activity too. We are dealing with a kind of professional interim or moratorium.

Altogether, readers of the *Reason* may be excused for finding in Milton's professional itinerary a somewhat confusing account of this crucial phase in the author's life, and in particular his debut as a prose pamphleteer. The entire passage is most unconvincing as Milton presents it in the *Reason*, thanks partly to the hypothetical and generic, third-person form into which he casts the entire discussion:

> For surely to every good and peaceable man it must in nature needs be a
> hatefull thing to be the displeaser, and molester of thousands; much better
> would it like him doubtlesse to be the messenger of gladnes and content-
> ment, which is his chief intended busines, . . . But when God commands to
> take the trumpet and blow a dolorous or a jarring blast, it lies not in mans
> will what he shall say, or what he shall conceal. [*CPW* 1:803][5]

"Would be a terror . . . surely . . . it must in nature be . . . would it like him doubtless to be": there is a vexing casualness in the knowing way Milton stresses the inconvenience of the decision to leave literature (or the "contemplation of truth," at any rate) for politics. Milton colors the whole passage with an unmistakable air of rationalization that is altogether different in effect from the unmitigated principles of the *Areopagitica*, say, or for that matter the anonymous *Apology against a Pamphlet* of two months later. As in those remarks about a career that might just *conceivably* marry "labor and intent study" with "the strong propensity of nature," Milton is neither remembering nor even thinking very immediately here. The prose is far from the kind of spontaneous eloquence that Milton called "eager" or "vehement"—the passionate kind of writing he had both practiced and discussed extensively during this period. To be sure, he offers additional, public motives for the decision to follow a literary vocation. But in fact, there is altogether too *much* motivation here. The *Reason*'s medial preface, with its antithesis of "prosing or versing," has long been accepted as Milton's considered view of his two careers and a reflection of the way in which he really thought about the discursive media. Actually, the *Reason* (somewhat like the letter of 1633) seems carefully designed to rehearse *all* the imaginable reasons why a "gentle nature" like Milton's could not conceivably have entered the prelatical controversy for vainglory, malice, or indeed anything "but the enforcement of conscience only."[6] In all this reasoning, the would-be poet seems to address us almost reluctantly, as though he were the Attendant Spirit of his own *Masque,* leaving the more congenial neighborhood of Jove's empyreal court. We have here, in short, a view of literature that is suspiciously close to late-nineteenth-century belletrism. And it is this argumentative pattern that the *Second Defence* rehearsed and considerably sharpened in 1654.

It is fair to say, indeed, that our most fundamental ideas about Milton's career and its development continue to be derived primarily not from the familiar letters or other primary materials Milton himself preserved for eventual publication, but from this rather late text and its evident original. Writers interested in Milton's early career are virtually invited to assume that discrepancies in the autobiographical record are negligible or misleading, or even that they conceal a consensus available somewhere behind the well-known documents from the period in question. As a result, their accounts continue to slight some interesting differences in the various biographical sources and downplay or ignore some significant misrepresentations on Milton's part. Both the *Defence* and the *Reason* present a prose variation on "Lycidas": the preparatory rituals of the dedicated swain have been cut off by hard mishap, the career interrupted (in the case of the *Reason*) by divine command—the only kind, as Milton's Samson was to recall so sharply, that can come with a "resistless" power. Given the reasons we may be dissatisfied with the *Reason*'s account, what are we to make of its most famous claims—and they are impressive indeed—that Milton had been "destined from a child" for the service of the Church but now finds himself "Church-outed by the prelates"; and, most astonishing of all, considering the *Reason*'s general lack of specific reference to past experiences, the claim that he had been "put from beholding the bright countenance of truth in the quiet and still air of delightful studies to come into the dim reflexion of hollow antiquities sold by the seeming bulk" (*CPW* 1:821–22; Hughes 671a). Do these references, or the surviving documents to which they seem so clearly to direct us, in any way explain how, in 1654, Milton was able to write that his father had always intended a professional life not exactly in "the service of the Church," but in "humane letters"?[7]

The young Milton's idea of vocation, wrote Arthur Barker in a learned and powerful book, was bound up with the phrases of "divine philosophy" together with the "ordered rhythms of classical poetry."[8] Both of the relevant familiar letters make it clear that we cannot accept without many reservations the *Reason*'s stark polarities in our continuing efforts to recover the authentic Protestant character of the poet's humanism. In the way they preempt the *Reason*'s argumentative patterns (especially the antithesis of literary and prose careers, remembered and sharpened in the *Second Defence*), the letters point to a complementary relation between the poetry and the politics of prose—between literature and the Church, or at least "the office of a pulpit." Neither letter quite prepares us for the *Reason*'s report (perhaps a scoff at his antagonists' shallowness) that Milton felt "Church-outed by the prelates." And the letter to Diodati in particular should encourage serious doubt about the related complaint that he had been "put from beholding the bright countenance of truth," that the actual encounter was anything like what he had proposed, or that he really thought nature and divine revelation or command were somehow pulling him in two different directions.

Milton's last surviving letter to Diodati (1637) shows us clearly just how close the affiliation could get between classics and divinity. More than any other early personal document, it accounts for Barker's important suggestion because it offers a kind of key to the writer's predicament in the form of what is arguably the central fragment of "divine philosophy" for the later Reformation. Here is a translation of what Milton wrote to Diodati:

> For though I do not know what else God may have decreed for me, this certainly is true; He has instilled into me, if into anyone, a vehement love of the beautiful. Not so diligently is Ceres, according to the Fables, said to have sought her daughter Proserpina, as I seek for this idea of the beautiful, as if for some glorious image, throughout all the shapes and forms of things ("for many are the shapes of things divine"); day and night I search and follow its lead eagerly as if by certain clear traces. [*CPW* 1:326–27]

Even more directly than in the letter to the unknown friend, Milton integrates the world of the fables with the Pauline texts concerned with the extension of the covenant or call, so crucial to the Reformers and to poets like Milton's beloved Spenser. Milton mentions a quest for ideal beauty, the practice of "Pegasean flight" in verse, and (in almost the same breath) the priestly calling to which he had been (as he would put it later in the *Reason*) "destined from a child." As a result—given his claim that there are "certain clear traces" now directing his quest—it is tempting to conclude (with Irene Samuel, for one) that the letter betrays nothing less than a "philosophic conversion" to something like Barker's and Bush's Christian humanism.[9] It is true that when Milton remembered this period of his life (remembered this *text*, we might almost say), he claimed that in joining the common effort to "lighten the difficult labors of the church" he had been "put from beholding the bright countenance of truth in the quiet and still air of delightful studies," a scene indeed reminiscent of the Younger Brother's appreciation of philosophy's charms. But as we shall see, he had already imagined the scene quite differently, and with no little humor, in "Il Penseroso"; and some would say that the Younger Brother, while coming along nicely, tells only part of the story. We may notice, however, that, Milton stops well short even of describing an actual encounter with Beauty or Truth. While he refers to a special talent mysteriously (but quite naturally) "instilled" in him, what he professes to feel, quite specifically, is a "vehement *love* of the beautiful" (my emphasis); he further stresses the plurality of the "shapes and forms" in which ideal beauty may theoretically reside, and the inclusiveness of his own search "throughout all" those shapes. He is far from claiming to possess anything like that "universal insight into things" of which he would speak almost familiarly in 1644.

It is in this enigmatic and plainly crucial conversation—made more so in retrospect, perhaps, by the deaths of his mother and Diodati himself —that we encounter Milton's first use of Euripides: the choral generalization πολλαὶ Υαρ μορψαὶ τῶυ Δαιμουἰωυ. As one of the annotations described it in the edition used by Milton, this was the poet's "solemn proverbial close"; it is the *quintessential* Euripidean conclusion, used in the final choruses of the *Bacchae*, the *Helen*, and the *Alcestis*, and remembered by Milton once again in the concluding measure of *Samson Agonistes*.[10] In the context of Milton's letter, the quotation captures almost perfectly the way in which some Renaissance scholars and artists had come to think of the historical function of the ancient poets. For a poet like Milton in search of methods alternative to "the office of a pulpit" (as he put it later), the Euripidean chorus represented one of the ancients' own best glosses on the manifold and fragmentary manner in which God had spoken in ancient times. The quotation thus represents the pre-Christian drama's deepest penetration into those mysteries remembered in the learned Apostle's great admonition to "prove all things, hold fast that which is good." In an appropriately veiled fashion, Milton's last letter declares a *poet*'s acquiescence to Paul's crucial text long before he employed it directly and strategically in the *Areopagitica*. It does so by linking the affective appeals of what would now be called "literature" to what Milton later declared to be "the special uses of these times."[11]

It is worthwhile to notice further the relation of the letter to the final milieu of that "prophetic strain" mentioned in "Il Penseroso" beyond the "studious cloister's pale," in an environment that more recalls the world of the desert Fathers or of the ancient prophets. The young Milton's quest for some shape of the beautiful requires a public venue; it goes on not exactly in a humanist's bower—certainly not the "quiet and still air of delightful studies," say—but emphatically outside this self-concealing (if also forti-fying) structure. Indeed Milton describes his own correspondence with Diodati as the siege of a kind of fortress; in the military idiom which pervades the letter he suggests that his friend, who is newly established in his medical practice and involved in some family disagreements, is not so much fortified as imprisoned within this "tyrannical citadel of medicine." In a way, the friend and only known confidant has taken the place of the unknown friend's correspondent inside the fortress; for in its guise of Pluto's helmet, the "citadel" was a place which Milton had imaginatively abandoned even as he revised the earlier letter; and certainly it was a differ-ent place from the "stronghold of wisdom" he had described in the Seventh Prolusion. Like the *Areopagitica*, the letter to Diodati confirms this reposi-tioning in such a way as to sketch a virtual prototype for the oration's great antihero, the "fugitive and cloistered virtue" that might well have been Milton himself. For when one considers the vocational tenor of the whole conversation, it is difficult to escape the impression that in Milton's mind the young Diodati's vocational choice and "stepmotherly warfare" have replaced a rather different kind of struggle, better pursued outside the citadel walls. Milton seeks someone who, "despising the warped judgement of the public, dares to feel and speak and be that which the great wisdom throughout all ages has taught to be best" (*CPW* 1:327), and intends to exert every "effort and labor of mine" to "rise to such glory and height of fame." The fascination with wisdom's consensus "throughout all ages" is coupled with an insistence upon the public expression of Milton's special brand of literary vehemence. However enigmatically and (one must con-cede) hesitantly delivered, Milton's outlook is very different from the situa-tion of the student in 1633, "as yet unserviceable to mankind."

Still, there is an important qualification. The dominant figure of the final letter to Diodati is neither the future poet of *Paradise Lost* nor the uncouth swain so artificially exhibiting his scruples in the way Milton had done with the unknown friend a few years previously. This speaker, we might say rather, is the writer or scholar who would be something more, a *speaker*. If Milton's ideal scholar would one day be "fraught with an universal insight into things," the present writer is still *reading*: reading, and practicing the writing, of "literature." And the self-conscious wanderer-among-the-Ethnicks concludes his letter by asking specifically for more books of history. As yet, he is the scholar who would complete the Seventh Prolusion's cycle of learning by becoming a "contemporary of time itself"; but there is a significant difference between the near mysticism of this last phrase and the seeming mundanity of Milton's request for more books of history. The letter to Diodati, in short, suggests not so much the actual encounter with "Truth's" countenance as the wish for a mere glance. As for the *Reason*'s kind of autobiography: what Milton was "put from" at the time he later recalled so variously was by no means the accomplished vision, a steady or "fixed" gaze at Truth's countenance. He had been interrupted in the scrupulously "self-suspicious" quest for one or another of Beauty's various "shapes." As we shall now see, the movement toward the later combination of personal history and recipe for social action may be difficult to chart, but it is significant and real.

Chapter Four

The True Poem *in Potentia:*
"L'Allegro" and "Il Penseroso"

But truly it is worth while, if our life is to be modeled on the example
of the Cherubic life, to have before our eyes and clearly understood
both its nature and its quality and those things which are the deeds and the
labor of Cherubs. But since it is not permitted us to attain this through
our own efforts, we who are but flesh and know of the things of earth,
let us go to the ancient fathers.
Pico Della Mirandola, *On the Dignity of Man*

The lie is in our understanding, and our darkness is so firmly entrenched
in our mind that even our groping will fail.
Dürer, some years after composing the *Melancolia* I[1]

For the various attempts to rescue an authentically humanist Milton, none
of the poems has proved to be more important than "L'Allegro" and "Il
Penseroso." Partly because of their date (safely prior to the dangerous
"Lycidas"), the twin poems of 1631 have long been thought to provide
crucial evidence for the "pre-Puritan" poet and by extension for the effects
of Protestant doctrines upon literary art. H. J. Todd summarized a long-
prevailing attitude in a general note on "L'Allegro" and "Il Penseroso": "No
man was ever so disqualified to turn puritan as Milton. . . . What very
repugnant and unpoetical principles did he afterwards adopt! . . . The
delights arising from these objects [Todd specifies the "studious cloisters
pale," the "high-embowed roof," the "pealing organ" and the "full-voiced

choir"] were to be sacrificed to the cold and philosophical spirit of Calvin-
ism, which furnished no pleasures to the imagination."[2]

The *Poems* of 1645 promises complexities of a kind altogether different
from the "trivial Airs" to be found in other books; this volume will involve
the more portentous question of "how harmonious thy soul is" (Sig.a4).
But "L'Allegro" and "Il Penseroso" have usually been considered free from
such deficiencies; and the poems' presumed attitude toward music, in
particular, has served as a kind of biographical key to the sensibility of
Milton the man. Small wonder, then, that the poems became a staple for
imitation and allusion during the century and a half after Milton had
written them, or that Richard Hurd (in a burst of enthusiasm to which we
shall return) could call *both* poems "airs," which (like Circe's music) "take
the prison'd soul, and lap it in Elysium" (Todd, p. 77).[3] This comes very
close to saying, as Coleridge was to put it in 1833, that if sublimity was
Milton's element, the "opposite qualities of tenderness and grace" were just
as authentic: "The same hand that armed the rebellious legions, and built
up the radiant domes of Pandemonium, mingled also the cup of enchantment in *Comus*, and strewed the flowers on the hearse of Lycidas" (*Conversations*, June 1833; Joseph A. Wittreich, ed., *The Romantics on Milton*
[Cleveland: Case Western Reserve, 1970], p. 275). Whether this virtuosity was evident within "L'Allegro" and "Il Penseroso," however, was
another question. And amidst all the early appreciation, Dr. Johnson's
reservations (published in 1779) are among the few comments directed at
important specific problems in the text. They are based largely on a passage
beginning eighteen lines from the end of "L'Allegro," when Milton's
speaker wishes to be lapped in "soft *Lydian* Airs / Married to immortal
verse." "Both his characters delight in music," wrote Dr. Johnson; "but he
seems to think that cheerful notes would have obtained from Pluto a
complete dismission of Eurydice, of whom solemn sounds produced only a
conditional release." And with this shrewd glance at a sense of history and
cultural authenticity apparently missing from the poem, Dr. Johnson
concluded that in general, "the colours of the diction seem not sufficiently
discriminated. I know not whether the characters are kept sufficiently
apart."[4]

I

Two episodes from the poems bring home the acuity of Dr. Johnson's
observations. About halfway through "L'Allegro"'s catalogue of "unreproved pleasures," one cluster seems to occupy our attention far longer than

has previously been the case; and Milton constructs the passage so as to display and advertise something new in his speaker, his activity *as a maker*. Initially, the poet's eye is said to "measure" the surrounding landscape (70), as though we were involved in the perception of an empiricist's object. But even as the speaker claims to have accomplished this, the passage is declared to be fictive (at "perhaps" in 79 and implicitly in what follows); and from this point, the speaker's vision actually becomes more precise, more particularly focused. Instead of the vague "some beauty," we have Phillis and her friends; conventionally rural, to be sure, but nonetheless individualized embodiments of beauty and mirth:

> Straight mine eye hath caught new pleasures
> Whilst the Landscape round it measures,
> Russet Lawns and Fallows Gray,
> Where the nibbling flocks do stray;
> Mountains on whose barren breast
> The laboring clouds do often rest;
> Meadows trim with Daisies pied,
> Shallow Brooks, and Rivers wide.
> Towers and Battlements it sees
> Bosom'd high in tufted Trees,
> Where perhaps some beauty lies,
> The Cynosure of neighboring eyes.
> Hard by, a Cottage chimney smokes,
> From betwixt two aged Oaks,
> Where *Corydon* and *Thyrsis* met,
> Are at their savory dinner set
> Of Herbs, and other Country Messes,
> Which the neat-handed *Phillis* dresses;
> and then in haste her Bow'r she leaves,
> With *Thestylis* to bind the Sheaves;
> Or if the earlier season lead
> To the tann'd Haycock in the Mead.
> Sometimes with secure delight
> The upland Hamlets will invite,
> When the merry Bells ring round,
> And the jocund rebecs sound
> To many a youth, and many a maid,
> Dancing in the Checker'd shade;
> And young and old come forth to play
> On a Sunshine Holiday,
> Till the livelong daylight fail. [ll. 69–99]

These details can best be seen, I believe, as pointing to original accomplishments of the speaker himself, like the earlier (and rather differently advertised) attribution of Milton's own genealogical material to "some Sager" authors (17). And the remarkable increase in the speaker's own energy is further enhanced in the passage immediately following, which Todd considered a "digression, perhaps disproportionately prolix" (p. 101). Milton fills in the account of *"Faery Mab,"* to the point that the pretense of that mere spectatorship involved in all poetic description yields to the lively sense of creative authorship:

> Then to the Spicy Nut-brown Ale,
> With stories told of many a feat,
> How *Faery Mab* the junkets eat;
> She was pincht and pull'd, she said,
> And he, by Friar's Lantern led,
> Tells how the drudging *Goblin* sweat
> To earn his Cream-bowl, duly set,
> When in one night, ere glimpse of morn,
> His shadowy Flail hath thresh'd the Corn
> That ten day-laborers could not end;
> Then lies him down the Lubber Fiend,
> And, stretch'd out all the Chimney's length,
> Basks at the fire his hairy strength;
> And Crop-full out of doors he flings,
> Ere the first Cock his Matin rings. [ll. 100–14]

Milton is far from belaboring the delicate matter of authorship here. His characters / tellers appear in orderly fashion ("She . . and he"), relating their tales of victimization or assistance by the faery creatures. The "Lubber Fiend" comes to dominate the account, even as he appears to grow in size; and the narrative of his departure in particular—he leaves just before the cock's reminder of morning duties—altogether transcends its initial status as just another of those "stories told." Almost imperceptibly, that strategically wielded "I"—the implicit "person" of the poem, Milton would call him in a moment of theoretic elation in 1642—joins the series of storytellers. Within the poem's terms, though, only L'Allegro could have told *this* story. The poet's abrupt restoration of his framing device ("Thus done the Tales" [15]) sets off this speaker's achievement as active singer/maker; there can be no mistaking this behavior for the anxious wooing of absent nymphs, much less the rural listeners' own creeping off to bed "By whispering Winds soon lull'd asleep" (116). I submit that the poem's nearest approach to quintessential, actual delight is this extensive encounter with Mercutio's vainly abused Queen Mab, the unseen creature mentioned to prove, of all things, that "dreamers often lie."⁵ And it is the relative immediacy of this small narrative that presents Mirth herself in the person of the lubber fiend. Milton virtually announces the Shakespearean heritage of this, his own most authentic moment long before he names his predecessor. Here is the Lydian air we truly *experience* in "L'Allegro."

As we approach the final movement of "L'Allegro" a dozen lines later, the poem appears to be marking time, its author gathering up this least problematic part of the work into a kind of cornucopia. "Such sights as youthful Poets dream / On Summer eves by haunted stream" looks back upon the entire poem to this point; and the ensuing "Then" takes us not to a subsequent or different locale, but to the same place, now wondrously inhabited by the true author of its allusive details, "sweetest Shakespeare, fancy's child."⁶ In this context, L'Allegro's striking request for Lydian airs is not so much a threshold as a bit of retrospective framing, a way of naming something we have been through already and asking for its extension. After the fact, so to speak, the poem's delights are not augmented, but summed up sub specie musicae.

> And ever against eating Cares,
> Lap me in soft *Lydian* Airs,
> Married to immortal verse,
> Such as the meeting soul may pierce
> In notes, with many a winding bout
> Of linked sweetness long drawn out,
> With wanton heed, and giddy cunning,
> The melting voice through mazes running;
> Untwisting all the chains that tie
> The hidden soul of harmony;
> That *Orpheus'* self may heave his head
> From golden slumber on a bed
> Of heapt *Elysian* flow'rs, and hear
> Such strains as would have won the ear
> Of *Pluto*, to have quite set free
> His half-regain'd *Eurydice*.
> These delights if thou canst give,
> Mirth, with thee I mean to live. [ll. 135–52]

It is only at this point, then, that our experience in the poem is called Lydian and thus given the rather uncomfortable clarity of a modal category.

Modern readers of the poem have been less willing than Dr. Johnson to consider the poem so closely, even where something presumably so clear-cut as musical references was involved. The particularity of Milton's built-in scholia here and elsewhere in the companion poems has provoked several expert scholarly investigations into the question of Milton's attitude toward the various modes of Greek (or medieval and Renaissance) music; and the consensus has supported a favorable reading of "Lydian" while ignoring Dr. Johnson.[7] In what is perhaps the most influential of these studies, James Hutton has argued that in the phrase "And ever against eating Cares," Milton was "merely reproducing" Cassiodorus, who had described the Lydian mode in a letter to Boethius as a source of "relaxation and delight, being invented against excessive cares and worries" (p. 46). Milton's only direct comment on the Lydians' proclivities dates from about ten years after the composition of "L'Allegro" and "Il Penseroso" and demonstrates the continuing importance of the poem's concerns into the period of the early political prose. In *Of Reformation*, he reproduces Herodotus' account of Croesus' instructions to Cyrus, who "learnt . . . to tame the *Lydians*, whom by Armes he could not, whilst they kept themselves from Luxury; with one easy Proclamation to set up *Stews*, dancing, feasting & dicing he made them soone his slaves."[8] Even without the specific mention of music, we are not far in this passage from the traditional view of Plato that the Lydian mode promoted "drunkenness, effeminacy, and inactivity."[9] In the pages that follow, I shall suggest that neither "L'Allegro" nor "Il Penseroso" fundamentally disagrees with this view of the Lydian mode's effects, even though in different ways each poem employs them. Our best guide to the poem's attitudes can be found in the subtle but discernible shifts in Milton's way of presenting the objects of his praise — or, more accurately, in the way he scrupulously *avoids* the actual manifestation of mirth and divinest melancholy for more than a glance. Thus (to return to Dr. Johnson) it is a mistaken L'Allegro, and not the pre-Puritan Milton, who supposes that the cheerful notes would free Eurydice completely. And the "colours of the diction seem not sufficiently distinguished" because Milton has constructed both speakers as creative but also awkward and anxious wooers. There is a difference between Milton's Penseroso and what he *would* be, a difference he shares with the aspiring L'Allegro. Neither speaker is conceived as really possessed of the ideal he seeks; both are inadequate or incomplete speakers in the sense that their presumed modes are dramatized as ideals, "tender stops": fragile, susceptible to outside influence, sometimes lucky in the attainment of an ideal voice. These are well-known characteristics of Milton's later poetry, but also of that emphatically "Puritan" document written and first published only six years later, "Lycidas."

II

The matter of our experience and its relation to the speaker's own verbal performance is crucial. And the rest of the poem shows how carefully Milton maintains his distinction between the narrative achievement of "secure delight" and his speaker's subsequent wish—entertained and dismissed at once, I believe—for a kind of hyperextended bliss which Milton decided not to stage as anything more or less immediate than the spectacle of "wishful thinking" in the strictest sense of both these words. From the request for Lydian airs until the poem's final couplet, we do not really hear the verse as being made up of discrete couplets pointing to self-sufficient delights; instead, what we encounter during lines 135–50 (as in the verse of *Paradise Lost*) is its "*sense*, variously drawn out from one Verse into another, not in the jingling sound of like endings" (Hughes, p. 210, my emphasis). And that sense has become remarkably sinuous and problematic in its articulation, "careful" in the forces exerted by its syntax. More than a temporary interruption in the dominant mode of the poem, these lines constitute the poem's single major shift, clearly signaled by "And ever against eating Cares."[10]

This arresting phrase, closer to Horace's *edaces curas* than to Cassiodorus' less vivid *nimias curas*, discloses more clearly than heretofore in the poem the chief rival to "secure delight."[11] Equally important, the phrase helps point, not to anything we have known already, but to something like an urgent desideratum—the specific kind of music that would serve a specific purpose, negatively defined. Under the proper conditions—and the variables are impressive in their abundance—this music would "lap" the speaker (he speaks in the first person as he has not done for sixty-seven lines) "against eating Cares." From this point on, we encounter the kind of difficulties in presentation that are usually associated only with "Il Penseroso." Judging from the poem's manner, we cannot confidently say whether the Lydian airs ever really accomplish their union (or their re-union?) with the "meeting soul"; certainly we do not experience such a thing in anything like the way we perceive the earlier "unreproved pleasures." As the request turns to the question of joy's duration, its object is made inaccessible syntactically. Not even "*Lydian* Airs" alone would accomplish joy's purpose; to do so they would have to be married to "immortal verse," an entity in itself involving an unlikely coupling, even for a poet of Milton's ambitions.

Furthermore (for we are compelled to proceed) Milton launches his description of this music with a dissociative "such":

> Such as the meeting soul may pierce
> In notes, with many a winding bout
> Of linked sweetness long drawn out,
> With wanton heed, and giddy cunning,
> The melting voice through mazes running;
> Untwisting all the chains that tie
> The hidden soul of harmony;
> That *Orpheus'* self may heave his head
> From golden slumber on a bed
> Of heapt *Elysian* flow'rs, and hear
> Such strains as would have. . . .   [ll. 138–48]

And on we must wend. Every word here adds to our distance from "secure delight." By sharpening the particularizing force of the modification (just what kind of music, of Lydian music—and so on—we shall need to "lap" us forever), each succeeding word necessarily removes us from the reality of delight. The music will have to pierce the soul in notes, but it can happen only if that soul is, literally, cooperative; the union cannot occur now, Milton suggests, unless it has somehow happened *in advance*—why pierce a soul that is well-met already?[12] The critique implicit in this near tautology is available elsewhere as we go on, as we try to determine, for example, the correct detail with which to place "with many a winding bout." Is the "wanton heed" the manner in which the sweetness is "long drawn out," or (in true careless fashion) should we put it in loose parallel with "with many a winding bout"? We may well wonder whether the near absoluteness of this clause is meant to embody its own grammatical subject, "the melting voice through mazes running." In any case, we are dealing with a local bit of disorientation; the considerable syntactic pressures exerted *upon* the absolute clause remind us what it would take to preserve the poem's delight forever. The soul of harmony will probably remain permanently imprisoned, we are likely to suppose (as a result of reading this sentence)—and it is not over *yet*. If all holds true, there are still more effects. Given the right conditions, Orpheus might hear . . . not Lydian music, surely (it is just the kind that would not keep him awake), but something refined enough to reunite a couple once married and now permanently separated by death.

The detail reminds us that the final segment of the poem involves in some definite sense a partitioning, beginning with marriage unconsummated and ending with marriage dissolved.

The harmless beginning to all this, "And ever against eating Cares," thus marks a false conclusion, and it involves the enthusiast's abortive attempt to extend delight into an indefinite future. It is the quality or nature of that delight that we are bound to forget as we proceed, and in particular the fact that it, too, is speech; for the narrative of the lubber fiend, like the more momentary pleasures which precede, is nothing less than the "honor due" which Milton's speaker had long before proposed as the necessary condition of his demonic company's arrival. The final couplet directs our view back toward those "unreproved pleasures free,"[13] but across no narrow frith; for we cannot well *remember* the pleasures, taken up as we have been lately with the twisting pathways of the poet's own discourse. The *singularity* of what this speech is getting at jars oddly with the unrestrictiveness of the penultimate line's "These delights"—*what* delights? Thus, with an abruptness which I think is deliberate, Milton recollects both our memory of this poem's momentary pleasures and the fact, for some time now forgotten, that from the beginning the poem has been an extended invocation, a request for joy and mirth whose effects are explicitly made contingent upon the speaker's own performance. In the intervening lines, far from offering us the *experience* of delight, Milton has restored our memory of the associations and conditions necessary for successful adjuration—and he does so virtually at the moment we have glimpsed Mirth herself, as though L'Allegro were oblivious to the actual accomplishment. As Milton thus reintroduces the poem's primary gesture of invitation-by-praise, he appears to restore the clearly *audible* couplet, now furnished with a density of scruple it has previously lacked. These last lines, with their severe medial caesura, emphasize what has already been "proven" in the seventeenth-century sense—the difficulties involved in the speaker's original task—and they also hint at the unlikelihood of success: "These delights if thou canst give, / Mirth, with thee I mean to live." Concluding as they do on the note of conditionality and with their stress on firm but unfulfilled intentions, indeed, the lines actually seem less straightforward than the corresponding verses in the reputedly more difficult companion-poem: "These pleasures Melancholy give, / And I with thee will choose to live." Milton all but concludes "L'Allegro" with the discursive manners of his pensive counterpart, whom Hugh Blair rightly found almost incapable of "unmeaning general expressions; all is particular."[14]

Stanley Fish has recently argued that Milton's languid Orpheus is the poem's perfect surrogate for Milton's reader. But Orpheus is mentioned precisely at the moment when Milton readmits to the poem the kind of difficulty which Fish believes to be excluded by the poem's subject. By pretending, in effect, that lines 135–50 never happened, the final couplet points up the significance of the pressures it seems to ignore. We never really displace or disturb Orpheus in this poem because—unlike the "Lubber Fiend"—he never appears. The arch-singer is mentioned distantly (and in the unwonted guise of spectator) just as we begin to work and worry precisely about "the resonances and complications which might be activated by another context," the context, as Fish would have it, of "Il Penseroso."[15]

III

As Johnson's perplexity suggests, "Il Penseroso" is not such a different poem—or so different throughout its length, at any rate—as we might have supposed. The corresponding moment to the lubber fiend's story occurs much earlier in the poem than does its counterpart; and to judge from the silence on this passage in the commentaries, it did not strike its early readers as a digression, much less an "episode," as I have called it. Yet it does offer a narrative vision of a particularly impressive kind. At line 52, there is a sudden glance at an actual presence attending this speech, "Him that yon soars on golden wing, / Guiding the fiery wheeled throne, / The Cherub Contemplation" (ll. 52–54). It is an odd moment, designed as though in fulfillment of the ideal conditions for true visionary experience described by Pico: we have before our mind's eye an actual cherub, even if we do not yet understand "its nature and its quality and those things which are the deeds and labor of Cherubs." And there is company for him. The mute Silence, Philomela, Cynthia, and her "dragon yoke" are here too, not just asked to come; and the poet actually addresses the "chantress" at line 63. In all this, Milton is clearly interested (once again) in the skewed relation between such an event and the speaker's own exertions, much as Dürer had written concerning the artist's pursuit of absolute beauty that "even our groping will fail." The dissociative pressures of Milton's syntax actually persist somewhat beyond line 52, as though the speaker had failed to notice the extraordinary arrival. Articulate recognition catches up with theophanic event in the charming familiarity of "'Less *Philomel* will deign a

Song," and as we first encounter corollaries of the remarkable narrative achievement—narrative events which enact the song of Philomela:

> But first, and chiefest, with thee bring
> Him that yon soars on golden wing,
> Guiding the fiery-wheeled throne,
> The Cherub Contemplation;
> And the mute Silence hist along,
> 'Less *Philomel* will deign a Song,
> In her sweetest, saddest plight,
> Smoothing the rugged brow of night.
> While *Cynthia* checks her Dragon yoke,
> Gently o'er th'accustom'd Oak;
> Sweet Bird than shunn'st the noise of folly,
> Most musical, most melancholy!
> Thee Chantress oft the Woods among,
> I woo to hear thy Even-Song;
> And missing thee, I walk unseen.   [ll. 51–65]

The only vehicle for narrative presence here would be Philomela's song, something of Milton's own construction (like the lubber fiend of "L'Allegro"). But in this poem the cherub arrives before the poet can properly summon him; and he differs in this vital respect from his faery counterpart, who is part of the speaker's own story, not somewhere outside it. Before Milton has the chance to build the lofty rhyme—to my ear, line 63 sounds as though it were constructed not as rapture but as ponderous *effort* to soar—we are put in the narrative presence of Cynthia's dragon yoke, checked (and "gently" checked) with the rhythms of Philomela's song, the only song which can make the oak "accustom'd." At moments like this, perhaps we can speak of an "inadvertent" success for the poet's own song (or that of a prevenient muse like Philomela), a success of the kind some readers have found in the invocations of *Paradise Lost*.[16] With the cherub before our eyes and (in "L'Allegro") the voice of harmony seemingly recaptured, we have momentarily achieved something which, according to Pico and others, is "not permitted us to attain . . . through our own efforts." And clearly Milton has not forgotten the traditional qualification. Instead of following Pico in turning "to the ancient fathers," however, he makes wooing itself a central and also a problematic activity in both poems; indeed, both poems capture, *then* woo (or continue to woo, as in "Il Penseroso") the object of their speaker's devotion. Milton distinguishes these two actions almost completely by the time the speaker has vanished

(1. 65) or is wishing for significant improvement in Orpheus' skills.[17] And by the speaker's own admission, Philomela gets "missed" only when she is wooed "the Woods among" (1. 65).[18]

From the outset of "Il Penseroso" (and perhaps even in the proem to "L'Allegro"), we are alerted to the qualifications attending the entire invocation—the overwhelming probability of summoning unsatisfactory alternatives to just the right kind of melancholy. The problem is established in starkest terms in the opening lines of "Il Penseroso" and recollected in line 123; the pleasures of this poem are perilously close to the gaudy shapes that might distract the "fixed mind." There is even the problem of getting the wrong kind of blackness (1. 17); and parenthetic bits of interpretive pushing remind us of eras and cultural achievements other (and better) than our own (ll. 25f., 101).[19] At times, the nearly self-defeating nature of the request is made amusingly obvious; Melancholy is to come—and yet keep her "wonted state"; come and yet remain fixed, with

> . . . looks commercing with the skies,
> Thy rapt soul sitting in thine eyes:
> There held in holy passion still,
> Forget thyself to Marble, till
> With a sad Leaden downward cast,
> Thou fix them on the earth as fast. [ll. 39–44]

There is the further traditional suggestion that the appropriate locale for the encounter may involve bad "Air," or the need of special charms to ward off "nightly harm" (1. 84). The landscape, too, may well suffer from the distracting noises of culture like the "rude Axe" (1. 136). And needless to say, there are other than "good spirits"—all those malign counterparts to "Faery Mab." Among such justling contingencies must Milton steer his poem's course; they account for the poem's difference in texture from "L'Allegro" (or from most of "L'Allegro"), and they serve as this poem's equivalent to the "eating Cares" of the companion piece. L'Allegro's mere mistakes, his anxious wishes, become a constant threat to the successful invocation of the pensive nun.

For all this, "Il Penseroso" by no means provides throughout its length those "resonances and complications" that Fish believes to be mandated by its very subject; the poem, indeed, may well lack a single context that would explain such a texture. The activities required of the reader of this poem are indeed demanding for long stretches of the pilgrimage, but there are occasional oases, as the persistence in this poem of "oft" and the non-directive "some" (or "sometimes") suggests.[20] Toward the end of the poem, indeed, the dominant manner of "Il Penseroso" seems to disappear altogether, as though it had been exchanged for that of its companion:

> There in close covert by some Brook,
> Where no profaner eye may look,
> Hide me from Day's garish eye,
> While the Bee with Honied thigh,
> That at her flow'ry work doth sing,
> And the Waters murmuring
> With such consort as they keep,
> Entice the dewy-feather'd Sleep;
> And let some strange mysterious dream
> Wave at his Wings in Airy stream,
> Of lively portraiture display'd,
> Softly on my eyelids laid.
> And as I wake, sweet music breathe
> Above, about, or underneath,
> Sent by some spirit to mortals good,
> Or th'unseen Genius of the Wood.
> But let my due feet never fail
> To walk the studious Cloister's pale,
> And love the high embowed Roof,
> With antic Pillars massy proof,
> And storied Windows richly dight,
> Casting a dim religious light,
> There let the pealing Organ blow
> To the full voic'd Choir below,
> In Service high and Anthems clear,
> As may with sweetness, through mine ear,
> Dissolve me into ecstasies,
> And bring all Heav'n before mine eyes.   [ll. 139–66]

We are as close as we ever get in "Il Penseroso" to the mere physical detail of "L'Allegro," perhaps altered (as Fish suggests) by the overlay of a supernatural "field of reference." Even here, however, it is difficult to read the word "There" (ll. 139, 161) as pointing to anything but a dislocation of the reader's experience from the speaker's desiderata. Furthermore, there are some vaguely anomalous features in Milton's final vision of things spiritual, some of them having to do, once again, with music. In view of the poem's abundance of scruple, is it really superfluous to decide whether the musician is "some spirit to mortals good, / Or th'unseen Genius of the Wood" (ll. 153–54)? (It is certainly critical that we see such a figure in the *Masque at Ludlow Castle*.)

Even if we have forgotten that "Stygian cave" of "L'Allegro," how can Milton's speaker be so casual about distinctions which have come to matter to us on the question of whether that music comes from "Above, about or underneath"? All comment, all criticism seems to have evaporated. The request for dewy-feathered sleep, in particular, for that "strange mysterious dream" (ll. 146–47) brings the poem uncomfortably close to the companion poem's rash plea for unconsciousness and the emphatically passive experience of cosmic amusement; the speaker at this point seems all too similar to that belated peasant (near the end of Book 1 in *Paradise Lost*) whose ear is charmed to the point that he cannot tell whether he sees or dreams.[21] The conjunctive "And as I wake," moreover, extends this projected passivity into waking life without substantially altering it. We would not feel the abruptness of this poem's conclusion, I think ("*But let my due feet . . .*"), did we not suspect that Milton's Penseroso was somehow letting go in the preceding lines. In any case, "Il Penseroso" ends not within the realm of Neoplatonic mysteries but with the wish that its speaker "never fail / To walk the studious Cloister's pale" (ll. 155–56). And we may suppose that this "never" matters for the acquisition of true insight. Like "There" in line 161, it points to the necessary conditions for what it mentions but scrupulously cannot enact: the dissolution "into ecstasies," the ability to "rightly spell," and of course that "Prophetic strain." These final lines, in fact, propose something rather different from the preceding—chiefly in the inclusiveness and conscious choice involved in the perception of its details. As we have seen, ecstasy of this sort is both postponed and otherwise distanced. (It would happen "there.") Unlike the dream—or, say, the kind of fascination exercised upon the Lady by Comus—it would be grounded in sense perception (within a visible and audible cloister/church) and perceived through the ear (the Lady's "best guide" in the Masque-world) and thence to "mine eyes." What Il Penseroso wants, for the present, is something like the "sober certainty of waking bliss," which Comus himself distinguishes from his mother Circe's music and hears in the Lady's song (*Masque*, l. 263). Once again, Milton has committed himself to a medium which does not and cannot point very directly to our experience as readers.

And may at last my weary age
Find out the peaceful hermitage,

The Hairy Gown and Mossy Cell,
Where I may sit and rightly spell
Of every Star that Heav'n doth shew,
And every Herb that sips the dew;
Till old experience do attain
To something like Prophetic strain.
These pleasures *Melancholy* give,
And I with thee will choose to live.   [ll. 167–76]

The concluding verses remind us once again that one of the poem's important "cares" is the abundance of inappropriate instruments of ecstasy, styles other than "due." If the right kind of melancholy could be summoned, there would have to be signs. Like his joyful counterpart, the speaker of "Il Penseroso" seems acutely aware of his mode and his prosodic vehicle above all; the chances are that Melancholy's arrival would change his behavior. In some apprehension, then, the poet would legislate the manner of that arrival: demure, decent shoulders decently covered; "Come, but keep thy wonted state, / With ev'n step, and musing gait" (ll. 37–38). In both poems, the most strenuous wooing involves us in a recognizable departure from this "ev'n step," as the claims of sense displace the intrinsic fascinations of its couplet form. (Milton had thought of "bondage" in connection with rhyme long before he wrote the note on the verse of *Paradise Lost*.) Far from possessing the ideals he would summon, the speaker of "Il Penseroso" concludes in the midst of things, where he began—another difference from this poem's companion. The poem ends by looking ahead to an insight located in an indefinite future—or rather at an end point ("at last"). Its insight would be a function of "weary age" and the product (one might suppose) of an education similar in kind to the one Milton proposed in the Seventh Prolusion (roughly contemporary with these poems and often linked with them): similar but more prolonged. The false arrival of "And may at last" is succeeded by "till old experience," and on it goes. Though described as something to be achieved only within the precincts of that hermitage beyond the more visible Church (or "studious Cloister"), the crown of this projected curriculum would be a style which veils its insight—or at least "something *like* Prophetic strain" (my italics). Clearly enough, as the commentary implicit in "my due feet" suggests, such a strain cannot enact our experience; what the poem gives can serve only as preliminary to what it mentions. This is the Jonsonian Milton, by and large; wary of those who would "take the prison'd soul, / And lap it in *Elysium*" (*Masque*, ll. 256–57). The prophetic strain is made no more available to us in "Il Penseroso" than the permanent effects of mirth are to the reader who negotiates the entirety of "L'Allegro."

For the reader of "L'Allegro," then, the request for *"Lydian* Airs" is important for the way the young (but hardly pre-Puritan) Milton entangles us in the pursuit of an elusive sense just at the moment his speaker attempts to prolong the experience of presence. Unlike the frequent appearances of mirth in the first poem's wonderfully varied landscape, harmony has become in his very next sentence a hidden and imprisoned essence, a mystery in the heart of a labyrinth. Milton means to stress the inability of mirth to perform forever—or in the "higher mood" of an Orphic rescue. And as I have tried to show, the situation is in some measure typical of Milton's fictional scenes, early and late. The extension of L'Allegro's request, the wish for mirth or Philomela to overextend herself—Is not the speaker here attempting forcibly to break the chains of harmony in a fashion similar to the "ventrous" but forgetful brothers' assault on Comus? There is something of a later swain's "uncouthness" in these lines. As we shall see, they provide a fascinating anticipation of the way in which Milton reported his own personal quest (as described in that crucial last letter to Diodati) for "this idea of the beautiful, as if for some glorious image, throughout all the shapes and forms of things."[22] In the way they also render the unlikelihood, in this "later age," of the Orphean quest for a plenary redemption, the lines also mark the boundaries of dispensations as well as musical moods and prepare for the stringencies of Sonnet 23, "Methought I saw my late espoused Saint," in which Milton stages a conspicuously labored attempt to remember just how his vision "came vested," and in doing so makes the speaker himself an energetic but patently limited counterpart to *"Jove's* great Son."

IV

Even more clearly than "Lycidas" and the twin poems, the *Masque at Ludlow Castle* testifies to the new potential Milton had discovered in the "air," a kind he associated with "sad *Electra's* Poet" and also (in its more conventional sense) with mere literary frivolity. The reader of the 1645 volume is warned of the possibility that "trivial Airs may please thee better"; the pages which follow are not merely "pleasing" but solid and substantial. The whole matter of this book involves the fitness of its audience: the question of "how harmonious thy soul is" (Sig. a4). But it seems evident that this had become a central theme in 1637–38, not only in *Justa Edouardo King* but in the published (or "national") version of Milton's *Masque*. And nothing in the masque clarifies the contents of that question better than the two Bridgewater brothers, seekers of their missing sister and would-be singers. Cedric Brown has recently reminded us that, like "the Lady," the brothers are fallible, perhaps the chief contributors to a moral realism that is potentially subversive of the very form in which Milton composed his entertainment. Certainly, the brothers are also responsive to the world in which they move. In a manner very different from the kind of simple allegory that might permit the identification of the Lady with a fixed value like "Mind," they seem to develop in consciousness and wisdom as they discover, then perform their parts—evidently including music, if they joined in singing the collective adjuration of Sabrina. And the Younger Brother in particular plays an active part in assisting Lord Brackley to discover the fullest import of their situation, including the very real need, in a world like the *Masque*'s, for "some good angel" (658). In keeping with the conventional significance of the Younger Brother as an adventurous but relatively unprivileged believer, Milton appears to activate the subordinate members of the work's various hierarchies in a way that anticipates Raphael's lecture on the activeness of the various spheres and kinds that make up the divinely ordained continuum of body and spirit.[23]

It has been suggested recently that the way in which the Younger Brother engages with Lord Brackley's initial assessment of the family predicament (at 343) involves an attempt to provide a complete family theory of some complexity (Brown, chap. 4, esp. pp. 79, 95). He seems to continue the Elder Brother's petition (addressed to the "faint stars" and "thou fair moon"), as though to provide the rest of the collective Bridgewater position on this matter. But generic expectations make it easy to miss the extent to which this position evolves within Milton's work and derives from a fruitful controversy of sorts. The Younger Brother fills in the literal level of their predicament. He anticipates (even if he does not quite understand) the Lady's mysterious frozenness in the customary chair. This should be seen as contributive to the masque's final vision, a step toward seeing the present occasion as contemplative in a sense neither brother understands as yet. Like the Elder Brother, he projectively defines the dilemma, helps to invent the masque's cast of characters, including the Elder Brother's reference to anyone who "hides a dark soul and foul thoughts" (383). (Both brothers have an engaging way of standing by what they have said. It is as though their courage is projected in the very way they have learned these lines.)

One could say, indeed, that the Elder Brother's second formulation on the powers of true virtue (454ff.) acknowledges and builds upon the Younger Brother's original contribution.

> Gods and men
> Fear'd [Diana's] stern frown, and she was queen o'th' Woods.
> What was that snaky-headed *Gorgon* shield
> That wise Minerva wore, unconquer'd Virgin,
> Wherewith she freez'd her foes to congeal'd stone,
> But rigid looks of Chaste austerity
> And noble grace that dash't brute violence
> With sudden adoration and blank awe?
> So dear to Heav'n is Saintly chastity,
> That when a soul is found sincerely so,
> A thousand liveried Angels lackey her,
> Driving far off each thing of sin and guilt,
> And in clear dream and solemn vision
> Tell her of things that no gross ear can hear,
> Till oft converse with heav'nly habitants
> Begin to cast a beam on th' outward shape,
> The unpolluted temple of the mind,
> And turns it by degrees to the soul's essence,
> Till all be made immortal. [445–63]

Here again, the Elder Brother makes appealing mistakes in the enthusiasm of moral exposition. It is the Lady, of course, who suffers something like the effects of that Gorgon shield she is supposed to carry in the form of her "virtue." But his "thousand Angels lackey her . . . And [speak] in clear dream and solemn vision" is recognizably an amplification of the Younger Brother's amusing "dragon watch with unenchanted eye" (6, 396). It is the developing conversation—not alone the brothers' complementary natures as the Elder Brother suggests somewhat misleadingly at 411—that moves us ever closer to the known outcome and (more immediately) to the exchange with Lawes-as-daemon-as-Thyrsis.[24]

The fact that the brothers are model listeners who become performers within the confines of the masque eventually involves them in the Lady's party; it brings them up to (and perhaps past) her level of accomplishment, just as the reader is invited to do in epilogue to the 1637, published version of the entertainment. The brothers' improvement during the masque involves putting together between them a view that in effect reconstitutes wisdom, including the reenactment of the Attendant Spirit's own invited appearance. The final instructions (a most inadequate word for this exchange) centralize in the masque design the extrafictional relation of Henry Lawes and his two younger charges in the Bridgewater family. Here again we are presented with a considerable adjustment of the hierarchy we might expect in court masques. For these true aristocrats, at least, there appears to be a kind of evolutionary breakthrough involved in the masque; Milton orchestrates the virtual amalgamation of his human group with the demonic or spiritual level, as though the family or ideological nutriment had changed the kind. The transformation is the effect of the continuity finally revealed (in the Epilogue) between the Attendant Spirit's destination and the world of the Bridgewaters as revised by the action of the masque and, in 1637, those readers whose "ears be true" (997). Still, the hierarchy we expect to discover in the world of Stuart masques is not entirely neglected. If the family structure seems dynamic, incorporating a kind of upward mobility to be observed especially among its subordinate members, this special group is also set off against ordinary mortals, including both the unlettered "hinds" and the courts of princes where courtesy is now "pretended" (325–26).

With this in mind we may turn to the hypothetical question of what would be accomplished if the brothers shared with the Attendant Spirit in the invocation to Sabrina.[25] Like other details, it would show the Bridgewater children themselves seeming to mature and specifically displaying the effects of Henry Lawes' tutelage; within the masque's fictional coordinates, this culmination to the boys' musical training—a figure for their training in virtuous aspiration—would be projected as an inventive response to Thyrsis's challenging questions and fabrications. In joining a collective adjuration, the brothers would complete a progressive action that begins with scrupulous and imaginative verbal exchange, ripens to a precariously conceived "divine philosophy" likely to issue in a falsely active kind of heroism (a little like what Uriel sharply calls Satan's "military obedience" in *PL* 4:955), and finally concludes in the aptly contemplative virtue of their accomplished sister's music, the performance of which finally carries them (at least as stylists) beyond the anxious couplet which qualifies the Lady's claim of freedom in mind and rind alike (663–64). In collaboration, at least, the brothers eventually improve in practical ways upon the results of the Lady's beautiful echo song.

If the published version of the *Masque* (1637) extends a call to the nation at large, the original performance too showed a widening sphere of influence for wisdom, the spread (or even the culmination) of virtue within the aristocratic family. And even discursively, there is an observable shift in the *form* of that wisdom. The youthful idealism of the Elder Brother is a "philosophy," eventually recognized as such. This is because his lore is increasingly codified and rhetoricized, something perhaps instinctively recognized in Comus's references to rigor and "grave saws," and perhaps also in the Younger Brother's amusing attempt to deny that they are "harsh and crabbed as dull fools suppose." (For all his protests of liberty, of course, Comus himself invokes "the canon laws of our foundation" and is eventually scourged specifically for his "dear wit and gay rhetoric.") This may help to explain the suspicion (common in readings of the *Masque*) that the Elder Brother may be safely viewed in isolation, that he functions as a simply conceived vehicle for Milton's own moral enthusiasm. If he seems anxious in the way he stands by what he has said and urges us all to lean on it safely, it is largely because this "happy trial" involves the kind of careful response provided by the Younger Brother. Lord Brackley's final speech, immediately before the reappearance of the Attendant Spirit, is made explicitly inauthentic in its charmingly naive assumption that the mere citation of "Antiquity from the old Schools of Greece" might induce agreement or belief. (The situation here recalls Nerissa's "good sentences well pronounced.") We shall encounter a somewhat different kind of scholarly candor in the Isocratic orator of the *Areopagitica*. It is important to recognize, though, that the punctuation to all this threatened testimony—all these scholarly marginalia—is first the Younger Brother's enrapt recognition of an argument beyond the textual surface, something inherently musical. He sets off the Elder Brother's extended exposition as musical entertainment, sees it (without quite understanding what he is doing) for what we know it is at a critical level of understanding. The response designates a threshold. We have reached an uncertain point when the Elder Brother's lore can either anticipate event (as in the Seventh Prolusions's description of the sage's powers) or "charm" us *in itself*. (This word, so common in appreciative discussions of the *Masque*, has its own dangers, to judge from Comus's memories of his mother's music as measured against the Lady's.) For a self-suspicious poet like Milton, even the divine philosophy could prove to be something like a "Lydian Air"—quite literally, an opiate of the Ludlow (or a national) elite. The Younger Brother focuses on the palate, and in this way on the readiness of an audience of which he is an exemplary member. The idea of that cloying "perpetual feast of nectar'd sweets" with the Younger Brother's own afterthought "where no crude surfeit reigns" (478–79) is aptly suggestive not only of the Elder Brother's final formulation on the eventual fate of "evil" (591–99) but also of Milton's educational theory of 1644, which was ever mindful of both musical discourse and the management of a "crudity." As we shall see, this theory was in itself a rather selective memory of the period, and even the year (1637) we are presently considering.

It is at this point, of course, that we have the entrance of the Attendant Spirit, recognized (with limited but this time sufficient accuracy) as "my father's" shepherd-musician Thyrsis. With this arrival we can mark the intersection of human with divine populations in the masque. And the encounter is identifiable as a continuation, not merely the kind of authoritative correction that would make the brothers obedient pawns, close relatives of that "Adam in the motions" which Milton was to mock two years after the closing of the theaters. It is the culmination of the brothers' own developing discussion of virtue. The Attendant Spirit's commendation "good vent'rous youth" compliments the brothers' joint recognition of an evil which will be separated from good ("Gather'd like scum") only eventually, "at last" (594). Doctrinally this is a step beyond the more magical views preceding this moment and also toward significant moral action: toward the active self-subordination of "*Thyrsis* lead on apace, I'll follow thee, / And some good Angel bear a shield before us" (657–58). In short, the brothers eventually join what they both perceive to be a "happy trial" (592); if evil cannot yet recoil upon itself in the fashion of those redounding flames of Hell, the masque does allow a rather unusual mixture of aristocratic mortal with divine natures, something like a hyberbolically presented realization of the Seventh Prolusion's ideals. And the joint summons would mark this intersection while centralizing the importance of musical art in the amalgamation of the divine level with this special, *melior natura*. What *Of Education* would call "poetry" (admittedly, in quite different public circumstances) is in the *Masque*'s world the literature missing from the rites and gestures of the "unlettered" country folk. As unorthodox as it would be generically, I believe that the brothers' collaboration in the invocation of Sabrina would fit with Milton's intention after all. Their well-supervised recital of those ancient analogues—original because apt, nothing like the marginalia of earlier suasive ventures—marks a fitting epitome of the aspiration "by due steps" mentioned by the Attendant at the outset as the essential condition for his own visit to the earthly pinfold. In the idiom of "L'Allegro," their performance expresses the "honor due" without which the masque's demon could not have appeared, preveniently, in the first place.[26]

V

The brothers' successful performance as singers is the dramatic effect of a magical plant which was pressed into multiple service between 1634 and 1637, both in "Lycidas" and indirectly, in what turned out to be Milton's final letter to Charles Diodati. The much-worried haemony of the masque was chosen from the Shepherd Lad's collection of simples. The bright golden flower mentioned by the Attendant Spirit is produced only "in another Country," not in the local soil where the dull swain, ignorant of the plant's nature and effects, treads on it daily (632–35). (Milton was to return to this matter of what could or could not be produced on English soil.) Initially in the Trinity MS of the *Masque*, this "small, unsightly root" is said to have been taken from among simples "of a thousand hews," but Milton replaced the variegated coloration with a multiplicity of names (a prominent feature in the brothers' shared adjuration of Sabrina). The original phrase of the Trinity MS, though, found its way into another "national" composition of that autumn in line 135 of "Lycidas," where "Bells and Flowrets of a thousand hues" is followed immediately by the call to "Ye valleys low" and then the famous floral catalogue, a passage once judged an excerptable Miltonic "beauty" and at least by one modern editor an "afterthought."[27] The final destination for the innocuous, almost formulaic, phrase is well worth considering, especially if (as Cedric Brown has recently argued) the masque's haemony figures the word of God (Brown, pp. 104–11).

The floral catalogue, of course, is a segment of the poem eventually designated as an indulgence in "false surmise," just as the entire poem is framed in retrospect as an expression of "eager thoughts." This pronouncement, which belongs with later wholesale dismissals of all things fabulous or fictive, looks back with considerable bitterness at a passage which began as a recovery from the Pilot's "dread voice" and its effects. If we remove Carey's "afterthought" from the poem, one result is that the bitter rejection of the swain's recovery (152–53) stands much closer to the phrase relocated from the manuscript version of the *Masque*. Only the call to the valleys intervenes, with its own disturbing mention of the "swart star." Thus viewed, the catalogue provides a more extended (and perhaps ultimately vitiated) indulgence in the "surmise" and more clearly *prepares* us for the judgment of falsity in such details as the lexical difficulty of a "white Pink," or the botanical improbabilities of a cowslip somehow able to hang its "pensive head" or a daffodil upright enough to fill its cup with tears. Though it is only a momentary effect, what gets blocked from our attention is the despairing association of the variegated flowrets themselves—the successors to the Shepherd Lad's valuable and efficacious "simples"—with self-satisfying fictions.

The effects of Milton's revisions here are more powerful if we recognize the "voice" of lines 113–31—and for that matter, the whole poem in Milton's later view—as an updated (and partly confirmed) version of the Old Testament prophecies heralding "the Day of the Lord." The voice that shrank the pastoral stream had called the corrupt shepherds "blind mouths," worse enemies to their charges than the wolf because of a mysterious connection between their "lean and flashy" songs and the sheep's diseased condition:

> The hungry Sheep look up, and are not fed,
> But swoln with wind, and the rank mist they draw,
> Rot inwardly, and foul contagion spread.   [125–27]

But in a real sense, this voice had preceded the formal arrival of "the Pilot of the *Galilean* Lake." Early on, the swain had mentioned the parching wind; the "heavy change" of the young shepherd's death had prompted the thought of "the Canker" and other enemies to youth of any species: frost, the taint-worm (37–49). And following the Pilot's speech too, there are clear reminders of the dread voice. Within the catalogue section, there are the dried streambeds, the effects of the "swart star," another mention of the tide ("whelming," corrected from "humming" in the Trinity MS)—all of these offset only by the mere promise of "fresh woods and pastures new" (193). And it is significant that the poem's core of vehemence is *prefaced* by the programmatic "Last came, and last did go" (108). In the concluding ottava rima, long after the Pilot's departure, the swain posits those "fresh Woods and Pastures new" despite an ambiguous leveling of "all the hills." When the prophet Joel warned of a renewed captivity for Judah and Jerusalem, he had specified earthquakes among other "wonders in the heavens and in the earth."

As Protestant readers commonly understood Joel's prophecy, details like this were to be directly associated with a ministry "cut off" from the traditional sacrificial offerings (1:5 and 1:9) and also with a potentially new venue and target for the divine word which Milton had figured as the haemony of the *Masque*. Joel laments the effects of the palmerworm, the locust, and the cankerworm; "the rivers of waters are dried up and the fire hath devoured the pastures of the wilderness." The drunkards of the land are urged to repent or "howl"; "the meat offering and the drink offering is cut off from the house of the Lord, the priests, the Lord's ministers mourn" (1:9; see also 1:13). In the heavens, "the sun and moon shall be dark, and the stars shall withdraw their shining" (2:10, repeated in 3:15). Joel asks for a trumpet in Zion, a fast and a solemn assembly, and he assures a general renewal to people and beasts alike: "Be not afraid, ye beasts of the field: for the pastures of the wilderness do spring, for the tree beareth her fruit, the vine and the fruit tree do yield their strength" (2:22). And he goes on to predict that "in that day [of the Lord], the mountains shall drop down new wine, and the hills shall flow with milk, and all the rivers of Judah shall flow with waters, and a fountain shall come forth of the house of the Lord" (3:18). Joel's prophecy is famous as the prediction of Pentecost, but a prominent feature of the text, especially for independent Reformers even of the early sixteenth century, was its focus on the call to the "remnant" and to the heathen. In particular the sectaries focused upon the characteristic Old Testament dislocation of familial and other hierarchies: the old men, Joel told them, would have dreams and the young see visions; it was the sons and daughters who would prophesy, the servants and handmaids who would receive the Lord's spirit (2:28). For spiritualists as early as Thomas Muntzer, Joel provided a justification for modern spiritualism of all sorts, a weapon to be used if necessary against the very founders of the movement:

> He will prepare it in the Last Days in order that his name may be rightly praised. He will free it of its shame, and will pour out his Holy Spirit over all flesh and our sons and daughters shall prophesy and shall have dreams and visions, etc. For if Christendom is not to become apostolic (Acts 2:16ff.), in the way anticipated in Joel, why should one preach at all? To what purpose then the Bible with [its] visions?[28]

Since the second phase in Milton's prose career involved a fundamental reconsideration of "fanatick dreamers" like the Anabaptists, Familists, and Antinomians, it is useful to consider briefly the details which "radical Puritanism" might have had in common with Milton's political and literary thought, the Protestant character of a humanism which produced the *Poems of Mr. John Milton* (1645) during the same period. It now seems clear that Milton was less embarrassed than some of his modern champions by the kind of humanism which was (and had long been) closely aligned with the sectarian and spiritualist Protestants who might initially seem hostile to "the classical tradition." Michael Fixler has argued in effect that these connections are accidental, and that Milton's lifelong "preference for a Christian humanistic aristocracy" in some ways resembling Calvin's theocratic experiment must be considered "distinct from and even opposed to [the radical sects'] political millenarianism" (pp. 134–35). But we cannot forget that the man who introduced Milton to the classics was after all a Protestant exile in Hamburg during the decade of the prolusions. Calvin himself had recognized at least the theoretical necessity of continued "prophesying" even by an uncredentialed ministry; and he offered an impressive explanation of the likely results of forbidding it: a "morose" antipathy to all doctrine from whatever source. The antagonists of the more established Reformers (like Milton's Presbyterian orthodoxy in the 1640s) habitually justified their actions by invoking Gospel-sanctioned Old Testament prophecies like Joel's, which so clearly sanctioned the dreams and visions of the young, the women, the servants and handmaids. Such texts had an obvious value to humanists like Thomas Young and Milton, or indeed anyone mindful of the principles of succession, whether familial, ministerial, or political. Muntzer's description of the Lord's "preparation" in the last days, including the banishment of Comus's dreaded shame and the generalized outpouring of the Holy Spirit, suggests the true reference for what the young Milton thought might flower with the completion or "perfection" of England's Reformation: not alone Milton's, but a rather generalized and even national "poetic" talent. And well before he undertook the business of pastorly rebuke to the prelates, the young poet was fond of dramatizing the "unanticipated" success of these aspirations, as well as glancing darkly at the well-known pressing needs; the would-be poet who in 1637 likened himself to Ceres, searching the barren earth for a daughter ravished from the vale of Enna, had complained in an earlier sonnet that his late spring showed no bud or blossom, even as the poem began to resound with an impressive bit of stanzaic closure.[29] Muntzer's question to the princes at Allstedt points to the central vocational problem of "Lycidas." As it happens, the monody's seemingly innocuous detail of "Bells and Flowrets" had originated as part of the swain's collection of "simples" in the masque at Ludlow. Deliberately excluded from the published (or "national") version of the masque, they reappear the next year in "Lycidas" instead, artfully arranged, strategically placed just before the poem's climactic discovery, and associated with the unexpected return of the pastoral mode itself. If Cedric Brown is right in associating the "unsightly" haemony with the divine Word, it seems likely that—placed where it is, after the "dread voice"—the request for the flowers' return to a landscape parched by the "swart star"—reflects the idiom of that other major document of 1637, the letter to Diodati. And the letter's allusion to a plural locus for "beauty" suggests the renewed aptness of a variegated and fragmented word in the light, not alone of humanism, but of a humanism sponsored by the millenarianism of the radical sects.[30]

As Northrop Frye has argued, such details constitute a norm or level of reference in the poem;[31] they present an enduring threat to the pastoral idiom similar to the way in which satiric "hoarseness"—or silence— threatens the epic intentions and theoretically comedic myth of *Paradise Lost*. From this point of view, the Pilot's voice involves a temporary incorporation, an attributed version, of what the poem will eventually call the swain's own "eager thought." (This is the kind of thing that happens implicitly, for example, in Triton's quite unquestionlike "Felon winds" and "each beaked Promontory" and the swain's distinctly *un*sage slip when speaking as Hippotades, at "that sacred head of thine" [91, 94, 102].) We can think of Frye's levels here as the "various quills" belonging to this poem's delicate instrument. The voice of the Pilot and the other participants in the obligatory procession is the prime reason Milton calls the reed's stops "tender"; one corresponding figure in *Paradise Lost* is the uneasy collaboration of the poet with his unruly, Pegasean steed of a poem (*PL* 7:17–18).

In light of this, it is fascinating that Milton's variegated bells and flowrets should replace the more clearly medicinal "simples" of the *Masque*. The fragility, indeed the "charm," of their beauty was reinforced by the addition of lines 142–50 and the rueful recognition of 152–53's "false surmise." More important, the passage presents an aptly skeptical version of Milton's own temper or inclination, so optimistically described in the privacy of his letter to Diodati the same year, a "vehement love of the beautiful." Thus prompted, and led on "by certain clear traces," he will pursue "this idea of the beautiful" in a world which presents a multiplicity of access or "shapes of things divine." Earlier, the sonnet commemorating his twenty-third birthday had suggestively qualified its own central complaint of belatedness. Now in 1638, he had transplanted and daringly modified an enigmatic plant, moving it to a publication containing at least the poet's initials. As it happens, the letter to Diodati is the destination of a closely related revision in the *Masque*, one even more crucial to the young Milton. In the Bridgewater and Trinity versions of the *Masque*, the Younger Brother had drawn a comparison of his sister, the lost "Lady," to Proserpina. A figure with clear affiliations to the "half-regain'd Eurydice" of

"L'Allegro," Proserpina was the object of Ceres' diligent search over a land made barren as a result of the girl's abduction from the fair field of Enna. The "ambitious" comparison, as Brown rightly calls it (p. 95), was deleted from the published *Masque* of 1637. In the final letter to Diodati it appears, with ambitions made almost explicit, in Milton's promise to search just as diligently as Ceres for "this idea of the beautiful."

Chapter Five

Monody Historified: The
Apology against a Pamphlet

And long it was not after, when I was confirm'd in this opinion,
that he who would not be frustrate of his hope to write well
hereafter in laudable things, ought him selfe to be a true Poem.
Apology against a Pamphlet

And by occasion foretells the ruin of our
corrupted Clergy then in their height.
Headnote to "Lycidas"

Of all the well-known "autobiographical" sources, the seldom-cited *Apology
against a Pamphlet* (April 1642) is an especially useful text for clarifying the
ways in which Milton's own autobiographical terminology has had the
unfortunate effect (only partly unintentional) of obscuring his career's most
interesting continuities. Together with the familiar letters of the 1630s, it
gives us reason to think that the texts which have encouraged conventional
Miltonic biography can too easily distort our understanding of Milton's
entry into the antiprelatical controversy, and of how he felt he had somehow led two separate professional lives, the works of his left and right
hand: the provinces, respectively, of politics and poetry. Of all the well-
known sources, the *Apology* seems most consistent with the primary materials upon which our biographical investigations must finally be based. In
the pages that follow I will argue that the *Apology* rather than the *Reason*
provides the true link between the familiar letters (and also the poetry of

the 1630s) on the one hand and Milton's subsequent work, *all* of it in his mind literary, at least through the prose of 1644. Like the letter to Diodati, the *Apology* reminds us that even if Milton sometimes assumed that (in the words of Michael Lieb) "the writing of tracts represented a lower order of endeavor than the writing of poetry," it was hardly a fixed principle; and for one brief but crucial—and poetically creative—period, he certainly saw things quite differently.[1]

As we have seen, Milton had presented himself in the *Reason* as a most reluctant *tuba domini*: someone of "green years" led by the genial power of nature to literature and to prose only by divine command, interrupted like the swain in his occupation of writing and study and speaking "out of mine own season" (*CPW* 1:806, 807). And Milton seems to have written his life in the *Second Defense* with clear memories of the *Reason*'s argumentative patterns, substituting only the humane letters for the Church as his parents' destiny for their gifted son. The anonymous Apologist strikes us as altogether a more impressive character than the John Milton of two months earlier. His manner and his retrospections point to a moral and vocational integrity that is never in question. He is here because a naturally "ardent" character underlies or anticipates both literature and the wars of truth.

We might say that a new idea of nature is at the heart of the difference. It has not been explicitly recognized, but the *Apology* records Milton's first public exploration of what became his philosophic materialism, that redemption of natural "matter" in which the *Areopagitica*'s great arguments from principle (however rhetorically deployed) find their common ground. At one point, in rather awkward fashion, the Apologist ventures into the theology of self-esteem, which he declares "cannot be asunder from the love of God itself"; in the process he offers psychological laws which the *Apology* presents as fulfilled in the evident morale, and perhaps even the discursive behavior, of its speaker:

> There is . . . a[n] . . . ingenuous and noble degree of honest shame, or call it if you will an esteem, whereby men bear an inward reverence toward their own persons. And if the love of God as a fire sent from Heaven to be ever kept alive upon the altar of our hearts, be the first principle of all godly and vertuous actions in men, this pious and just honouring of our selves is the second, and may be thought as the radical moisture and fountain head, whence every laudable and worthy enterprize issues forth. And although I have giv'n it the name of a liquid thing, yet it is not incontinent to bound it self, as humid things are, but hath in it a most restraining and powerful abstinence to start back, and glob it self upward from the mixture of any

ungenerous and unbeseeming motion, or any soile wherewith it may peril to stain it self. [*CPW* 1:842]

This may not be the kind of writing for which Milton continues to be read; but for all the wooden candor of its venture, consider the scrupulous disengagement of a natural principle from merely personal nomenclature; the passage acknowledges the possible inadequacies of the terms "I have given it" and calls attention to the argumentative intentions somehow intrinsic to his metaphoric materials, the ordinary natural properties of "liquid things."

Throughout the pamphlet, indeed, it is hardly an exaggeration to say that the Apologist is a celebrant of nature; if we remember the tone of that last letter to Diodati, the word has clearly recovered a good measure of the meanings it so conspicuously lacks in the *Reason*'s account of its author's predicament. A benevolent "nature" largely accounts for the pamphlet's impression of authorial expertise and even becomes the matrix of autobiography, allowing the Apologist to retrace what Milton elsewhere called the "smooth course of history" leading toward the present moment. In the following passage, Milton provides a background for the speaker's very presence in the form of a moment of decision:

> These reasonings [that he "who would . . . write . . . ought himselfe to bee a true Poem"], together with a certaine nicenesse of nature, and honest haughtinesse, and self-esteem either of what I was, or what I might be (which let envie call pride) and lastly that modesty, whereof though not in the Title page yet here I may be excus'd to make some beseeming profession, all these uniting the supply of their naturall aide together, kept me still above those low descents of minde, beneath which he must deject and plunge himself, that can agree to salable and unlawful prostitutions. [*CPW* 1:890]

In the context of the *Apology*'s passionately unified nature, we can guess at all Milton meant by suggesting that a paradise could be lost by breaking "union," or that Satan might have destroyed himself by *thinking* himself impaired. As close as we may well be to a kind of self-analysis here, the power of the *Apology* stems from what can only be called its sense of authority, the way in which autobiography of a sort is fused with grand assertions, ventured on the basis of an "undefiled" nature, about such matters as the divinely ordained pedagogy, in which no man is to be "forc't wholly to dissolve that groundwork of nature which God created in him, the sanguine to empty out all his sociable liveliness, the cholerick to expell quite the unsinning predominance of his anger; but that each radicall humour and passion wrought upon and corrected as it ought, might be made the proper mould and foundation of every mans peculiar gifts and vertues" (*CPW* 1:900). The insistence on natural innocence is everywhere apparent here, as in the writing of the next several years; what Sirluck took to be a seemingly irrelevant afterthought ("marriage must not be called a defilement") shares its idiom with the Miltonic canonist's conclusion, recalled in the preface to *Samson Agonistes*, that an "ethnic" presence in the divine Word had been justified by the learned Apostle himself: "Paul . . . thought it no defilement to insert into holy Scripture the sentences of three Greek Poets, and one of them [Euripides, as it happens] a Tragedian" (*CPW* 2:508). It is as though—in the narrow space of two months—Milton had come to experience those special circumstances in which "God and nature bid the same," as Abdiel tells us they do when "he who rules is worthiest" (6:176–77).

According to the *Reason*, as we have seen, Milton had entered the antiprelatical disputes under quite different circumstances. Requiring a method for obeying the divine command to "blow the trumpet," he had found a precedent for his own vehement expressions in the "method that God uses." To justify his vehement manner, he appeals to "the Spirit of God, who is purity it selfe, [and] abstains not from some words not civill at other times to be spok'n" (*CPW* 1:901–02). Milton's style is viewed clearly as a strategy, chosen (as in the *Animadversions*) to implement Christ's "rule and example" (*CPW* 1:662). Our reexamination of *An Apology* allows us to see this appeal as something of an anomaly. For as we have seen, Milton had invoked something like the *Apology*'s language (of "liquid things") in 1637 when speaking to Diodati of his vocational condition. Employing the very metaphor Hobbes was to find so alarming, Milton had written, "He has instilled into me, if into anyone a vehement love of the beautiful" (*CPW* 1:326). The Apologist now reverts to that earlier Miltonic idiom, with the important difference that the divine pedagogy, even a rudimentary but daring theology, is his explicit context. The Apologist finds his model in Martin Luther, that comparatively recent Christian teacher whose example "may stand for all."[2] But Milton is remembering a specific situation: Luther before Charles at Worms in 1521. He faithfully records Luther's striking claim that he had attacked Rome "not of revelation, but of judgment," a motive that sounds like Milton's own reference (in the *Reason*) to a chosen, strategically selected style, orchestrated in deference to a divine command. But the rest of the passage makes it clear that Milton is primarily concerned to deny or displace the *Reason*'s kind of argument. For the ground of Luther's style, as in the last letter to Diodati, is something like a naturally "instilled" vehemence, an ardent nature also possessed by the Apologist and governing his speech for some time now. The *Apology* leaves it to Luther himself to clarify the motivational differences from the *Reason*'s account of its latter-day reformer. The model reformer defends his polemical eagerness on the grounds that he was "of an ardent spirit, and one who *could* not write a dull stile" (my emphasis); and the Apologist is sufficiently impressed with Luther's "ardent spirit" to "looke to mine own." In keeping with his nature, the Apologist admits that he has not examined Luther's writings with sufficient thoroughness to "know how farre he gave way to his owne fervent minde" [*CPW* 1:901] —this is no mere scholar. But he does not mind elaborating on Luther's distinction (that he had attacked Rome "not of revelation"), specifically rejecting the view that direct inspiration is the only warrant for reforming zeal, and venturing to deny even that the prophets or Christ himself "had immediate warrants from God."

Indeed, the Apologist's new manner and personality—the whole feel of this climactic entry in the antiprelatical struggle—depend upon something more far-reaching than Christ's presumed method or an obscure appeal to scriptural "reasons that imply themselves." Milton's new terminology and the way it virtually repudiates the appeals of the *Reason* seem especially striking and pervasive in the *Apology*'s ventures into divine history and a kind of prototheological speculation. Even Christ becomes a relatively secularized figure, a sort of literary virtuoso uniquely situated: "With all gifts in him," Milton writes, Jesus could "expresse his indoctrinating power in what sort him best seem'd. Sometimes by a milde and familiar converse, sometimes with plaine and impartiall home-speaking regardlesse of those whom the auditors might think he should have had in more respect; otherwhiles with bitter and irefull rebukes if not teaching yet leaving excuseless those his wilfull impugners" (*CPW* 1:899–900).[3] In the context of the *Apology*, indeed (the specifically religious propriety of the vehement style in controversy), Milton's emphasis may seem surprisingly pragmatic; he reports that Luther "thought it Gods will to have the inventions of men thus laid open, seeing that matters quietly handled, were quickly forgot" (*CPW* 1:901). And Milton concludes that this is "as any other virtue, of moral and general observation" (901). Indeed, the Apologist's portrait of Christ and his unique times might well be considered a self-consciously adventurous consolidation of the inchoate theology Milton had implied in the letter to Diodati; in similar fashion, it returns to the Second Prolusion's description of Pythagoras and adapts it to a much more specific sense of the times. We are dealing, after all, with the very different, more specialized state of affairs obtaining in any period subsequent to the life and ministry of Christ; it is a time when men necessarily encounter teachers whose more limited stylistic talents express only collectively "what was all in him." By the same token, there are different ages to be considered: "times of opposition," to take the example of the Apologist's own day, when the traits and talents of an earlier period no longer work, when "this coole unpassionate mildness of positive wisdom is not enough to damp and astonish the proud resistance of carnall, and false Doctors." It is in times like these—and I shall return to Milton's evident suspicion that they may well recur—that Zeal "ascends his fiery Chariot," and indeed actually "drives over the heads of Scarlet Prelates, and such as are insolent to maintain traditions" (*CPW* 1:900). Can there be any doubt that now is such a time?

We have postponed the discussion of a critical feature in Milton's argument, the vigorous denial that he has indulged in the rankest kind of hindsight, the risky argument from "divine testimony." The artifice of separating these issues is the price we pay for noticing the seductive power of Milton's appeals to a most innocent nature, as in that seeming afterthought that the Apologist had freely consulted with himself "by every instinct and presage of nature, which is not wont to be false." Buried though it is syntactically, this ringing affirmation points to an authorial motive and a metaphoric ground of explanation that is virtually new in the Miltonic canon of this antiprelatical period. Its rather sudden appearance in the canon hints at its value for the developing author as well. In light of nature's quarrel with divine command in the *Reason*, we may be right to think of this moment as a major development in the body of Milton's thought,[4] perhaps a prime source for his later thoughts on the "one talent which is death to hide." But the *matrix* of Milton's affirmation is the Apologist's insistence that he had entered the pamphlet wars freely, having "thought with myself" prior to the events in public life which have lately confirmed his prejudices. And this insistence indeed goes far to explain two central points of Milton's literary theory in the *Apology*: the requirement, first, that the would-be author himself be a "true Poem, that is, a composition and patterne of the best and honourablest things"; and even more striking, the thought that the complete or "perfect" speaker is someone whose intentions flow almost immediately into external events: "His words (by what I can express) like so many nimble and airy servitors trip about him at command, and in well-order'd files, as he would wish, fall aptly into their own places" (*CPW* 1:949).[5] The casual reader of the *Apology* may well get the impression that everything has combined to produce the speaker's morale and the general ambience of the moment; the speech embodies the marriage of "reasonings," instincts, a certain kind of nature, and some opinions. Best of all, though, it involves the external confirmation of one of those opinions in the realm of "events"—just the sort of happening (in the *Areopagitica*'s terms) that might turn knowledge "in the making" into the thing itself. It is in these circumstances that we first encounter the prophetic vocabulary which Milton remembered generically as "insight" in *Of Education* and which he particularized once again at such important junctures in *Samson Agonistes.*

In Milton's soaring, self-consciously "poetical" references to the times when Zeal "ascends his fiery Chariot," Milton's contemporaries cannot have failed to see allusions of the most immediate and topical kind to such sensational developments as the Bishop's Exclusion Bill, the imprisonment of Archbishop Laud, the fate of Strafford, and (most recently) the "miraculous and lossless" suppression of the Irish rebellion. Here and elsewhere in the *Apology*, Milton comes close to invoking that indispensable prop to hindsight, the argument which the logic handbooks called "divine testimony"[6]—something seemingly independent of the merely personal or private observer and a collective possession to be assessed (in the words of the *Areopagitica*) by "the general instinct of holy and devout men." As the Seventh Prolusion helps us to see, however, the immediate, local one-upmanship of the pamphlet wars has been disguised in the *Apology* as an essential part of wisdom; far from viewing such events as contributing to a momentary advantage in an ongoing struggle, the Apologist can just point to historical facts and their self-evident "reasons." More specifically, the events have become the heroic acts, and not just the perceptions of a collective group, the Parliament, not just a more or less isolated sage. The "fatal block" itself—the most inconvenient of Milton's allusions—is made implicit in what Milton calls "the force of so much united excellence [met] in one globe of brightnesse and efficacy" (*CPW* 1:924). And the sudden victory in Ireland is urged as proof that the purely military tactics of ordinary deliverers have been superseded; Parliament has expelled the oppressors of the "inward persuasion" *without* mere force, "while two armies in the field stood gazing on" (*CPW* 1:925).[7] What has destroyed this latest "shape" of tyranny, in fact, is the new, generalized form of "majesty": an almost magical combination of wisdom and power, something very like the 1633 letter's scholarly, obscure "weaponed creature in the word":

> With such a majesty had their wisdome begirt it selfe, that whereas others had levied warre to subdue a nation that sought for peace, they sitting here in peace could so many miles extend the force of their single words as to overawe the dissolute stoutnesse of an armed power secretly stirr'd up and almost hir'd against them. [*CPW* 1:925–26]

In Milton's account the very audience of the present tract have become the authors, or at least the immediate agency, of the accomplishments it celebrates. Having triumphed over the "teachers," like David and the young Jesus, the Lords and Commons of the *Apology* have become at once the spiritual and rhetorical heirs of Luther and kindred spirits of the chronicler himself, possessed of that special kind of authority whose virtue, Milton writes, "should be neither obscure in the opinions of men, nor eclipst for want of matter equall to illustrat itself" (*CPW* 1:924). And the circumstance, so oddly conveyed in Milton's reflexive verb, is significantly unclear as to our own historical orientation as readers; it seems that we are dealing with the sort of thing (and with the kind of speech) that occurs in *any* "times of opposition," and such times come and go—up to a point.

"Despite the hyperbolical haze," Michael Fixler has suggested, "[Milton's] panegyric of Parliament presents us with probably the sharpest picture of his aristocratic ideal as he imagined it in practice" (p. 135). Apart from its function as a latter-day chronicle, the prose of the *Apology* often specifically realizes the effects which Milton and his colleagues had so frequently anticipated during the antiprelatical controversy, as in the following well-known passage from the conclusion to *Of Reformation*:

> Then amidst the Hymns and Halleluiahs of Saints some one may perhaps bee heard offering at high strains in new and lofty Measures to sing and celebrate thy divine Mercies, and marvelous Judgements in this Land throughout all Ages. [*CPW* 1:616; italics deleted]

As every reader of the biographies knows, Milton was believed to have promised his national (or a Christian, or a Protestant) epic almost from the moment he wrote such passages; thus did he become, in the minds of some enthusiasts, the most single-minded of all English literary careerists. The *Apology* allows us to make better sense of these arguments, including as it does the cultural theorist's insistence, for example, that the extended portrait of the Long Parliament (Milton's first of several) is a perfectly decorous encomium designed to embarrass his antagonist Joseph Hall (here become a sort of literary Witwoud). The occasional sublimity of his Apologist, however, is something very like the the angel chorus of *Paradise Lost* 3, or the "unanimous" raptures of Eden—in prose or numerous verse, we may recall—and appropriated into the latter-day, fallen world. The breathless recommendations of spontaneous prayer are here partly to advertise the performance of a speaker whose thoughts, like those of the great epic's bard, could almost "voluntary move / Harmonious numbers" (3:37–38). But unlike some of his readers, Milton was well aware that there were potential uses for such strategies of "disorientation," however they may be reassessed later—even, in some cases, by the author himself. In a phrase like "this cool unpassionate mildness of positive wisdom" (the kind that's "not enough" when one is dealing with "carnal, and false Doctors") we have virtually arrived at the converse of *Of Education*'s famous definition of poetry as "simple, sensuous, and passionate." If the Apologist's assurance also looks backward to the formulations of academic *ludi*, it can do so only by revising them into the general territory of "divine history." Milton's new-found ability to justify the vehement method in controversy "with more success" thus involves the transformation of a bit of recent news into the probable aftermath of wisdom in verbal action, a chronicle of deeds which speak loud the divine doer. In Milton's mind, that is to say, the Apologist's assurance is premised not so much on hindsight as on the more general credentials of the "author" in the fullest sense of that unstable word.

For in fact, there had been a long-term preparation for this critical moment; or, to put it more accurately, the present situation confirms or "historifies" a scene imagined with playful enthusiasm almost a decade earlier. In the Seventh Prolusion, Milton had described the learned man as someone who through contemplation could virtually experience an "eternal life"; to his public, as it were, this mere observer will appear to be an actual author: "Truly he will seem to have the stars under his control and dominion, land and sea at his command, and the winds and storms submissive to his will. Mother Nature herself has surrendered to him. It is as if some god had abdicated the government of the world and committed its justice, laws, and administration to him as ruler" (Hughes 625). The student of history as well as of the timeless laws, Milton's sage would live "in all the epochs of history . . . and . . . be a contemporary of time itself . . . [he will] extort from Fate a kind of preliminary immortality." He would be an "oracle to many peoples," one whose home is a very shrine or *templum* chiefly, it seems, because almost nothing can happen "without warning or by accident" to a man securely possessed of what Milton calls "the stronghold of wisdom." Essential to the oracle's experience as an observer of the world, then—and responsible for his reputation as a virtual manipulator of event—is the lack of any surprise in what is called (mistakenly, of course) "accident." For such a person, it would be a damaging admission to suggest (as Dalila does in *Samson Agonistes*) that a given action "more evil drew / In the perverse event than I foresaw" (736–37); a "perverse event," indeed, is a contradiction in terms. In this view of things, the vulgar notion of hindsight becomes part and parcel of what Michael Fixler has called "triumphant wisdom," the history of what Milton would eventually style "insight."[8]

If the *Apology against a Pamphlet* announces and performs a new literature of the Church, we may speculate that it can do so largely on the strength of Milton's having discovered a precedent in the more recent past. In the 1645 headnote to "Lycidas," we may recall that Milton was to speak with some generic precision of a monody and of two distinct kinds of literary "occasions": the death of the learned friend and (more interestingly) the act of composition itself. By this second occasion, Milton writes, the author "foretells the ruin of our corrupted Clergy, then in their height." With the *Apology* in mind, we can more readily see that Milton's headnote identifies the success of a certain kind of poet, the sage to whom nothing comes as a surprise, whose high words so perfectly coincide with the "height" of the victim's present fortunes. But there is a less speculative connection between the *Apology* and the great elegy. In the poem itself, we may recall, the speaker is discovered to be at once an uncouth swain *and* a poet rather suddenly (and after the fact) in the poem's final eight lines. At "He touch't the tender stops of various Quills" (188), we are offered a generic accounting for that confusing mix of voices that, to this point, has been the poem; only here does Milton offer a definitive and, what is more striking, a *single* attribution. Evidently this author in "uncouth" dress is capable of controlling "various Quills," if indeed he cannot manage the entire range of literary effects—the reason, perhaps, for the "Mantle blue" awarded him in the penultimate line of the poem. This account of the poem's conclusion ought to strike any unbiased reader of the poem itself as forced; the point is that it is the *kind* of reading to which the *Apology* points. If Milton keenly felt the loss of that hapless youth and the unripe talents of his surrogate the swain in the act of composing the poem and remembered them when writing "out of mine own season" in the *Reason of Church Government*, the Apologist clarifies—or perhaps he belatedly invents—its triumphant other dimension: the fragility of its tender stops and the profound accomplishment of its "various Quills." As we have seen, the poem's final eight lines themselves are a clarifying memory of these things; but the *Apology* recollects them once more with the sharpened, explicitly Christological focus of individual talents that somehow constitute "what was all in him." And the Apologist's bit of doctrine is rooted in the thoughts Milton chose to preserve in the prolusions and the familiar letters of the 1630s, notions he would again display parabolically ("as the poets use") in the *Areopagitica*'s fable of Isis and Osiris. Among many other things, the personal, historical, and literary revisionism of the *Apology* is the 1645 headnote to "Lycidas" writ large, a sort of poetics-after-the-fact for what has turned out to be (in its author's eyes) his first "true Poem."

Certainly, Milton practices a similar kind of critical reading within the *Apology* itself, finding in the Apologist's own recent work a signal case of temporary but nonetheless radical generic indeterminacy involving a central genre and rhetorical situation in the last days. One of Milton's most interesting defenses of the unpremeditated style is prompted by Joseph Hall's complaint about questionable decorum in what he took to be a prayer in the *Animadversions*. Defending this bit of vehemence, Milton insists that the passage in question was not a prayer after all, but "a hymne in prose frequent both in the Prophets, and in humane authors; therefore the stile was greater than for an ordinary prayer" (*CPW* 1:930). Milton may have been actually embarrassed here; but there are suggestions elsewhere in the *Apology* that he supposed Hall's error (of mistaking a collective "hymn of the faithful" for a common prayer) to be symptomatic; it is a time, he may have thought, when the exquisite fit of poet, subject, times, and audience can all too easily be transformed into a "false Doctor's" kind of misconstruction. The *Apology* is full of expressions which seem to presuppose a sense of radical historical fulfillment. Our richest source for the theoretic formulations of Milton the artist is also an enactment, its central character manifestly gifted with those all-important "free and unimposed expressions" (*CPW* 1:941). But the very assurance of the Apologist—the entire context of Miltonic theory—can easily be misunderstood. Like "Lycidas," the *Apology* is a curiously discontinuous document embodying the inconsistencies and tensions that would inform all of Milton's subsequent work. It includes momentary oases of "vehemence" or (as he would call them in *Areopagitica*) "sentence[s] of a ventrous edge," but it is hardly limited to such sublimity (*CPW* 2:534). The grand style we find here and there in the oration may be considered not so much a program for the speaker's authority as an occasional epiphany, in the manner of Il Penseroso's sudden encounter with the cherub Contemplation. In the idiom of the *Areopagitica*, we have witnessed the carefully staged intermittent expression of "Truth's own method," necessarily working in a fruitful tension, like Patience, the muse or prevenient Grace itself, with the more mundane "pace and method of [ordinary] discourse."[9] There is every sign that the *Apology* was constructed as one more proof that we live in a special time. But it seems equally clear that the millenarianism which affects Milton's writing during the antiprelatical period has been somewhat qualified here, perhaps in a manner appropriate to that uncertain period prior to the period of millennial fulfillment. What, then, is the relation of the present tract to that moment when (in Chrysostom's words) "we all meet together into the unity of faith, and knowledge of the Son of God, unto a perfect man"?

In the *Apology*, Milton is at some pains to suggest that his speaker is by no means restricted to the stylistic expression of his own ardent nature; in a time of "perfection," a given speaker's personal tendency is not to be identified with the entire literary program or the contingencies of the composition in question. More often than not, indeed, the ardent reformer speaks in urbane or witty fashion, occasionally offering learned generalities about literature, ecclesiastical history, and even theology. In view of the specifically religious grounds of the pamphlet's argument (this is another illusory limitation to be countered by well-staged cosmopolitanism), we should be impressed with the grace and good humor he shows, for example, in treating topics like the variety of character types or the history of God's pedagogical ways with men. Altogether, the Apologist seems the almost fully developed progenitor of the *Areopagitica*'s orator. There is a distinct sense of *rebellious* modulation when the expert in literary and historical laws suddenly reverts to the ancient "manifold" method Milton had pondered in the 1630s, or begins to "soar awhile as the poets use":

> In times of opposition when either against new heresies arising, or old corruptions to be reform'd this coole unpassionate mildness of positive wisdom is not enough to damp and astonish the proud resistance of carnall, and false Doctors, then (that I may have leave to soare a while as the Poets use) then Zeale whose substance is ethereal, arming in compleat diamond ascends his fiery Chariot drawn with two blazing Meteors figur'd like beasts, but of a higher breed then any the Zodiac yeilds, resembling two of those

four which *Ezechiel* and S. *John* saw, the one visag'd like a Lion to expresse power, high authority and indignation, the other of count'nance like a man to cast derision and scorne upon perverse and fraudulent seducers; with these the invincible warriour Zeale shaking loosely the slack reins drives over the heads of Scarlet Prelats, and such as are insolent to maintain traditions, brusing their stiffe necks under his flaming wheels. [*CPW* 1:900]

Even as he speaks so coolly of the styles appropriate to the various kinds of age, the Apologist is caught up in an ecstasy or "holy rapture," and we seem to move out of history altogether; the ardent virtuoso seems prompted by the sage's mastery of "event." Looking at this prose with our much-diminished notions of literature, we have become accustomed to refer such passages to the norms, presumably more congenial, of Milton's verse, and with good reason. Like the "unexpressive nuptial song" of "Lycidas" or those glances ahead in *Paradise Lost* to "ages of endless date," a passage like this accomplishes that "baroque" conflation of future with present which Lowry Nelson has noticed in the final section of the Nativity ode.[10] We seem to move out of time altogether into that perfect place described in the *Reason*, where the "paths of honesty and good life . . . appear to all men both easy and pleasant" (*CPW* 1:818).

To say that Milton moves *us* out of time, though, is to recognize the ways in which the *Apology* attempts to incorporate its own reception. In Milton's way of writing history and declaring its laws, he generalizes the experience of his speaker. The Apologist's present isolation becomes the vehicle of rhetorical consolidation; at the very moment he claims to have been once a "member incorporate into that truth whereof I was perswaded" (*CPW* 1:871), our mere spectatorship may well convert to something like sympathy or, better, participation. Even as the prophetic historian informs us as to what really happens in "times of opposition," his individuality virtually disappears; the parenthetic "that I may have leave" becomes the Apologist's final bit of ordinary conversation. In effect, he is displaced by the figure (at length the armed figure) of Zeal; but this requires a more general realignment among the various elements in the scene. In one of his more modest moments, the Apologist proposes to be useful to the "bystander" who has happened upon this conversation with Joseph Hall —for, like the *Areopagitica* of two years later, the *Apology* is no mere "text." The ordinary relation of author to "lay" audience is revised so as to include us all *as speakers*; it is as though we had become that nation of prophets with which Milton was to identify the listeners (or the right-minded listeners) of the *Areopagitica*: "of a quick, ingenious, and piercing spirit, acute to invent, subtle and sinewy to discourse, not beneath the reach of any point the highest that human capacity can soar to" (*CPW* 2:551).[11] This is what is involved in supposing, as we are asked to do, that we are hearing "the absolute voice of truth and all her children" (*CPW* 1:850). It is one of those special times, Milton would have us believe—and the *Apology* ought to convince us that they occur in mid-speech as they sometimes do in life—when "I do not conclude that Prelaty is Antichristian, for what need I? The things themselves conclude it" (*CPW* 1:850). The author steps forward not so much to argue a case as simply to urge us to look and see—to observe the "reason," the self-evident Presbyterianism, say, of church government. He appears to be driven by a style, but strictly speaking, it is not quite his own. "High authority" has become relocated, "presage and instinct of nature" for the moment a *generalized* possession, and we are listening to ourselves, as embodied in the armed figure of Zeal. Remove the individual author in this fashion from the right kind of epic poem, and the work will remain unaltered as to kind, since questions of genre will ultimately be determined not by authorial "intent" but by a style—or rather a "higher Argument"—outside any poet, an argument "sufficient of itself to raise / [The] name" of heroic poem or age.

The last pamphlet in the antiprelatical series posits a curiously defined middle ground between past and future; the imagery of Revelations and its sources has been accommodated to a more open-ended sense of history. Moreover, it seems as though the future has opened up again. There is an ample prospect for speculation, where earlier we had faced the oft-rehearsed scenario of the last sessions. The silencing of the false oracle here is a future and emphatically hypothetical possibility; it is viewed almost with fatigue as the kind of thing that would put to an end the entire period of controversy. For all his Apologist's professional urbanity Milton concludes the *Apology* by assuring prophetic powers to those who adopt Luther's (and the Apologist's own) manner:

> Ye shall soon discerne that *Turbant* of pride which they weare upon their heads to be no *helmet of salvation*, but the meere mettle and horn-work of Papall jurisdiction; and that they have also this guift, like a certaine kinde of some that are possest, to have their voice in their bellies, which being well-drain'd and taken downe, their great Oracle, which is only there, will soon be dumb, and the *Divine right of Episcopacy* forthwith expiring, will put us no more to trouble with tedious antiquities and disputes. [*CPW* 1:953]

In his concluding promise as elsewhere, Milton deliberately maneuvers toward the imagery and tone (in a word, toward the specific "quill") of his attack upon the clergy in "Lycidas"—something like the tone Milton gives to the Father in Book 5 of *Paradise Lost*. The fact that the Son so helpfully characterizes this tone (lest we miss the nuance) is testimony to the difficulty we may well find in distinguishing Fatherly derision (or was it the pure embodiment of Reason?) from Miltonic disenchantment. In any case, we have a very different view of things from the 1645 headnote's remarkable declaration of "occasion." In asking the nation to continue the practice of zeal—if indeed he is not demanding its resumption—Milton comes close to performing another function of the vatic poet, seemingly antithetical to the quasi-choral hymns of celebration: "deploring and general relapses of kingdoms and states from justice and God's true worship." Reprehension too was an appropriate rhetorical activity of the poet as Milton conceived his office; but it is a different activity from what Milton came to call prophetic "insight," and one suited to different circumstances—to an "age too late" for epic, among other things.

Together with other texts of the period we are considering, the *Apology* is remembered and re-presented in *Of Education* as a repository of "insight." But the final pamphlet in the antiprelatical series is insistently retrospective in itself. Far from looking ahead to anything so remote or hypothetical as the epic project mentioned in the *Reason*, the *Apology*'s kind of history and autobiography was meant to point scrupulously to promises already kept. More faithfully than the *Reason*, it revisits the 1630s in detail and makes explicit the concerns of the familiar letters, sometimes virtually in the language of theological doctrine. Among its various functions, this pamphlet serves to consolidate a Miltonic and public past of great complexity.

Necessarily, all this will entail a substantial misrepresentation of the Miltonic and public past alike. In the manner of the 1645 headnote to "Lycidas," the *Apology* indirectly attributes almost magical powers to the young, literary-minded correspondent (that "obscure" but conscientious seeker among truth's many shapes). But it also domesticates those powers; it reduces their disturbing and even violent potential into comfortable and misleading terms sometimes erroneously considered exclusively modern in their implication—like "insight" and "poetry"—into all those vague and conflicting meanings we pack into the word "literature." The young Milton's "vehement love of the beautiful" has become "instinct and presage of nature"—a "prophetic" term, clearly enough, but now something with familiar roots in nature; and the Apologist is bold to add that nature is "not wont to be false." "Instinct and presage of nature"—and with this such other terms as "zeal," "vehemence," and "Truth"—will shortly be recommended to Samuel Hartlib as the deceptively brief and modern "insight," itself an aspect of the more all-encompassing (and safer-sounding) "poetry." Here as in other instances of principle and psychological law giving, we are moving toward the pedagogical recommendations in *Of Education*, published a year before the *Poems* of 1645 and reprinted, together with the earlier academic exercises, as part of *Poems . . . Upon Several Occasions* (1673). In this way, works like the twin poems and the prolusions became part of the paradigmatic itinerary that has so frequently been mistaken for Milton's own prospectus. Like the letter to Diodati, the *Apology* shows how this "play" was remembered as something grander: as a moment of imagination released and somehow recorded, Urania and Wisdom at play in the "presence of th' Almighty Father," as Milton put it in recasting the Psalm in *Paradise Lost* 7. Thus viewed, the final antiprelatical pamphlet becomes a crucial moment in the development of that conjunction of word with event which Milton came to call an "occasion." It is with good reason that the *Apology* turns our attention so directly to the prophetic author and all that is involved in his potential influence. In doing so, it helps us recover the setting and the full intentions of that obviously congenial figure, whose function in Reformation history had perhaps been obscured by the rhetorical necessities as well as the historical circumstances of the *Reason*.

Here is a text, then, which in many ways seems premised on a sense of vocational fulfillment, and even something more—for Milton seems well on the way to recommending to his own successors the study and practice of "poetry." This study is conceived pedagogically—not as an ornament or accomplishment but as a crucial step in the phase of a curriculum devoted to the national sage's return to society from a scholarly retirement "fraught with an universal insight into things," and so prepared to speak "in parliament, council, or pulpit" (*CPW* 2:506). And the *Apology* presents itself as a model. Its anonymous but *representative* speaker and his discursive situation are the realization of earlier Miltonic ideals, from the nearly impossible academic vision of the prolusions (or "Il Penseroso") to the more evidently sectarian visions and prayers of the earlier pamphlets of the current series. Moreover, these are conditions which the Apologist now insists he took pains to stage quite consciously in the *Animadversions*; for, as we have seen, the Apologist is also equipped with a personal and vocational past. That exemplary encomium of the Long Parliament displays its author (and we too are theoretically involved in the act) not just as a better arguer and would-be policymaker but also as divine historian, singer, and sage. It is from a distinctly new vantage point that we *all* look back upon a collective victory for the vehement or ardent personality Milton had come to think of as his own. In this context, almost accidentally, we encounter the fullest and most adventurous of Milton's literary theorizing.

Considered as a reading of "Lycidas," the *Apology* is ultimately faithful to the entire poem, as much to the swain's sense of isolation as to his vehemence and literary virtuosity. For the most striking prose in the *Apology* is nostalgic, like Samson's early thoughts of the Timnite or his misunderstood retirement at Etham. It looks back to a time when spectacular event flowed immediately from prudence and the practice of a zealous wisdom; when it seemed that the Parliamant's own members had virtual command at once of both the "refluxes" of thought and "that which is called fortune from without"—those twin objects of tragic mimesis as Milton had described it in the *Reason*. Hall's reading of the prayer / hymn seems fair enough and perhaps inevitable, given the kinds of tensions which permeate this pamphlet. He may also have noticed that the flights of rapture we find here and there in the *Apology* are self-consciously personal rather than corporate or collective; and in their tones and effects they anticipate the momentary and illusory choric songs that seem to take us so ambiguously beyond time in Michael's narrative as we approach the conclusion of *Paradise Lost*. In this context, it is most significant that the Milton of April 1642 is a personal as well as divine historian, and that his Apologist recalls a better time, when I "conceiv'd my selfe to be now not as mine own person, but as a member incorporate into that truth whereof I was perswaded, and whereof I had declar'd openly to be a partaker" (*CPW* 1:871).

Moreover, the actual subject of Milton's most eloquent theorizing—what he so passionately calls "the greatest decency" of spontaneous and unpremeditated expressions—is a much diminished thing here; a speaker divorced from the sphere of "event" and thus seemingly removed from the completest of Miltonic authorial scenes, imperfectly received in the sense that he is limited to the expressions of the lyric mode, "which from a sincere heart, unbidden come into the outward gesture" (*CPW* 1:941). At least potentially, this way of describing the matter divides Milton's speaker from those events which could once again confirm his wisdom, even as it separates him from the heavenly chorus that both accomplishes and celebrates heroic deeds. By contrast, what Milton wishes to recover by speaking as literary and political adviser to "them in authority"—what seems to be now *missing*—is precisely the rest of the ideal scenario as he now supposes it to have existed in 1641: a "vertuous" wisdom in the primitive sense of the word, by which Parliament (and he himself in "Lycidas"?) extended for so many miles "the force of their single words" (*CPW* 1:926). In the way its theory isolates Milton's Apologist against a background of potentially hostile "accident," the *Apology* offers an early and revealing glimpse of Milton in a kind of personal and professional limbo and lays the groundwork for tragedy of a kind different from Milton's favorite Protestant model.[12] And what of Milton's reception by an earthly audience, whether fit or otherwise? Summing up the issues of the anti-prelatical controversy, Milton wrote that "the functions of Church government ought to be free and open to any Christian man though never so laick, if his capacity, his faith, and prudent demeanour commend him" (*CPW* 1:844). Within the rhetorical framework of the *Apology*, as we have seen, Milton the hymnist can sometimes simulate the removal of that "wall of separation" dividing the priestlike Apologist from the readers who have happened to overhear this quarrel with Bishop Hall. As for the London of 1642, however, Milton's "ought to be" is as telling as Shelley's ill-concealed concessions concerning the social power of the poet as an "unacknowledged legislator of mankind."[13]

Chapter Six

Trying All Things
in the *Areopagitica*

Encountering the great passages in Milton's prose (and especially, perhaps, in the *Areopagitica*), we would never guess that its author, much less its speaker, found the world to be in bondage to custom, and particularly subject to the tyranny of scholarly and even linguistic usage. But for all the profound optimism of the great oration, it is here that Milton also writes that we have become "the latest and the backwardest Schollers of whom God offer'd to have made us the teachers" (*CPW* 2:553). Books may be the lifeblood of a master spirit, but they are more commonly composed of "stale receits" and as a result are a "stark and dead congealment of wood and hay and stubble forc't and frozen together." For all this they are not so much merely read and heard as consulted, like recipes or the fundamentalist's holy books. We can easily form the impression from reading the *Areopagitica* that "authorship" in general has become abortive scholarship, as though we were facing something like a radical crisis of authority and canonicity; an author's works appear in the oration as fragmentary, barely remembered quotations, not really *speeches*.[1] To be sure, it was not always thus. We are told that the English isle once provided a point of departure for "the school of *Pythagoras*, and the *Persian* wisdom," had served all mankind, indeed, as a cultural source, a cathedral of philosophy.[2] But the delightful fantasy is displayed only as a tale of which "Writers of good antiquity, and ablest judgement have bin perswaded" (551). And in fact, the prevailing burden of the *Areopagitica* is the striking claim, repeated and

varied throughout the oration, that "we have lookt so long upon the blaze
that *Zuinglius* and *Calvin* hath beacon'd up to us, that we are stark blind
(*CPW* 2:550). At the outset of the antiprelatical disputes, as Georgia
Christopher has reminded us, Milton "is impatient because the Reformation had not yet been reformed in England" (*Science* 217–18). In the
Areopagitica, it is as though the Reformation itself had become bound by
"human traditions" (550).

Nor has our speaker himself escaped the infection. The ringing eloquence for which we cherish the *Areopagitica* is in fact something we encounter much less frequently than the enthusiasts of Milton's prose care to
admit. Much of the time, its speaker seems to be a discursive isolate—the
solitary private man: bookish, at times hardly capable of speech, at best
only potentially the man of copious fancy he seems to admire. We may
picture him, I suggest, as the "pupil teacher" Milton seems so fond of
mocking: citing, translating, furnished with the paraphernalia of those
"sober graduatships," in general completely immersed in the busywork of
scholarship. The would-be orator is consistently "in a private condition,"
and there is a corresponding sense of alienation for the reader of this work.
More often than not, the rhetorical situation of the *Areopagitica* is emphatically dissociated in something very like Eliot's sense: as readers we feel
uninvolved with any of Milton's pronominal or other communal reference
points, disengaged from his "I," "you," or "the realm" alike. The *Areopagitica* becomes eloquent—and we encounter those arguments from
principle which make it so irresistible to students of Milton's thought—
when the ordinary, disjunctive relation of author and listener is revised so
as to include us all *as speakers*, not just those "bystanders" mentioned in the
Apology. In these, the oration's greatest moments, the several constituents
of the rhetorical scene seem to merge into a national or supranational
community not unlike the mysterious "country" to which Samson refers
(*SA* 894).[3] In the following passage, for example, the public and collective
"I" of the oration seems to represent a stage of social consolidation even
more complete, for example, than those experiential appeals to what "we
know" elsewhere in the speech:[4]

> Good and evill we know in the field of this World grow up together
> almost inseparably; and the knowledge of good is so involv'd and interwoven
> with the knowledge of evill, and in so many cunning resemblances hardly to
> be discern'd, that those confus'd seeds which were impos'd on *Psyche* as an
> incessant labour to cull out, and sort asunder, were not more intermixt. It
> was from out the rinde of one apple tasted, that the knowledge of good and

evill as two twins cleaving together leapt forth into the World. And perhaps this is that doom which *Adam* fell into of knowing good and evill, that is to say of knowing good by evill. As therefore the state of man now is; what wisdome can there be to choose, what continence to forbeare without the knowledge of evill? He that can apprehend and consider vice with all her baits and seeming pleasures, and yet abstain, and yet distinguish, and yet prefer that which is truly better, he is the true wayfaring Christian. I cannot praise a fugitive and cloister'd vertue, unexercis'd & unbreath'd, that never sallies out and sees her adversary, but slinks out of the race, where that immortall garland is to be run for, not without dust and heat. Assuredly we bring not innocence into the world, we bring impurity much rather: that which purifies us is triall, and triall is by what is contrary. [*CPW* 2:514–15][5]

Barker observes that the greatest expression of Milton's Independent Puritanism also displays the tone of a humanistic document.[6] For Barker, the *Areopagitica*'s emphasis upon the classical learning of the early Christians, its frequent use of Plato, Bacon, and Spenser, its many reminders of the tradition of Erasmus and Hooker are impressive testimony that Milton, like Lord Brooke, represented a "liberal rationalism" which was roughly consistent with Puritan principles. And this is the significance, Barker concluded, of the fact that the speech incorporates

> proportionately more references than any of the other controversial tracts (except *Of Education*) to those pagan writers "with whom is bound up the life of human learning," that the Parliament is urged "to imitate the old and elegant humanity of Greece," that Adam and Psyche are mentioned in the same breath . . . ; "divine and human learning" were together "raked out of the embers of forgotten tongues." [81]

In determining the biographical and historical context for the *Areopagitica*, Barker focuses on the relatively immediate controversial antecedents of Milton's oration, and he leaves the impression that the humanism of the work punctuated Milton's relatively sudden break with Puritan (or Presbyterian) orthodoxy—and more specifically, derived from "the shock of his matrimonial mistake and the condemnation of his divorce tract" (p. 84). If these experiences brought him close to the tolerationism of Chillingworth, Hales, and Falkland, it is fair nevertheless to ask whether earlier antecedents, more elusive but just as personal, anticipate these ideological affiliations or illuminate the question of just how deeply these bonds run. For example, Milton's early allusions to vocational matters—addressed, like the *Areopagitica* to the question of Apostolic learning—suggest a more emphatically Protestant classicalism than we might have supposed, and help to prepare us in some detail for the socially engaged but also distinctively literary Puritanism of the *Areopagitica*. Recent investigations have tied Milton's humanism more closely to the less rational side of Puritan polemic than Barker's account; but we still need a fuller picture of the immediate vantage point from which Milton restores the Parliamentary memory and pretends to share the common human principles. In the pages that follow, I will argue that the *Areopagitica* points to an original and experimental accommodation between a coalescing Independent Puritanism, on the one hand, and the long-standing claims of the antique world to which Thomas Young and others had introduced the young Milton many years earlier. Nothing in the speech suggests this more immediately, I submit, than the way in which the *Areopagitica* displays its learning and stages its humanistic oratory; in a real sense, the eloquence of the oration is *itself* something conspicuously remembered and even "raked out of the embers of forgotten tongues."

The authority of Milton's speaker first becomes an interpretive issue in the *Areopagitica* during a narration which occurs a little more than a page earlier than the great critique of the "fugitive and cloister'd vertue." Here is the passage:

> *Dionysius Alexandrinus* was about the year 240, a person of great name in the Church for piety and learning, who had wont to avail himself much against hereticks by being conversant in their Books; untill a certain Presbyter laid it scrupulously to his conscience, how he durst venture himselfe among those defiling volumes. The worthy man loath to give offence fell into a new debate with himselfe what was to be thought; when suddenly a vision sent from God, it is his own Epistle that so averrs it, confirm'd in these words: Read any books what ever come to thy hands, for thou art sufficient both to judge aright, and to examine each matter. To this revelation he assented the sooner, as he confesses, because it was answerable to that of the Apostle to the Thessalonians, Prove all things, hold fast that which is good. And he might have added another remarkable saying of the same Author; To the pure all things are pure, not only meats and drinks, but all kinde of knowledge whether of good or evill; the knowledge cannot defile, nor consequently the books, if the will and conscience be not defil'd. For books are as meats and viands are; some of good, some of evill substance; and yet God in that unapocryphall vision, said without exception, Rise *Peter*, kill and eat, leaving the choice to each mans discretion. Wholesome meats to a vitiated stomach differ little or nothing from unwholesome; and best books to a naughty mind are not unappliable to occasions of evill. Bad meats will scarce

breed good nourishment in the healthiest concoction; but herein the difference is of bad books, that they to a discreet and judicious Reader serve in
many respects to discover, to confute, to forewarn, and to illustrate. [*CPW*
2:511–12]

Milton boldly advertises the sources of his story, Dionysius' "own Epistle,"
in such a way as to interrupt the narrative continuity. Indeed, Dionysius
himself, we are told, was the more ready to trust his experience, that
"vision sent from God," on the basis of its compatibility with 1 Thessalonians 5:21. Up to a point, Milton carefully distinguishes Dionysius' words
and thoughts from Paul's and his own, at least until he remembers the
saying which the pious and learned man "*might* have added" (my italics). In
fact, of course, the entire tale of Dionysius is the carefully articulated
culmination of a long and scrupulous parade of witnesses for the defense of
reading. Dionysius is introduced into the speech quite hypothetically, just
in case we agree to "be try'd by visions" (a most unlikely case, given *this*
author). The experience is presented as a "vision recorded by *Eusebius*." It is
a vision (we are further told, in case we should be susceptible to traditions)
of greater antiquity than the classic story Milton has just recounted—in
high satiric fashion—about how "the Divell whipt St. *Jerom* in a lenten
dream, for reading *Cicero*" (*CPW* 2:510). In view of the well-known
experimental bias of the *Areopagitica*, it is the text centeredness of all this
that is so striking, as though Milton's own authority in the oration were to
arise from an anthology of proverbs.

On the other hand, Milton maintains this scholarly candor only up to a
point. The tale of Dionysius leads him inevitably to the Pauline text which
more than any other licenses the *Areopagitica*'s entire battery of arguments,
1 Thessalonians 5:21. When we first encounter Paul, the force of the
Apostle's words is vitiated by being presented as just one of the "remarkable sayings" of this author, diligently collected by the writer and set off
against his own seemingly original pronouncements ("Books are as meats
and viands are"). With this central text, however, there occurs an important shift, the effect of which is to alter—momentarily, but radically—the
evident unoriginality of the entire discourse.[7] Milton's speaker starts to
participate in Dionysius' decision (grounded, as we have seen, on a vision as
well as a text). He now abandons the habit of scrupulous footnoting and
attribution, proceeds to fill in Paul's text with another from Titus 1:15,
and he even improvises "original" Pauline material. The moment involves
what seems to be, at last, an integral speech delivered in propria persona. It

is from this crucial point that *John Milton* proceeds to that testimony from the Parliament's own John Selden and thence to what "I conceive" and to the passage with which I began: a recapitulation and creative extension of authorities, "reasons and theorems almost mathematically demonstrative" into that most adventurous field of learning, ecclesiastical history and its principles (*CPW* 2:512–13). The entire passage thus moves toward—and through—the kind of appeals for which we read the *Areopagitica*. But the speech (or what is not much different, the speaker) seems to become whole only here, as he appears to throw off his thraldom to maxims and other sources, divine and otherwise. Without the signposting that has characterized his procedure to this point, Milton's discourse becomes, in a manner of speaking, seamless. Uniting all voices (in the Latin sense of "speeches"), he has achieved authority, something he calls elsewhere "the life of teaching." If the text from 1 Thessalonians produced a mind, we now encounter a mind that produces (or at any rate remembers) all texts, including classical ones. The word "unapocryphall" seems to put a whole method behind us; but a great deal is *included* in what we are told "God said without exception": in that "unapocryphall vision" of the Apostle Peter. All those remembered texts, potentially capable of unlocking the most fundamental mysteries of the human predicament, enter into the seeming originality of the orator at this point. Milton has engaged in the deliberate construction of a dramatically *masterful* moment, in which a complete and apparently collective memory becomes part of a more all-encompassing authority, a "universal insight into things." It is from this point that the speaker of the *Areopagitica*, until now conspicuously the scholar/reader, becomes an orator and in some literal sense an "interpreter."[8] And it seems clear that a specific Pauline text validates that authority, actually releases that eloquence.

As I have suggested, this kind of clarity is a temporary accomplishment, momentarily permitting free (and evidently subversive) play to what Milton will subsequently call "the ingenuity of Truth." By the time we have arrived at the work's finest and most sustained bit of eloquence a page or so later, it seems that its context virtually requires an extensive indulgence in citations and translations of others' texts, the information from Solomon, the traditional scholarly considerations of "the Syriack" and of those conventional distinctions (between public and private matters, between voluntary and other kinds of actions). The threshold is familiar. It is only upon mentioning some books of magic burned by St. Paul's converts that Milton's orator begins to speak for us once again, as though we had all suddenly become part of a "knowing" community. It is the distasteful thought of a recipe for implicit belief or programmatic action that seems to spark this vehemence—a clear descendant of the polemic Milton had been so busy trying to describe and defend in the antiprelatical pamphlets of 1641–42, and a drastic change from the tones of the arch scholar to whom we were listening just a moment ago. Our speaker's appeals have become distinctly more "simple, sensuous, and passionate," as in that relaxing and seemingly familiar reference to "the field of this World"; a gesture which puts the earth back beneath our feet and provides the scene with a bit of vegetation. It is simply but insinuatingly done; the plant soon grows double, and eventually we are led to recognize the Tree of Knowledge itself. In general, it seems that what "we know" in this and other such passages derives from a combination of intensive metaphor and elaborated fable— from what Milton took to be the procedures of the ancient poets. Like its predecessor the tale of Dionysius, the passage suggests that throughout the *Areopagitica* we are dealing with an orator whose varying relation to his material (whose occasional "originality") is a central part of Milton's design. And as we shall see, there is a philosophic component to the orator's insight as well. Ernest Sirluck has shown that this authority involves "arguments from principle," principle ostensibly based upon experience.[9] And the *Areopagitica* is perhaps unusual in the extent to which it relies upon these arguments; Sirluck's introduction is especially valuable for its demonstration of how they provide a kind of appeal which Milton had begun to find indispensable during the composition of the divorce tracts. But it is important to stress that the poetry and the authority alike are recognizably canonical. I would claim that the appearance of the seemingly original or poetic orator is itself the function of yet another principle, in effect: that the "argument from experience" in these two early instances is dramatized as a memory sparked by a text. Peter's vision—or at any rate the attenuated memory of that experience related in Acts 10:9–16— comes close to serving as the heart of this work, in close conjunction with Paul's "Prove all things, hold fast that which is good." To a remarkable extent, I believe, the learned Apostle is made immediately responsible for the eloquence, and even the learning, of Milton's Isocratic oration. It is on this account—a matter of rhetorical ethos—that we are told of St. Paul's skill, shared with his predecessors Moses and Daniel, "in all the learning of the Aegyptians, Caldeans, and Greeks." It is something, Milton adds pointedly, which "could not probably be without reading their Books of all sorts" (*CPW* 2:507–08).[10]

For Milton and other Protestants during the Reformation, 1 Thessalonians 5:21 and the closely related account of Peter's vision in Acts 10:9–16 were cornerstones for Protestant discussions of vocation, and also of special developments in the divine pedagogy to be manifested during the last days. If the recollection of Paul's advice seems to spark the memory of material wholly "unapocryphall" in Milton's speech, it was Peter's experience that had provided the decisive historical breakthrough. For the commentators, the story of Peter's trance, the vision of the "great sheet" holding "all manner of fourfooted beasts of the earth, and wild beasts, and creeping things, and fowls of the air" (AV), and the command to "Rise . . . kill, and eat" involved nothing less than the threshold dividing two whole eras and dispensations. Calvin regarded this vision as an assurance of Peter's special calling, which was to remove "the wall of separation" between Jew and Gentile: "Now God made the covenant of the life common to all the whole world, which he had shut up in one nation, as in a treasure."[11] A member of Milton's contemporary audience in the *Areopagitica* further explained that the liberty to eat flesh was assigned to "the days of Messias, which now first taketh place at this vision of Peter and forward."[12] And he went on, "This is the very first beginning or dawning to the kingdome of heaven; . . . here Peter hath the keyes of the kingdome. . . . It was he that first and onely opened the doore, and the doore being once opened, was never shut, nor ever shall be till the end of the world" (236–37; italics deleted). Thus does John Lightfoot, the orientalist and member of the Westminster Assembly, define the place of this Apostle in ecclesiastical history: "And how little this concerneth *Rome* or the Papacy, as to be any foundation of it, a childe may observe" (ibid.). Viewed in this way, the text concerns one of those mysteries "hid from the beginning of the world," the way in which the Gentiles were ultimately made "partakers of the same salvation with the people of God, and ingrafted into one body," as Calvin explained it (420). And because there was a clear contradiction between the divine vision and the Law in which Peter was nurtured, the Apostle stood in need of special confirmation, Christ's explicit commandment to preach the Gospel to the Gentiles notwithstanding. "There was such and so great difficulty in the novelty itself, that [Peter and his fellow apostles] could not acquaint themselves therewith by and by . . . when they come to the push, they doubted nevertheless, being stricken with the strangeness of the thing" (421).

Luther may well have considered 1 Thessalonians 5:21 as his basic justifying text when he declared at Worms that he could not lawfully revoke "the word of God which I have alleged." He had treated the passage as a virtual epitome of God's word in an earlier dispute concerning the question of canonical books and ecclesiastical authority.[13] In seventeenth-century England, this appeal proved to be a two-edged weapon, realizing the potential which had been recognized by Calvin long before. With evident reluctance, Calvin had argued that it is essential to the health of the Church to maintain the line of prophecy, particularly in the latter days. Even where "all do not speak precisely according to set rule, we must nevertheless, form a judgment, before any doctrine is condemned or rejected."[14] Calvin was in a good position to recognize the special danger provided in this text to "external preaching" (or what Milton calls the "outward callings of men"); he is most concerned to vindicate the alliance between "prophecy" and the common ecclesiastical functions, and he points squarely to the sectarians who stand to profit from the text: those fanatic libertines who think "no one . . . spiritual unless he is a despiser of doctrine" (299). Still, Calvin finds the risk worth taking, and even necessary:

> Paul . . . may seem here to give too great liberty in teaching, when he would have *all things proved*; for things must be heard by us, that they may be proved, and by this means a door would be opened to impostors for disseminating their falsehoods. . . . As, however so great diligence can never be exercised as that there should not sometimes be persons prophesying, who are not so well instructed as they ought to be, and that sometimes good and pious teachers fail to hit the mark, he requires such moderation on the part of believers, as, nevertheless, not to refuse to hear. For nothing is more dangerous, than that moroseness by which every kind of doctrine is rendered disgusting to us, while we do not allow ourselves to *prove* what is right. [301]

For the Independent author of *The Ancient Bounds* (1645), the "exonerating times" had removed the need for Calvin's doubts; the liberty to prove all things "is as worthy the vindication as any," and he explicitly attaches the freedom to a "liberty of profession." To hinder this, he writes, "were a most tyrannical usurpation over that connection which God hath made between the act of the understanding and the will . . . and indeed to violate the law of God and nature."[15]

Milton too thought of Peter's vision as having purified "every beast and creeping worme," in a formulation which brings him strikingly close to the central reversal in Coleridge's "Rime" (*CPW* 1:844).[16] That moment had provided a definitive removal of the Old Law's "distinction of clean and

unclean"; the distinction once abolished, "all living creatures were sancti-
fy'd to a pure and Christian use, and mankind especially, now invited by a
generall call to the covnant of grace" (*CPW* 2:261), no matter what might
be said to the contrary by Peter's ecclesiastical successors. Milton's discussion of Peter's vision takes some pains to downplay the historicist dimension of this and the Pauline texts which explained how "God, who at
sundry times and divers manners spake in times past unto the fathers by
the prophets, Hath in these last days spoken unto us by his Son," as the
authorized translators rendered Hebrews 1:1. After all, Peter's experience
was part of a virtual release from history for all believers. It was the divine
son himself who now spoke "in divers manners." Hence the presence, in
Scripture, of those more open-ended Pauline texts, which (like the *Areopagitica* itself) urged the "richly variegated" (AV's "manifold") nature of
truth in any era (Ephesians 3:10), and perhaps particularly in the last days,
when (as Bale, Mede, and others had remarked in expounding the vision
of Revelations) the enigmatic and "manifold" method of divine instruction was once again appropriate (as it was not for more rational-minded
audiences). This much seems clear, for example, from Milton's prominent
deployment of 1 Thessalonians 5:21 in his first antiprelatical pamphlet:

> If we will but purge with sovrain eyesalve that intellectual ray which *God*
> hath planted in us, then we would beleeve the Scriptures protesting their
> own plainnes, and perspicuity, calling to them to be instructed, not only the
> *wise*, and *learned*, but the *simple*, the *poor*, the *babes*, foretelling an extraordi-
> nary effusion of *Gods* Spirit upon every age, and sexe, attributing to all men,
> and requiring from them the ability of searching, trying, examining all
> things, and by the Spirit discerning that which is good. [*CPW* 1:566]

Clearly enough, the way was well prepared for that central argumentative
principle of the *Areopagitica*, "For books are as meats and viands are" (*CPW*
2:512). But just as clearly, *Areopagitica*'s "humanism"—whatever we may
think of it—is not so much an ideal outlook or principle of the emerging
poet as it is an ad hoc organizing strategy, a poetics for the special times.[17]

I

For all its emphasis upon a "masterful" authority redeeming flawed materials and tools, then, there is every reason that the *Areopagitica* should differ
from *Paradise Regained* in persistently refusing to present its speaker, so to
speak, "in isolation," as a kind of rhetorical spectacle. The kind of cultural

recall seemingly achieved by the Son of *Paradise Regained* is something which Milton thought the divine Son, the historical model for his epic champion, had in effect made obsolete, or at any rate practically unattainable. Significantly too, that kind of mastery, and with it the Son's pivotal victory, occurs prior to the Son's public ministry in Milton's epic. In the context of the *Areopagitica*, such a gift is the momentary possession of a very different (and recognizably Pauline, as distinct from Messianic) kind of character. No less than the young correspondent of 1633, the *Areopagitica* is a deeply "self-suspicious" work, implicitly dedicated to the proposition that its own discursive constituents, like the Law itself, are at least potentially "methodical" or "syntagmatic"—self-referring, self-aggrandizing, in every way "systematic." In keeping with the divine Author's use of maxims (a form calculated, like parable and perhaps the poet's fables, to free us from these perils), the oration is a frankly artificial and even nominalist text, a work whose central strategies serve to counter the view that a book—or for that matter, a poem—is in any way a self-sufficient object. As a whole, the *Areopagitica* reveals how consciously Milton sought, in part through the "poets'" own procedures, to convert the detritus of controversy—for many contemporaries the sign of social and religious collapse[18]—into the materials of truth and beauty. He redeems the process of error, just as he would the "Law" for which books and even language provide a prime source of analogy.[19]

In the *Areopagitica* as in the final letter to Diodati, beauty is a central preoccupation. In the oration it has become a collective and cultural problem rather than the object of a personal quest to be conducted, apparently, among books and in the composition of poetry; but the focal point, once again, is the walled structure identified here with the Temple at Jerusalem and sharply distinguished from from the ideal body of truth, which Milton calls "*homogeneal* and proportionall" (*CPW* 2:551). In the fallen world, the separation of wheat from tares is a practical impossibility, and it is in any case the "Angels Ministry at the end of mortal things" (*CPW* 2:554–55). Hence we are faced with a kind of interim aesthetic and ecclesiastical paradigm: a Temple which is consistently described in terms of elements which "can but be contiguous in this world." The symmetry which "commends [this] whole pile and structure" actually derives from "many moderat varieties and brotherly dissimilitudes that are not vastly disproportionall" (*CPW* 2:555). The true poem, Milton had written in the *Apology*, inheres in the person of its poet (*CPW* 1:890); here we are to encounter works whose "uncouth" appearance is likely to be "more unsightly and unplausible then many errors, even as the person is of many a great man slight and contemptible to see to" (*CPW* 2:565–66). We have virtually arrived at the full content of *Paradise Lost*'s preference for "th'upright heart and pure" before "all Temples" (1:17–18).

Sirluck reminds us that Milton's analogy with the "person" of some great men is particularly apt to Paul, and we might add Isocrates and Moses as well. The point I would stress, however, is that—whatever Milton may have meant in calling the *Areopagitica* a "regular speech" several years after the fact—he deliberately composed it as an "irregular" and largely discontinuous structure, as though to anticipate Raphael's remark that things are most regular "when most irregular they seem" (5:624).[20] With the important exceptions we have noticed, Milton's references to "brotherly dissimilitudes" and "contiguity" provide a fitting description of the state of learning and language as we experience it more or less normally in the *Areopagitica*: properly viewed, the building of the Temple in Jerusalem can serve as an epitome of Milton's own method in the oration, a method appropriate to the age in which we live. For Milton locates us consistently in an era like Peter's, when "the strangeness of the thing" is a foremost consideration. With a critical articulateness that sets off his perspective from the more engaged millennialism of the antiprelatical pamphlets— with an eye to the future—Milton describes it as a time for "men of rare abilities." And Milton had particular reason to add that there are problems peculiar to such times, problems involving the reception of new kinds of authority: "Neither is God appointed and confin'd, where and out of what place these his chosen shall be first heard to speak; for he sees not as man sees, chooses not as man chooses, lest we should devote our selves to set places, and assemblies, and outward callings of men" (*CPW* 2:566).

In a real sense, the *Areopagitica* is conceived not so much as a text-cum-audience as a kind of conversation, a conception employing what is perhaps the most important domestic and social ideal developed during the period of the divorce pamphlets: "What ever thing we hear or see, sitting, walking, travelling, or conversing may be fitly be call'd our book, and is of the same effect that writings are" (*CPW* 2:528). This emphasis upon effect is why Milton can call a book a "universall thing" (*CPW* 2:528) and also claim that the bagpipe, rebec, and fiddler's "gammuth" make up "the Countrymans *Arcadia's* and his *Monte Mayors*" (*CPW* 2:525). If there is a touch of condescension in Milton's advocacy here, there is no doubting that the point holds true when considering the plight of authority in places more bookish, or more embattled, like London itself.

The emphasis is clear when we recall that *Areopagitica* everywhere implies a major shift in Milton's attitude toward the Anabaptists and Familists, those prime beneficiaries (to Calvin's way of thinking) of the texts which had originally been counted among the chief weapons against Rome and which have become the catalysts to Milton's own eloquence in the *Areopagitica*. As late as 1643, Milton had written that the sectaries were possessed by "fanatick dreams";[21] now, increasingly associated by his orthodox critics with these same "libertines," Milton links them (in most unCalvinist fashion) with the province of the "special ministry," a category long associated with the progressive extension of the "covenant" beyond the visible ecclesiastical establishment—itself in turn the counterpart of the Jewish temple. Some of the *Areopagitica*'s most engaging prose, indeed, seeks to realign our sympathies for the sectarians in whom Milton had recently found the portraiture of his own authorial cause. Here again, they are disguised as those special authors "able to manage and set forth new positions to the world." And the authors are in turn wayfarers and warfarers alike:

> And were they but as the dust and cinders of our feet, so long as in that notion they may yet serve to polish and brighten the armoury of Truth, ev'n for that respect they were not utterly to be cast away. But if they be of those whom God hath fitted for the speciall use of these times with eminent and ample gifts, and those perhaps neither among the Priests, nor among the Pharisees, and we in the hast of a precipitant zeal shall make no distinction, but resolve to stop their mouths, because we fear they come with new and dangerous opinions, as we commonly forejudge them ere we understand them, no less then woe to us, while thinking to defend the Gospel, we are found the persecutors. [*CPW* 2:567–68]

The passage powerfully captures and marshals Milton's lately discovered suspicions about "zeal" which he later enshrined in some severe and revealing pages of the *De Doctrina Christiana*; and it does so in part by avoiding a stable reference for "we" and "they." Dangling there as it does between rhetorical supposition and outright recrimination, that nearly autonomous "As we commonly forejudge them ere we understand them" makes brilliant use of what may well have been a major deflection in Milton's intellectual and professional life. It presents the final proof that the defensively systematic warrior can be an actual enemy of the truth he seeks, that in a world where all of "us" are wayfarers and warfarers alike it is especially difficult to distinguish the "troublers" from the special warrior / authors. At times (and in texts) like these, readers and authors are ultimately or potentially interchangeable, equally members of a new subcommunity in which "obscure" or "private" scholarship (or merely "writing") is tantamount to Christian warfare, in the specific Pauline sense to which Milton had first alluded in 1633:

> Behold now this vast City; a city of refuge, the mansion house of liberty, encompast and surrounded with his protection; the shop of warre hath not there more anvils and hammers waking, to fashion out the plates and instruments of armed Justice in defence of beleaguer'd Truth, then there be pens and heads there, sitting by their studious lamps, musing, searching, revolving new notions and idea's wherewith to present, as with their homage and their fealty the approaching Reformation: others as fast reading, trying all things, assenting to the force of reason and convincement. [*CPW* 2:553–54]

Again the text occurs, this time in a way which points directly to Milton's own ideological reassessments. But in a more important sense, Milton's city is recognizably the community comprising his own readership; like the "national digression" as a whole, the passage points to the fait accompli that is the *Areopagitica* itself.

For all the work's emphasis upon a "perfected" knowledge, it is important to recall once again the actual texture of the *Areopagitica*, in which the great moments arise from the work's own dust and heat. As we have seen, the speaker of the oration spends a good deal of time in the role of the stumbling reader, making his way through the "rubbish of Canonicall ignorance" (*CPW* 2:224). Nothing in the oration makes this aspect of the text clearer than the dramatic incident involving "Truth," the subject of this work's most impressive bit of "poetic" fabling. Just a few pages before the conclusion of the speech, Milton constructs the historical background of our epistemological predicament in an etiological myth with unmistakable affiliations to the story of Ceres and Orpheus.[22] Once Truth came into the world with her "divine Master"; and she "was a perfect shape most glorious to look on," like the figure of *scientia nuda* in *Ad Patrem*. Torn to pieces by a "wicked race of deceivers" (this happened, Milton tells us, after Christ's ascension and the "sleep" of the Apostles), her body was scattered through the world:

> From that time ever since, the sad friends of Truth, such as durst appear, imitating the careful search that *Isis* made for the mangl'd body of *Osiris*,

went up and down gathering up limb by limb still as they could find them. We have not yet found them all, Lords and Commons, nor ever shall doe, till her Masters second comming; he shall bring together every joynt and member, and shall mould them into an immortall feature of loveliness and perfection. [*CPW* 2:549]

Strategically located as it is, just a few pages before the conclusion of the speech, the story solidifies the truth that in our middle era we are, like Thales and other predecessors, necessarily involved in gathering Truth's fragments: that what looks like a pilgrimage has taken the place of the more straightforward methods of Christian warfare.

By the time we have thus discovered our origins, we have long forgotten that Truth herself has already put in a brief but impressive appearance in the *Areopagitica*, in one of the most fascinating recoveries from the speaker's customary forgetfulness. As so often, Milton's speaker is not at his best in the conspicuously "argumentative" prelude to the recovery; he is almost too organized in his wooden, "methodical" fashion. His objections come forth as sayings, caveats undigested into real argument or speech, as though they were badly machined standard parts, not so much fitted together as merely adjacent. It is all spoken with lips rather un-Miltonically pursed:

'Tis next alleg'd we must not expose our selves to temptations without necessity, and next to that, not imploy our time in vain things. To both these objections one answer will serve, out of the grounds already laid, that to all men such books are not temptations, nor vanities; but usefull drugs and materialls wherewith to temper and compose effective and strong med'cins, which mans life cannot want. The rest, as children and childish men, who have not the art to qualifie and prepare these working mineralls, well may be exhorted to forbear, but hinder'd forcibly they cannot be by all the licencing that Sainted Inquisition could ever yet contrive. [*CPW* 2:521]

This is the speaker as performer-of-tasks, working with discrete precepts, "reasons," and the other tools and materials of dialectic. It is at this point that Milton virtually presents Truth herself as a kind of built-in antagonist to the scholar-author, as a *character*, something like the Cherub who suddenly appears on the scene in "Il Penseroso." He partitions his orator from the argument—or at least from his rival author's *kind* of procedure—and the Isocratic speaker joins us once again as the witness and celebrant of Truth's ingenuity in anticipating or "preventing" his own lesser kind of authority, like Patience in the nineteenth sonnet, or the gracious muse herself:

> [But all this—Milton's text employs the cooler "Which"] is what I promis'd to deliver next, That this order of licencing conduces nothing to the end for which it was fram'd; and hath almost prevented me by being clear already while thus much hath bin explaining. See the ingenuity of Truth, who when she gets a free and willing hand, opens her self faster, then the pace of method and discourse can overtake her. It was the task which I began with, To shew that no Nation.. . . . [*CPW* 2:521]

Clearly enough, the overall performance by no means corresponds to the neat but wooden execution of "the task which I began with." Thanks to the metaphoric strategy that is central to both argument and design, Milton's parts or components once again become a kind of garden; the single answer that "serves" both objections is presented figuratively as something which grows "out of the grounds already laid." This is one of the many references in the *Areopagitica* to a kind of substratum for "truth" conceived as a "material" thing rather like the Chaos of *Paradise Lost*.[23] To the likely question "*What* 'grounds already laid'?" Milton's impersonal construction provides the answer that their appearance was not exactly of the speaker's own devising: of itself, the next topic "hath almost prevented me by being clear already while thus much hath bin explaining." The celebration of Truth's ingenuity in finding her own seekers is another moment of pure "interpretation" in the literal sense, a moment involving the entrance of the demonic muse independently of the author's own exertions, catching him just at the instant of inadvertency. It can also be taken as a sort of distant premonition of the New Criticism's poetics, a way of saluting discourse somehow ideally performed, caught in its purest, "uncontrollable intent": when a text or book becomes *real* speech, Truth has gained "a free and willing hand, [and] opens her self faster, then the pace of method and discourse can overtake her." Coming as it does in the absence of the catalytic text which had released the orator's talents earlier, the passage represents an even more radical interruption on the part of that "same Author"; and it clarifies the point that such encounters with true authority cannot be achieved exclusively through the "grand style" or what Milton had called "vehemence." The kind of authorial abdication which insists that the discourse in question cannot succeed "if all be mine" provided an enduring and effective matrix for the prophet's words, and Milton's best answer to the haunting suspicion that he is, after all, a "Jesuit of an artist."[24]

II

The *Areopagitica* is a true companion of the letter to Hartlib with which it has often been published: that educational plan designed to produce speakers "fraught with an universall insight into things" and prepared to "speak in Parliament or counsell" (*CPW* 2:406). Those speakers, we may recall, would engage in strategically timed reviews, "sometimes into the rear of what they have been taught, until they have confirm'd and solidly united the whole body of their perfected knowledge, like the last embattelling of a Romane legion" (406–07), a retrogressive ritual and military image paradoxically appropriate to the conditions of learning in this special day and age. Like the reviews of Milton's scholars, the *Areopagitica*'s flights of eloquence involve a temporary but radical recuperation of authority, a recovery based on the notion of the ideal speaker as the potential "recapitulator" of all human culture; forgetting nothing in pagan or his own cultural experience, potentially capable of all reference, ready to declare who, behind all the appearances, is the "true wayfaring / warfaring Christian" —and resisted by those who, like the "fugitive and cloister'd vertue," are enclosed within a kind of citadel:

> When a man hath bin labouring the hardest labour in the deep mines of knowledge, hath furnisht out his findings in all their equipage, drawn forth his reasons as it were a battel raung'd, scatter'd and defeated all objections in his way, calls out his adversary into the plain, offers him the advantage of wind and sun, if he please; only that he may try the matter by dint of argument, for his opponents then to sculk, to lay ambushments, to keep a narrow bridge of licencing where the challenger should passe, though it be valour anough in shouldiership, is but weaknes and cowardise in the wars of Truth. [*CPW* 2:562]

In a sense, the kind of social realignment we find in the *Areopagitica*'s moments of supreme confidence represents an ideal ending for the young Milton's quest for beauty, an ending with more than a casual anticipation of the Son's decisive victory in Book 6 of *Paradise Lost*.

For all Milton's emphasis upon the effects of conversing, for all the dramatic immediacy of the *Areopagitica*, of course, there is an irreducible difference between speaking and writing for publication.[25] Even this unlicensed speech in favor of the "liberty of unlicensed printing" is in cold print and has the outward form of a slender volume in our hands; there can be no denying the sense in which even this book is a *partly* dead thing. A host of comments about the specifics of printing, book-making and -selling are premised on jokes like this: those satirical references to "dangerous frontispieces," to the "wet sheets" of a weekly court pamphlet, to the low "salary of presse corrector." All of this, however, becomes part of an extensive ontological proof, which Milton pursues with fine tact, conflating distinctions between printed texts and "writing" and (in one instance) working them into an amusing speculation on the problem of a printer when dealing with an author particularly "ingenious":

> What if the author shall be one so copious of fancie, as to have many things well worth the adding, come into his mind after licencing, while the book is yet under the Presse, which not seldom happ'ns to the best and diligentest writers; and that perhaps a dozen times in one book. The Printer dares not go beyond his licenc't copy; so often then must the author trudge to his leav-giver, that those his new insertions may be viewd; and many a jaunt will be made, ere that licencer, for it must be the same man, can either be found, or found at leisure; mean while either the Presse must stand still, which is no small damage, or the author loose his accuratest thoughts, & send the book forth wors then he had made it, which to a diligent writer is the greatest melancholy and vexation that can befall. [*CPW* 2:532]

The physical existence of the book—and the essential fact that its reader is even now legally tainted—becomes one of Milton's chief arguments that licencing cannot, practically speaking, be *managed*.

As it happens, an apparently minor textual crux located at the heart of the *Areopagitica*'s most famous passage adds considerably to the force of this point and also to his claim about the effects of conversation. In five presentation copies of the first edition, the printed text's "wayfaring" has been emended, perhaps in Milton's own hand, to "warfaring."[26] It seems likely that the printed version of Milton's illegally published text has almost instantly become a "variant" in at least five of its "shapes"; and editors and readers have obligingly weighted the alternatives, almost as though the printed "y" and script "r" provided a paleographic rendition of good and evil, those two "twins cleaving together." Is one of the alternatives, in the *Areopagitica*'s own idiom, "truly better"? If we assume that Milton altered the word thus slightly, the change would redeem the word "wayfaring" —long associated in Milton's mind with the methods of the ancient poets—by pointing to the union of Isis's search for the fragments of Osiris with the Christian armament of Paul and the commentators. At the moment, its author is on the verge of preferring the meandering Spenser to straightforward Aquinas, and preferring him specifically as a teacher into the bargain; for himself and perhaps for the recipients of the five copies, such a revision might declare that oration and author have fulfilled the conditions, first mentioned in 1633, for that ideal union of scholarly and literary "obscurity" with public authorship. The alternatives are potentially collapsible.

Our acceptance of "warfaring," however, need not depend upon proof positive that Milton was responsible for the emendation. Whoever made it, the change is a telling indication of what Milton supposed must happen "if we think to regulat Printing" (*CPW* 2:523); and it testifies to the kind of potential Milton found in the Isocratic form, something to be read aloud or (better) acted out.[27] Unlike the eloquent passages of the *Areopagitica* to which it is related, the emendation is in the Miltonic sense an "event" or aftermath. Like other, more casual, details in the oration ("By the very sound of this which I shall utter . . . ," *CPW* 2:487), it points to the sounds of a new speaker, one other than John Milton. However slight the physical alteration of the page, the "reading" is thus also a speech and involves the activation of another author, a living reader to whom textual authority may in this special case defer. Indeed, it is not so much a revision as a further completion of Milton's text and may serve its purpose as the germ of another one, even more freely evolving; it is a *living* trophy of England's liberty. Only this kind of speech—once it is published—can so literally entail the multiplication of speakers and publics to which Milton refers in his allusion to the dragon's teeth of Cadmus. The work's ultimate play on the fixity of the printed text also offers its final proof that books indeed do "contain a potencie of life in them to be as active as that soul was whose progeny they are" (*CPW* 2:492).

Chapter Seven

Paradise Regained and
Milton's "Other" Satan

Daemon. Far other arms, and other weapons must
Be those that quell the might of hellish charms,
He with his bare wand can unthread thy joints,
    And crumble all thy sinews.
Elder Brother.   Why, prithee Shepherd,
  How durst thou then thyself approach so near
    As to make this relation?
      A Masque, 612–17

Almost from the moment of publication, it was commonplace for readers to
patronize or even ignore the Satan of Milton's brief epic, primarily because
he did not quite measure up to his splendidly eloquent predecessor. Here,
he was a depressed and world-weary figure who all too clearly reflected the
misfortunes or mistakes of his author. Somehow he has arrived too late to
pose anything like an adequate or even interesting test for Milton's divine
Son, whose heroic victory consequently rings a little false. As though
continuing the supposed degeneration of Satan in *Paradise Lost*, the Son's
enervated antagonist is often thought to become even more demoralized, if
this is possible, as the work proceeds. Milton had clearly silenced his own
greatest character, went the argument of this stage in the poem's critical
history. Gone, surely, were the days when even the most dedicated of
Milton's readers would be stirred to action (or awaken, for that matter) "if
once they hear[d] that voice" (*PL* 1:274).

From the standpoint of the Reformation theology which informs Milton's epics, of course, it is irrelevant to consider Satan simply as a character or dramatic spectacle. We know that Milton's illustrators were driven to combine some unlikely traditional iconographical formulas in order to portray the Miltonic hero / villain; and it seems inevitable that something like the same combinations were necessary to produce the original "wild work" (*PL* 5:111–12). But whether the character turned out to be an amalgam of epic hero, melodramatic villain, heroic rebel, what you will, the poet / Reformer's immediate problem was the fact that the Satan is within us; uncircumscribed by the bounds of any fiction, he waits "day and night for [man's] destruction" (2:505). Perhaps more openly than its predecessor, Milton's brief epic addresses the problem of putting Satan within us, of suspending disbelief in its most radical form: the kind of resistance to personal engagement that the Reformers thought was built into any "story."[1]

In some well-informed recent scholarship, Milton's second Satan has shown some signs of recovering the Antaean strength he had possessed for Luther and the other reforming authors. He can now be taken seriously again, it is argued, either because there is more of his predecessor in him than we might have thought, or (more promising) he is a fit antagonist after all, a dialectician more or less in command of his strategies and seeking to undermine the very identity of his opponent. In fact, there are important connections between the Satan of *Paradise Regained* and his progenitor, together with some signs that Milton has deepened his conception in at least one respect. But in order to explore these connections, we need to consider much more directly the implications of this "other" Satan's presumed *weaknesses* in *Paradise Regained*.[2]

Satan had begun his career in Milton's work as a deeper rendition of Comus, the figure of the rhetorical virtuoso now masking an inner conflict. Belatedly revealed (following the rhetorical grandeur of the first two books), the tormented character who admits that "my self am Hell" is doomed to remain perpetually locked within the contrarieties that constitute that self, to reason within (not, as in Adam's later case, "through") mazes.[3] From various sources within *Paradise Lost*, we gather that his original perception of the divine love involved something like instinctive denial, and that it was expressed in a fundamentally revisionist manner, reducing love to an arbitrary but binding force indistinguishable from hate: "Love or hate, to me alike, it deals eternal woe" (4:69–70). As Helen Gardner has observed, the poem suggests no different prior condition; an extraordinarily tolerationist poem in its way, *Paradise Lost* does not contradict Satan's claim (directed at the isolated resister Abdiel) that "We know no time when we were not as now."[4] His initial speeches, which so rightly impressed readers of the early nineteenth century and later, suggest a kind of Stoic heroism. But the vantage point provided by the soliloquy of Book 4 denies his actual *possession* of a "fixed mind" and suggests further that the eloquence that had made him so attractive and "famous" is "evasion vain" (as Adam calls his own similar efforts in Book 10); it is talk specifically designed to suppress the thought "both of lost happiness and lasting pain." Because Satan is condemned to observe the fruits of "all his malice," his deepest needs include the kind of oblivion recommended by Moloch in the council debate, and also the verbal or visual bedazzlement proposed by Belial and Mammon, respectively, that might make the painful going a little easier. Full of hypothetical and lyric indulgences of the kind Milton had signaled in his early prose with fictive signposts like "a kind of" and "perhaps," Satan's verbal behavior is not altogether removed from the uncouth swain's impulse to suppress the crucial memories: "For so to interpose a little ease / Let our frail thoughts dally with false surmise" ("Lycidas," 152–53).

And the impulse is shared by the Bard himself. In the invocation to the third book of *Paradise Lost*, the poet looks back upon his "obscure sojourn" in Hell and an escape "through utter and through middle darkness borne / With other notes than to th'*Orphean* lyre" (3:15–17). The poem begins by identifying this obscurity with the primeval Chaos and with what is dark within the poet himself. As though to prove that complete escape is impossible, Milton allows us to hear adversarial complaint in the very core of the invocation; and Book 4 opens with the conflicted soliloquy on Mount Niphates, the lines Milton may well have written while *Paradise Lost* was still projected as a tragedy. Looking around him "in prospect of Eden," Satan *sees* nothing but hell:

> for within him Hell
> He brings, and round about him, nor from Hell
> One step no more than from himself can fly
> By change of place: Now conscience wakes despair
> That slumber'd, wakes the bitter memory
> Of what he was, what is, and what must be.   [4:20–25]

As we have seen, *Paradise Regained* also provides complex framing for that descent into self with which the narrator virtually identifies the action of the poem; the brief epic presents nothing like the antiphonal conflict that seems to have provided Milton's original conception of the Satanic state of mind. But in a curious and subtle way, *Paradise Regained* helps us see more clearly that in both epics a prime function of Satan's well-known literalism, his propensity for lyric particularity, is the wish to escape, to drown all memory in Lethe (as at 3:221–22). As in *Paradise Lost*, Satan would abstract himself from his own evil and so be "stupidly good" (9:465). Hence, in *Paradise Regained*, he gladly dreams on (in rather conspicuously Fletcherian fashion) about the angels' "mild seats" as a species of heaven, and he postures grandly about his fear of a "ris'n" enemy (2:125, 127); he will speak of the Fall from Heaven as though it never *really* took place; and he gets picky about the historical agenda and the providential means by which "that fatal wound / Shall be inflicted by the Seed of *Eve* / Upon my head" (1:53–55). The last example, like many others, suggests once again that Satan literally cannot forget his "hated habitation" (1:47) any more than he can escape himself, here or in *Paradise Lost*. There is a sense that all these distinctions and hypotheses—the well-known nitpicking of the poem—could never suppress the whole truth for Satan, however distracting or confusing it might be for the poem's readers. His talk is "poetry" in the sense of escapist fiction; it is *evasion*, a term both Adam and Samson use to describe similar efforts. And evasion is the point of Satan's curiosity about time too, or the exact manner in which "that fatal wound / Shall be inflicted by the Seed of Eve / Upon my head." It is a wonderfully apt stroke that within this bit of chitchat, Milton would enclose the poem's first reminder of the one thing Satan would most like to forget, the poem's prime "source" in Genesis 3:15 and, more immediately, Milton's open-ended history of the oracle's "verification" in *Paradise Lost*. Until that moment in the tenth book, Milton withholds the text which theoretically contains the poem's entire "great Argument"; but it began with Satan's nagging "thought" (1:54ff.), and the same thought torments him "now." As befits the prime member of a Miltonic exegetic council, Satan flounders and literalizes at 1:60–63, 70–75. And this very characteristic and well-known behavior seeks to suppress the whole notion of "mysterious terms," substituting in their place a terminology appropriate to our visible world: the kingdom or "empire" of earth and air, Mammon's realm. Far from making Satan's overweening memory and lyric "imagination" the occasion for pathos, Milton makes it conceptually and stylistically central; it becomes the brief epic's *idea* of Satan. What seems merely left over from the Adversary of *Paradise Lost*, so to speak, is in fact retroactively clarified within it.[5]

From the first publication of *Paradise Regained*, readers have noticed the peculiarities in this "other" Satan's perceptions and memories. His very first speech is full of an airy verbosity that is appropriate to the location of his movable council. There is more than ample confirmation, too, of all that we had ever thought about the well-known Satanic literalism. We know, for one thing, that hell is not a place situated somewhere "in the air." In speaking (several times) about Alexander (the "Pellean conqueror"), Satan seems most impressed with visible or "outward" signs of recognition like the "triumph." He is associated with such props as shrines (1:438), temples (449), and the panoramic views of Athens and Rome. And while we are shown an "imperial city," what Satan notices seems rather different: an "imperial *palace* (the Capitol upon the Tarpeian rock) aspiring [like himself, of course] "above the rest." Crude as it now seems to say so, Satan really *does* seem fascinated with spatially prominent structures, defensive and "impregnable"—with anything that is "adorned," "gilded," "conspicuous," "glittering," and "fair." And this way of looking at things extends into metaphorical territory, as when he speaks, for example, of the "perfections" of Aaron's robe, or "graces divine," "gifts," or (most difficult, perhaps) "glory." If Satan is a strategically skillful speaker, we must also account for a new and evasive verbal *honesty*, an almost compulsive need to keep on talking, as though he were Samson in the old "effeminate" days; he tends to translate and revise his speech, often in the direction of the ringing bon mot. If he is no longer the grandly titled "Father of Lies," he is a talker, a chatty sophisticate like Comus or Belial, but with a stronger instinct for truth telling of the sort to be found in *Paradise Lost* only in the "unpremeditated" speech of first awakening, or the semiprivacy of Mount Niphates. This is the kind of hedging we find, for instance, in a line like "in manner at our will," where (quite characteristically) Satan cannot seem to help giving away the entire qualification. It is as though Milton has deliberately developed to the fullest extent a whole "soft" side of himself, noticed by Coleridge and perhaps missed by Blake, Shelley, and later readers wishing to promote the "stronger" Satanic stuff in the great poet.

Consider the moment in the first book of the brief epic, when Milton reveals what is left of his greatest Adversary. In an extraordinary overture to the Son, Satan catches himself using the word "love," and engages in a bit of onstage editing. Asking to "approach" the Son, he takes back the word "love," as though in the interest of perfect accuracy:

> Though I have lost
> Much luster of my native brightness, lost

To be belov'd of God, I have not lost
To love, at least contémplate and admire
What I see excellent in good, or fair,
Or virtuous; I should so have lost all sense.
What can be then less in me than desire
To see thee and approach thee, whom I know
Declar'd the Son of God, to hear attent
Thy wisdom, and behold thy Godlike deeds.   [1:377–86]

Ever the revisionist, Satan flattens the distinctions between what is "good" and what is "fair"; in his final (and very sociable) apology there is little to choose between "virtue" and appetitive or merely vegetable "sense," something Milton had called "vigor" in the earlier epic. The passage takes us as close to Satan as we ever get in *Paradise Regained*, and perhaps in both epics. Underneath its surface is the painful recognition, more fully developed than anywhere in the first book of *Paradise Lost*, that after all he *has not* "lost all sense" and perhaps cannot do so. (See *PL* 1:54–55, 213–20). It is Satan's *fate*, it seems, to experience that "desire / To see thee and approach thee," just as he had done alone in the garden. This, paradoxically, constitutes "reprobation," immediately experienced as a "pain of longing unfilfulled"; it is what Samson will call so specifically "the *sense* of Heaven's desertion." Clearly enough, Milton's Satan cannot love and knows it—knows that his "punisher" knows it (*PL* 4:103). And in *Paradise Regained* this erotic hollowness is projected as a kind of aestheticism. If this Satan has suffered a falling-off, the spectatorly distance remains intact; there is still an ability to "contemplate and admire" what he sees "excellent in good and fair." And this pursuit of aesthetic "excellence," that lingering talent so different from the young Milton's quest for the many "shapes and forms of things divine" which constituted ideal "beauty," is the reason the conquered Satan of Book 4 falls just as he does, "smitten with amazement."[6]

In *Paradise Regained*, Milton directly confronts the problem of the New Testament's "uncertain keeping," in part by insisting on the pre-textual secrecy of the Son's heroic deeds. He further claims that the Son's accomplishments were "unrecorded left through many an age," even though these temptations in the wilderness were of course the subject not only of Luke's and Matthew's Gospel accounts but also of the numerous retellings cited by Mackellar.[7] John Carey has argued that this means something like "unsung, uncelebrated" (p. 1078). But *Paradise Regained* appears to involve a somewhat different focus from the earlier epic's emphasis upon an argument "more heroic" than its predecessors. If *Paradise Lost* corrects the record on the matter of true heroism in its "higher argument" as yet unsung, the Son's deeds are *"above* heroic." It is as though such deeds can be heroic only *if* done in secret, without the contamination of the various media or even a text.

But Milton has not forgotten Raphael's dictum that "process of speech" is a necessary vehicle here; even immediate acts of God like the verification of His oracle must be "So told as earthly notion can receive" (*PL* 7:179). Consequently, Milton makes the Son's heroic deeds "secret" in an additional sense by enveloping them in tradition, something the poem clearly regards—and demonstrates—as all pervasive. If Satan has been silenced as an effective voice, he survives as a chatty attendant. His "talk" is a kind of listening-without-hearing, a virtual definition of tradition as Milton understood it. The crucial innovation of *Paradise Regained* is the way in which Satan is not so much the Bard in disguise as a sort of public for the divine critic. His "corporate" side, noticed acutely by Malcolm X, has also taken a different turn in the brief epic.[8] If he stood for a kind of worldly orthodoxy in *Paradise Lost*, there was always the hint of internal dread and disaffection; for all that "firm concord" worked out during the Council, Milton's original hell is a place of anarchic but also potentially vital individualism. There is no such resistance to be found in the world of *Paradise Regained* except in the most abstracted and isolated form. Satan never seems quite distinguishable from that quasi-ecclesiastical "council or consistory" that must authenticate his thoughts; he is surrounded by an enveloping cloud (or better, a "globe") of make-believe listeners and collaborators. It is as though the conflict which Milton had originally located within Satan has been rearranged, reassigned, with the result that the demonic entourage is much more cooperative: *Paradise Regained* makes it clear that the audience *is* Satan. With less political and social tension by far than Prospero's island, the wilderness of *Paradise Regained* features not so much the chaotic energy of the first epic's hell—that swarming of bees in springtime—as collectively orchestrated, animated puppets, agents marching in formation, a "chosen band" offered to the Son as "thy gentle Ministers" (2:375). Satan provides an all-too-effective model for human audiences too, whether on- or offstage; his entire function can be summarized by the words of the narrator, immediately following the first of the several accounts of the Baptism at Jordan: "That heard the Adversary." The initial two words here force a convergence between the poem's adversarial and ourselves, its offstage readers. In this way, the Satanic corporateness established by his frequent consultations includes any reader, and we watch even the "red letters" of Matthew's Gospel get taken up (at 1:29–33) by the Adversary, as though mistaken interpretation had attended the unmediated occasion itself. Thanks to a new kind of Satan, the moment seems familiar because it comes across as a kind of media event. Like the Chorus and other visitors to Samson, the Adversary serves as a kind of built-in memory—a source of our "thoughts," if not quite the Son's. But much more important for the reader of *Paradise Regained*—the late Reformation, non-Messianic, or otherwise "gentle" reader, at any rate—Satan serves an additional function as the prime onstage recipient and echo of the emerging author's words. In vocalizing and expatiating upon the Son's recollections (and early consciousness in general), he stands for the early public of the divine (or otherwise "extraordinary") protagonist, a prominent character in both poems of Milton's final volume.

Thus viewed, the scene of *Paradise Regained* becomes what Milton considered to be the narrow verge between the tradition-bound antecedents of this crucial moment in human history and its equally traditionalizing reception. In it, Milton writes the history of the inner "motions" which precede and eventuate in the Gospel. But the design of *Paradise Regained* involves the incorporation, *within this Gospel scene*, of a worldly, ecclesiastically defined church. And the poem presents this structure as the origin of a literalist, merely verbal tradition, something made out of what Satan has "seen, or by relation heard" (2:182). In a sense, *Paradise Regained* is more wide-ranging than its companion partly because it seems to incorporate that future conversation with the "gentiles"—in effect with *us*—to which the Adversary refers toward the end of the poem. Like the book of Judges for *Samson Agonistes*, the familiar source of Milton's myth is synecdochically included within the work, a distant aftermath, we might say, of the authentic (or "unapocryphal") events we witness, a creation of the early public to which I have referred. It is as though, in keeping with the way he presents history in the concluding book of *Paradise Lost*, Milton had coupled Luke and Matthew with an epitome of Acts, say, or Paul's Epistle to the Galatians.[9]

The epic encompasses the early, but for Milton perhaps also a kind of paradigmatic, history of the Church in the world; its real contention is between the maturing but still questing Son in the third book of *Paradise Lost* and an antagonist who seems to be the "textualizing" repository of an *emerging* Gospel. We may be privileged observers as in the *Masque* and so often elsewhere in Milton's poetry, in on revolutionary events performed "in secret" and consequently "unrecorded left through many an age" (1:15–16). In reading the poem, we witness nothing less than the divine Son's glimpsing of providential "means," including the fact of his own Job-like human suffering. But there is considerable challenge here too, a sharp ambiguity in our advantaged position. For in a sense, Scripture is "uncertainly kept" even here. What we observe is emphatically not the unblemished form of chastity, nor are we made privy to what the young Milton had called the "shapes and forms of things divine." Instead, we have the spectacle of something like a separatist movement. Milton calls the divine Son a king at the very moment he disaffiliates from "the brethren," a group bound to remind us of Milton's own Presbyterians and called by the Son "distinguishable scarce / From Gentiles" (3:424–25).[10] This is the oracle the world "would not receive." The poem does not shrink from alluding ironically to the eventual "fame" of Andrew and Simon, and fame (we will shortly be reminded) is "double-mouth'd" (*SA* 971). Throughout this work, in short, we are in the close company of tradition's own special (and very durable) guardian, the "White Devil."

As Luther had described it in developing his doctrine of the two Gospels, the "White Devil" was the keeper of tradition and the expert in their strange powers of fascination. Indeed, fascination was the primary technique of the "White Devil," a bedazzlement consistently described in visual terms. "He stirs up the dust, hoping to raise a cloud before our eyes so that we cannot see the light. In the cloud he dazzles us with will-o'-the-wisps to mislead us."[11] He seeks to "lead us off our path by his flying brands and flames" (*Luther's Works* 40, p. 70). Under such circumstances—and especially in a church—it is the Christian's difficult task to "receive [God's] Word without stopping to gaze at its external beauty or equipment," for "[God] permits no false prophets to attempt anything except something external, such as works, and subtle minute discoveries about external things" (*LW* 20:73; 40:80). Luther's name for the keeper of traditions was meant to distinguish him from the "black" devil, the relatively easy mark who wears the kind of label ("Error" or, say, "The Apostate Angel") that makes him less a threat than a cartoon figure: the devil as an ass. The true Adversary, of course, "does not want to be as black as he is painted," Luther had written; "he would like to shine in the beautiful garment of God's Word" (*LW* 24:264). Satan consequently "adorns himself with such an angelic, yes, such a divine form and appearance, just as he makes a god of himself when he speaks to Christ in Matt. 4:9" (*LW* 24:312). Taking his seat "not in a stable or in a pigpen or in a congregation of unbelievers, but in the highest and holiest places possible, namely in the temple of God," the white devil is a specialist, as Luther sees it, in custom and the impossible claims of the Law—in general, the whole area of spirituality, where he "peddles his deadly poison as the doctrine of grace, the Word of God, and the Gospel of Christ, in the guise of an angel or even God himself" (*LW* 26:25). And this last "angel" was the one Milton and Luther thought of in connection with an especially fervent passage by Paul in Galatians 1:8: "But even if we, or an angel from heaven, should preach to you a gospel contrary to that which we preached to you, let him be accursed."[12] If the Satan of *Paradise Regained* were conceived along these lines, it would explain the extraordinary extent of his involvement or overlapping with the whole range of the work's characters, including the Son—an artistic development with interesting and perhaps not altogether manageable implications for the role and actual behavior of the epic historian himself.

In his own consideration of the "double scripture" in chapter 30 of the *Christian Doctrine*, Milton wrote that the "external scripture of the written word" (and especially the New Testament) "has often been liable to corruption and is, in fact, corrupt," thanks chiefly to the "various untrustworthy authorities" assigned to its care. For Milton, who draws his general conclusion by invoking the mysteries of divine provenience, the textual situation is a virtual proof of the primacy given to the second, internal "Scripture of the Holy Spirit": "I do not know why God's providence should have committed the contents of the New Testament to such wayward and uncertain guardians, unless it was so that this very fact might convince us that the Spirit which is given to us is a more certain guide than scripture, and that we ought to follow it." It is on the evidence of Scripture itself, Milton thought, that "all things are eventually referred to the Spirit and the unwritten word." This is the very source *Paradise Regained* seeks to reconstitute in presenting deeds performed "in secret" and "unrecorded left through many an age" (*CPW* 6:587–88, 589, 590).[13]

For Milton, a central part of the literary problem was inherent in the very nature of his scriptural materials, in the various ways in which the Bible "spoke all things" (in Chrysostom's phrase) even at a moment, like the temptation of Jesus in the wilderness, when it seemed to be recounting biography. Part of the Son's well-known "coldness" as a literary character—including his tendency to anticipate what Satan "should have said"—involves a perfectly traditional point for which Milton felt a special affinity: that in his exchanges with the Pharisees, for example, Jesus had addressed not just the words but the thoughts of his antagonists. In a well-known passage of the *Advancement of Learning*, Bacon had described it thus:

> For it is an excellent observation which hath been made upon the answers of our Saviour Christ to many of the questions which were propounded to him, how that they are impertinent to the state of the question demanded; the reason whereof is, because not being like man, which knows man's thoughts by his words, but knowing man's thoughts immediately, he never answered their words, but their thoughts. Much in the like manner it is with the scriptures, which being written to the thoughts of men, and to the succession of all ages, with a foresight of all heresies, contradictions, differing estates of the church, yea and particularly of the elect, are not to be interpreted only according to the latitude of the proper sense of the place, and respectively toward that present occasion whereupon the words were uttered, or in precise congruity or contexture with the words before or after, or in contemplation of the principal scope of the place; but have in themselves, not only totally or collectively, but distributively in clauses and words, infinite springs and streams of doctrine to water the church in every part. And therefore as the literal sense, as it were the main stream of river; so the moral sense chiefly, and sometimes the allegorical or typical, are they whereof the church hath most use: not that I wish men to be bold in allegories, or indulgent or light in allusions; but that I do much condemn that interpretation of the scripture which is only after the manner as men use to interpret a profane book.[14]

In effect, the Son of *Paradise Regained* is not really speaking to Satan or to many of us; our relation to this scene is something like the potentially interested bystander to the Apologist's quarrel with Joseph Hall.

Students of Milton are indebted to Barbara K. Lewalski for the fullest explanation of how Milton's poem can be said to refer us, in Milton's words, "to the unwritten word." In her study *Milton's Brief Epic*, Lewalski makes the fascinating observation that at certain points in the epic we have momentary "imaginative recreation[s] of the Son's heavenly existence before his incarnation."[15] As in the "Nativity" (which this poem echoes at 1:109 and frequently elsewhere), there is the distinct feeling of points in time collapsing or telescoping, of a new kind of timeliness, the suggestion of a fundamental dehistoricization of the Son that is accomplished in our minds as well as his, despite considerable resistance. The poem as a whole seems to conflate several distinct moments in the Gospel accounts, as scholars have long noticed. Northrop Frye has suggested, for example, that the action of *Paradise Regained* involves a recognizable displacement of the Harrowing of Hell. And there are thought to be "proleptic" references to the Crucifixion, including, most notably, the Son's mention of a "crown of thorns." In addition, of course, there are the poem's many references to the Annunciation, itself a collection of earlier texts like the oracle in the tenth book of *Paradise Lost* (see 1:59, 133). It seems clear that the Son's now complete command of the Law and the Prophets is part of a more generalized memory here, harking all the way back (for all we know) to that primeval council of the gods, mysteriously inclusive of "the Satan" and uniquely recorded in the Babylonian original of the Job story—the very "beginning," so to speak, of *Paradise Lost*. Fundamental to the poem is the idea of historical synecdoche which would link the "strangeness" of the early Gospel era (as Calvin had called it) with a more radical kind of historical (or posthistorical) revolution. We are dealing, in short, with the sort of conquest over Gospel "story" for which Revelations offers the main paradigm.

To the extent that we are time- (and story-) bound readers, it seems hard to imagine that we will be much different, as critics, from Comus, who wonders why the Lady is "vext"—what has made him (or Milton, more likely) so anxious? What so many readers regard as protomodern "anxiety" here seems to involve the Seventh Prolusion's contemporaneity with "time itself." It pertains both to that long-term memory (the one Lewalski thinks "returns"), going all the way back to the beginning, and also to the ability to address himself (as Milton put it in the *Areopagitica*) "to aftertimes." In this light, remarks that *have* to sound just testy to mortal men ("I never liked thy talk", or "I *told* you") acquire real point: in fact, Satan does remember, but pretends not to. Hence the seeming "inhumanity" with which the divine Son shows the sort of mastery so differently displayed (as "Pauline") in the *Areopagitica*. Hence, too, the ease of misunderstanding the point of the Son's seeming weariness—all those "he who's" and the impression that this is *always* the way it works. After all, it is in the widest possible context (virtually against the backdrop of the extratemporal divine "prospect high") that Milton locates the historical part of his fiction, the culmination of the Son's "private" phase of education.

With some very topical recollections indeed, Milton had explored this new kind of time most recently in the tenth book of the earlier epic, in dating (or rather refusing to date) the moment of verification for the "oracle" of Genesis 3:15.

So spake this Oracle, then verifi'd
When *Jesus* son of *Mary* second *Eve*,
Saw Satan fall like Lightning down from Heav'n,
Prince of the Air; then rising from his Grave
Spoiled Principalities and Powers, triumpht
In open show, and with ascension bright
Captivity led captive through the Air,
The Realm it self of Satan long usurpt,
Whom he shall tread at last under our feet.   [10:182–90][16]

Quite specifically—in a moment like "So spake our Morning Star, then in his rise" (1:294)—*Paradise Regained* records the "ascension bright" mentioned here. And other details, however easily forgotten (because presented, necessarily, without spectacle), similarly point to this radical conjunction of such diverse points in time: the Son rose from his grave / ascended into heaven precisely *when* Jesus saw Satan "fall like Lightning down from Heav'n." Now, then, was that the day of the final temptation over there in wilderness X, or the day (mentioned at *PL* 3:392–96) when He drove his "flaming Chariot wheels" over the necks of "warring Angels disarrayed"? Just as the word "wilderness" in *Paradise Regained* becomes unspecific or generic, so the word "day" has been drastically altered from early on in *Paradise Lost* and before that in the ode "On the Morning of Christ's Nativity."

Given these obvious recollections of the heady early 1640s, it is remarkable to what extent an earlier retrospection also clarifies the poem's sense of vocational and intellectual closure. Behind *Paradise Regained* is the theological notion, intimated in the Second Prolusion and fully developed in the *Apology*, of the divine Son as the "recapitulator" of the human species. Coupled with this very early preoccupation is a central idea from *Of Education*—soon to reappear as an appendix to the *Poems* of 1673—that intellectual "perfection" can be approximated through the procedure of scholarly review. On the threshold of what *Of Education* had called a "universall insight into things," the Son is engaged in one of those periodic reviews which Milton had required of his hypothetical scholars: retirements, as he had called them, "for memories sake" to be undertaken until they have "confirm'd and solidly united the whole body of their perfected knowledge, like the last embattelling of a Romane legion" (*CPW* 2:406–07). At such a point in the cycle of learning, an educational quest can easily become the defense of a citadel; the underpinnings of divine contemplation—the whole ladder of the earthly sciences, so to speak—can be kicked away at last, or pulled in behind you, as Robert Frost put it in his variation on the theme.[17] The moment had a considerable history in Milton's thought even before its compression into that modern-sounding term "insight," and there can be little doubt that he had originally devised his curriculum, including its meticulously described last phase, with relation to traditional Christology. Borrowing from the early portrayal of Pythagoras, his Apologist had described the Son (and other teachers of the Church) in the specifically literary terms appropriate to the *recapitulator generis humanae*, who possessed all literary gifts and commanded the whole range of styles otherwise divided among the teachers of his church. A prime model for the Shakespearean prince, this Son was *literally* composed "of all humors that have showed themselves humors since the old days of goodman Adam to the pupil age of this present." Milton had distinguished his stylistic omnicompetence from the limited means of Luther or his own Apologist. A single or dominant style (like these Reformers' vehemence) would signal a character altogether different from one in literary as in other ways "perfect"—a literary person possessed, in a sense, of no character at all. Hence our impression that the Son's literary talents remain almost completely latent, our sense of mere parodic echo when he deviates into Satan's kind of lyricism while remaining "unmoved," beating Satan at his own dazzling game of verbal microscopy. And the Son's historical consciousness, too, is "recapitulatory." In the brief epic and *Samson Agonistes* alike, the repeated word for the protagonist's behavior is "revolve"; a kind of review (or in Milton's idiom a "revolution") seems to precede the self-defining acts of each hero. Like Samson, the Son of *Paradise Regained* is "revolving" all these traditions, literary and prophetic texts alike, to the point of mastery, or the kind of authority occasionally attained by the speaker of the *Areopagitica*. By the same token, we are clearly well beyond the ideological claims of these texts—beyond "politics"—when he can speak of them as mere books or say of them, so remotely, that "I have also heard, perhaps have read" (4:116). His much discussed "Think not but that I know these things; or think / I know them not" (4:286–87) consequently points to something much more specific than a reticent or reserved nature. There are undoubtedly gaps in the hero's information as to how he should throw off his obscurity and (in his seemingly incomplete phrase) "openly begin" (1:288), as to how he might complete the haunting parallel with "Uzzean Job." But our nearest approach to the raw consciousness, say, of Satan's soliloquy on Mount Niphates is the long retrospections of Book 1. It is an interesting and difficult passage—for the Son, no doubt, a recurrent flashback like Eve's memories of her own reflection in that "crystal mirror."[18] But as the bystanders to the present encounter, we are denied this kind of history in *Paradise Regained*. We seem to witness the ritualized postlude to a biographical struggle never really enacted here; the real temptation was over before the present poem began. So far as the Son is concerned, Satan just refines and clarifies matters already resolved, matters consequently just rehearsed during the poem proper. He knows "these things" already, a prime reason this poem's Satan seems almost dutiful in playing out the play. In a fundamental way, indeed, the entire work can be regarded as aftermath; we are at least twice removed from any existential or psychological reference for that "descent into himself." This phrase may work with others like it to align the particular historical moment with that other matter of Descent, Ascension bright, all the mysterious lore of "verification." For better or worse, the work remains faithful to the uniquely recapitulatory consciousness of its subject, someone in the process of becoming (as Milton had put it in 1632), "a contemporary of time itself."[19]

Unfortunately for Milton—or readers who prefer warmer literary humors, at any rate—the Son sounds the part. As with the Lady at Ludlow, his very "freedom" seems to involve a lack of style, and even the denial or qualification of an impressive lyric talent. As we have seen, he is meant to be a far more imaginative and rhetorically talented character than he can show; certainly, he need not be thought of as the exclusive practitioner of any one style, even Milton's own late "plain" or spare one.[20] One of his speeches late in the poem, usually considered an anomaly, is useful in this context. Interrupting Satan's presentation of the world's kingdoms, the Son becomes marvelously, some think uncharacteristically, inventive; for the briefest of moments, Milton brings us as close as he ever gets to the lyric virtuosity of Jonson's Sir Epicure Mammon:

> Nor doth this grandeur and majestic show
> Of luxury, though call'd magnificence,
> More than of arms before, allure mine eye,
> Much less my mind; though thou should'st add to tell
> Thir sumptuous gluttonies, and gorgeous feasts
> On *Citron* tables or *Atlantic* stone;
> (For I have also heard, perhaps have read)
> Their wines of *Setia*, *Cales*, and *Falerne*,
> *Chios* and *Crete*, and how they quaff in gold,

Crystal and Murrhine cups emboss'd with Gems
And studs of Pearl.   [4:110–20]

It is an almost gratuitous bit of authorship in Satan's own manner (the "Office mean," Milton had called a similar indulgence in *Paradise Lost* [9:39]): a passage which permits us not even a distant prospect of architectural configurations, but an almost dizzying close-up of the materials and adornments of drinking cups. He is an expert in antique porcelains, we discover to our surprise, and he proves it by scrutinizing what Michael had called the "Arts that polish Life (*PL* 11:610).

For the critic, the difficulty of the moment is suggested in Milton's parenthetic "I have also heard, *perhaps* have read," and the implications of "unmov'd"—that awful programmatic word for the speech and (some would say) the whole poem. This strangely expository figure seems cold and disengaged ("bard-like") because he is beyond us; it is virtually inevitable that we draw conclusions which are unrelated to the Christology that informs the poem, or even to the actual range of the Son's performance. The poem itself insists on the question of the Son's (and God's) relation to us when Satan observes (no doubt enviously) that "all men are sons of God" or that "relation stands." There is good reason for the scholarship that focuses on the vexed matter of his divinity, historical uniqueness, or theological typicality. Still, though he may be unique, the Son does not appear to mean anything very mysterious in a phrase like "I as all others," for example. The "as" here is surely unintensive, the Son less committed to his "recapitulatory" function than, say, Richard II at Pomfret, playing in one person many people. And the poem is full of other examples. The Son clearly does not mean as much as he says when he observes that the Baptist "knew me" at 1:275. A curious feature of the 1671 volume is the way in which both its protagonists, although clearly extraordinary figures, generalize their predicament, suggesting that anyone could perform similarly wondrous deeds. Just as God may dispense with "me or thee" in *Samson Agonistes*, so the Son's "he who" becomes a kind of formula here, referring to anyone possessed of "Light from above, from the fountain of light" (see also 4:318, 322f., 517–20). It is easy enough for *him* to say it is not a question of special talents. Our instincts were right; the problem is his lack of character, his seeming remoteness or mysteriousness or secrecy. The problem of carrying on with the naive and questing voice of *Paradise Lost*'s redeemer becomes critical when we overhear the Son at the moment of "insight" or recognition, when he takes the first step forward to speak in this poem's version of pulpit or council.

It is at just such a moment—the juncture of a private, contemplative descent into self and the subsequent, active ministry—that the narrative dilemma seems almost insoluble, and we inevitably pose the old questions about whether the Son is tempted as God or as man. Obviously, there is specific point to the Father's early suggestion that the present encounter is a kind of exercise preliminary to the ultimate conquest (just as the Harrowing, say, is a preliminary)—that here the Son will be enabled to "lay down the *rudiments* / Of his great warfare" (1:155–60; italics mine). But if "Humiliation and strong Sufferance" are to be the eventual trial for the Son in his mortal form, the brief epic's rudiments seem to consist too specifically in the activity of textual collation and (as we shall see) an almost simultaneous process of demonic deconstruction. He begins at the level of allusion and collation, following up important quotations (like John 18:37 and Ps 12) with an effect of complete mastery of the Reformation Bible.[21] As unspectacular as all the checking seems, furthermore, this is the poem's way of getting at the spiritual sense of Scripture, not just its "history": the speech we have just heard—and not, say, the "historical" emergence of Jesus from the river Jordan—constitutes the actual rise of the Son, who is consequently called "our Morning Star." The designation, like others in *Paradise Regained*, aligns the poem with the kind of scriptural consummation that occurs in Revelations 22:16 (and of course throughout that culminating book), when Jesus himself draws all prior identities together (even "from the beginning") in the phrase which provided Lancelot Andrews with his meditation on "A star never seen before."[22]

In moving toward what Milton regarded as a scriptural consummation, though, a large part of the Son's job is to check Satan's memory, so to speak, by picking out "the text" or, better, its "reason" from the rest of the Adversary's verbiage. The issue of "textuality" is clearly central to the poem. The result, almost inevitably, is a character who strikes us (not just Satan) as "difficult and nice"—a "precisian," as the Puritans were sometimes called. At 3:394, the Son seems almost to mimic Satan's part, opposing it with a very precise memory of 1 Chron. 21:1 (407–12). (Elsewhere, the Son duplicates, and *improves on*, Satan's self-pity, in this way literally practicing self-despite.) He can also fill in on the experience of the "happy place," merely mentioned by the Adversary, to the point of displaying the Bard's own kind of doctrinal clarity.[23] But the very precision of the Son here is part of a character that is meant to seem far more imaginative and inventive than he is willing to show; relatively speaking, the Son seems much freer than Satan from what "is written." Paradoxically, his way of matching texts (as at the climactic "Also it is written") involves a *freedom* from "textuality" in Satan's trivial, pedantic sense; by arresting Satan's words he makes *them* the text in question, gives back to these recognizable voices the kind of indifference or "materiality" that can lead us through the mere words to the sense or reason of this moment in Gospel history. By the time we hear about the "spirit and judgement equal or superior" which the Son would have us bring to the reading of classical authors, are we meant to have recovered something very similar in the presumably different territory of sacred history?

Chapter Eight

"With Curious Eye":
Setting and Structure
in *Paradise Regained*

Vain wisdom all, and false Philosophy:
Yet with a pleasing sorcery could charm
Pain for a while or anguish, and excite
Fallacious hope, or arm th'obdured breast
With stubborn patience as with triple steel.
PL 2:565–69

In the special circumstances Milton provides in the brief epic, it seems misleading to think of Satan as essentially the same old friend of *Paradise Lost*: grand but tattered, unfairly dogged with the divine (or more likely the poet's own) wrath. There can be little doubt that, seen specifically as a character, the Satan of *Paradise Regained* is denied much of the sympathy which bathes him in the earlier epic. He is pronounced "foil'd in all his wiles" more often and more variously than many readers care to remember. But Milton walks a fine line here. For all his conceptual rigor, Milton knew as well as Shakespeare that there was much to be said on behalf of his Falstaff. In fact, the *real* Satan of *Paradise Regained* is nothing a reader can be done with quite so soon—or indeed, at any point—in the narrative. Well-informed and skillful readers continue to argue that in *Paradise Regained* the Son has indeed been "fully tried" in a typological sense that may include the reader as a third Adam; that the work can point mysteriously to (and beyond) those central incidents in the ancient faith, the Passion and the Harrowing, and so can involve the ultimate verification of Scripture's central promise. One thinks of the young Ellwood accepting the manuscript of *Paradise Regained* (or the whole project of 1671) from the famous blind poet and taking some of the credit for rounding off the great apologetic enterprise. But we may also permit Milton a rueful smile at his earnest friend, even if we stop short of adding *Samson Agonistes* to the pile of papers he handed to the young Quaker who had somehow failed to locate "Paradise Found" within *Paradise Lost*. It is not just that the Son's unique "talent" is literary death to hide in *Paradise Regained*. Milton's very conception of the antagonist, together with the structure of the brief epic, permits a brilliant and surprising resilience: an extraordinary degree of influence over the characters and presenter of the poem, and consequently the disturbing sense of an aftermath to that seemingly definitive fall from the pinnacle of the Temple.

Satan is usually discussed as the provocateur (however inept) of the Son's tart replies, or else as an ineffectual respondent; and I have perpetuated this convention. With Satan's "sensuousness" (or "Epicureanism") in mind, however, we are in a better position to understand the very interesting nuances, the ways in which he serves the poem's readers as a sort of raw, unheroic memory. In the Adversary's initial speech, Milton suggests that Satan provides our contact with the human "ages" now being reviewed in such different fashion—in an uninvolved way none of us could possibly manage—by the divine Son. He claims to have witnessed the Son's entire career, in and also prior to history; he has heard the prophecies of the Messiah, of the Annunciation, and of course the early "private" career, to which the present encounter serves as culmination; "From that time seldom have I ceased to eye / Thy infancy, thy childhood, and thy youth, / Thy manhood last, though yet in private bred." It is ironic, but certainly no accident, that he also offers the poem's first reminder of Genesis 3:15 and the "oracle" so embarrassing to himself (1:53–55).

Within the work too, Satan is the original witness. The poem's first sustained use of Scripture occurs during the Son's memory of his mother's speech, where—together with some perfectly innocuous shepherds and a "glorious Choir / Of angels"—we discover, of all things, a "vested Priest" standing right there before "just *Simeon* and Prophetic *Anna*" (1:242, 244, 255–57). Here as in *Paradise Lost*, the sources of tradition are located "fast by the Oracle of God" (*PL* 1:12) and its practice is entangled in false worship "with Temple, Priest, and Sacrifice" (*PR* 3:83). And whether

Satan is considered as a character, a mode of behavior, or an institution, Milton's version of the White Devil is its vehicle. It is he and not the Son himself who ventures to quote the "Sovran voice" at Jordan (1:84–85; Matt. 3:16–17), while we are scrupulously denied access to this text. (This has not deterred intelligent readers from accepting the quotation as authentic, and even attributing it to the Son—one of the many interesting lapses in the poem's critical history.) A copy who would be the original, this poem's Adversary is composed entirely of what he has "seen, or by relation heard" (2:182), a creature of tradition; and the pervasiveness of tradition is a central preoccupation of the poem. Satan's entire function can be summarized in the words of the narrator immediately following the first account of the Baptism: "That heard the Adversary" (1:33). And however illusory it may be, he has plenty of assistance from those intelligence reports and "councils"; from the behavior of the earliest "believers"—the various personages who joined the Son at Jordan, considered specifically as historical characters; and even, I will suggest, from the poet himself.

I

Granted, there is something to be said for the thoughts of Andrew and Simon, who are given intimations of Revelations in their "fiery wheels" (2:15), and trust in the Son's "coming again to judge the quick and dead." The detail allows Milton to picture the temptation in good synecdochic fashion as the dawn to a new, posthistorical "day." But if we recall the Apologist's use of a similar phrase, this zeal may seem premature, and the echo of the creed somehow inappropriate to a moment so much *earlier* than, say, the crucifixion. This, surely, is temporal displacement carried too far. There seems to be a general fear that a relatively minor disappearane on the Son's part is tantamount to full-scale abandonment; their "belief" seems to depend upon the physical presence of the Son, not exactly on the evidence of things unseen. As though bound to a script, they insist upon the "expressness" of the messianic designation, and there are times when even the structure of Milton's sentences (as in "Therefore" at 2:18, or "Sometimes they thought . . . as once") suggests their bondage to precedent and tradition—to what Luther might have called the Law in the Gospel. If it is possible, the rather nationalistic Christianity of the "new-baptiz'd" seems *premature*; it is in any case rooted in an implicit faith in experiences and associations prior to the public ministry. At times, their tone seems almost suspiciously pathetic (as at 2:9–10). Despite the apparent familiarity of the new baptized with the conventional sites of inspiration, their poetry seems escapist, self-fascinating, facile. Though it is a complex portrait, Milton appears to suggest the fallibility of these early believers who trust the "high Authority" of divine pronouncements they may never have heard; there is a limit, after all, to what "talk" and sharing quarters can impart. And if we consider the almost programmatic issue of the poem-as-true-record, it is not promising either that they are so clearly linked with the canonical Andrew and Simon, "famous after known . . .—though in Holy Writ not nam'd" (2:7–8). They help Milton point to Peter's experience, resolved by the vision of Acts 10:6, that is, the ordinary human difficulty of modifying in the face of new or revolutionary developments, and specifically that resistance to new teachings which Milton found often reenacted in England's history (according to the Digression in the *History of Britain*). Together with the fishermen and even Mary, they provide those "thoughts from without" from which the Son must extricate his own conscience before he himself can become the "voice divine" in action.[1]

"Meanwhile," in Milton's disjunctive phrase, there are the bystanders to this dispute: the readers of the poem, for better or worse the guardians of the brief epic's crucial Gospel incident. As many of them have publicly testified, it is not always easy even to get the attributions straight, to sort out these overlapping characters. The difficulty of the Son's predicament is manifested partly in the problems we so frequently have in determining basic questions of syntactic agency; Milton's sentences often seem as permissive as the divine will. In retrospect, the celebrated instance near the poem's conclusion (when, as William Kerrigan observes, Satan and the Son inhabit the same pronoun) proves to be symptomatic.[2] Much earlier (at 1:319), Milton has forced a conjunction between the Son's "thoughts," often incorporating another character's voice, and Satan, who turns out to be the primary voice in question. The "he" of 319 *turns out* to be the Son, but some work is required to *avoid* identifying this "he" with the "who" just three words farther down the line.

> But now an aged man in Rural weeds,
> Following, as seem'd, the quest of some stray Ewe,
> Or wither'd sticks to gather, which might serve
> Against a Winter's day when winds blow keen,
> To warm him wet return'd from field at Eve,
> He saw approach; who first with curious eye
> Perus'd him, then with words thus utter'd spake.   [1:314–20]

The uncertain agency of this moment (or at 1:36, say) is the effect, for the particular-minded reader at any rate, of Satan's character: the Adversary's deep-seated need to "approach" the Son or indeed to *be* "the exalted man" himself. Like Whig historians of the sort Milton became in 1642, we get the story straight only after the fact. Even as the Son discovers the fullest contents of the divine will, Satan attends him as the semi-inner author in charge of "glib[bing] with lies" the tongues of Ahab's "flattering Prophets" (375), as close to this divine source as the toad at Eve's ear.

The originating incident of the Baptism provides the poem's most extensive evidence of the intent to make "Sons" of all readers; here Milton seems acutely aware of the paradoxical fact that his own text involves the inward, "unwritten" territory of the spirit. For us, the Son's own memory of Jordan is the last of three separate accounts; and it involves significant corrections of the record, including our own, presumably immediate memories of the event itself. There is a considerable interval between the almost fragmentary cries of the Baptist and the poem's first speech; and yet Milton seems to insist on the continuity of his poetic action with the true, inwardly scriptural record. In presenting the original incident of the brief epic, indeed, Milton seems determined to avoid the trappings of what Raphael calls "process of speech." The descent of the Spirit instantly punctuates the Baptist's recognition of the Son; for this wonder there is no question of any presenter's credentials, no onstage author. The Father's voice is heard even as the dove descends, not disjoined by one of those very theatrical "meanwhiles"; so far as we can tell, the dove's descent *is* the Father's voice. (Consistently in *Paradise Regained*, "knowing" seems to be a quiet, unspectacular affair, like that remarkable but easily neglected awakening of the poet in Sonnet 18.) And on the other hand—equally part of the poem's world—there are the very different memories of the Baptism, each of them significantly revisionary.

In details like Heaven's "Crystal Doors," Satan's account recalls the odd particularity of that vision of Jacob's ladder in the third book of *Paradise Lost* (510–15). There is a lively curiosity about the mechanics of that perfect dove's descent "on [the Son's] head"; the whole scene is reminiscent of those electronically simulated national leaders speaking out on the issues at amusement parks. And this is part of a generalized attempt to fascinate, disguised as honest interpretive puzzlement as to "whate'er it meant" (1:83). In the authentic account (heretofore "unrecorded," we have been told), it was quite simply "Heaven" which opened, and "the Spirit" which descended, however incomprehensibly to Satan, "in likeness of a Dove"—

all this while the Father's voice from "Heaven pronounc'd him his beloved Son" (1:32). Satan's crystal doors are missing from Milton's (the evangelical?) account; nor is there any concern on his part, it seems, to locate "Heav'n" relative to "the Clouds" (1:81). Milton seems to take pains to deny us anything, in Satan's terms, "express." It is Satan, in fact, who alone quotes the "Sovran voice" in *Paradise Regained* or, rather, who would become the voice divine by *mis*quoting, inventing: "This is my Son belov'd, in him am pleas'd" (1:85). (Considering what we have already said about Satan as a character or "person," much may depend upon our noticing his confusion as to who was doing what to whom at Jordan [1:80–83], his reluctance to ascribe vocal sovereignty to another voice, his constitutional inability to restore the true "I am.")

The last of the poem's historians restores (and even improves upon) our own treacherous memory of this poem's originating moment. He speaks very casually of Heaven's "eternal doors" (1:281; Samson will refer similarly to God's "ear"), incorporating Ps 24:7. Perhaps to our surprise, he applies the phrase "like a dove" to the verb "descended": he cancels the disjunctive, hypostatic word "likeness", because after all it is the *motion* that was "dovelike," not (as Satan would have it) the spirit's *shape*, as in the vulgar illustrations. (Satan's "whate'er it meant" had further suggested that the "meaning" of this event was something other than shape or motion alike.) It is in keeping with this kind of precision that the brief epic's Son is remembered for his silence during the work.[3] His definitive putdown of Satan is quite frankly "inauthentic" in the sense that it is cited as something written and just opportunely remembered; this heroic deed is a quotation. Throughout he engages quite freely—almost precisely in the attitude of the Lady in *Comus*—in the recognition of a source and center outside himself. He insists on affiliation, the "filial freedom" that involves the subordination of "his own" acts to the "I am"; as he says so precisely, "I seek not mine, but his who sent me, and thereby witness *whence* I am." In this way, the Son can "stand" (and "succeed" in more than one sense of the word) precisely by insisting on his subordinate place in the divine family. In this context, it is significant that the Son chooses not to quote the Father's own "voice" at Jordan, just referring to it instead as "the sum of all" (1:283). This is one of the many lingering (if also revised) signs of Milton's social and theological principles, to be found as early as the *Masque at Ludlow Castle*.

At a point like this, it becomes clear that we share something of the difficulty the Son finds in locating, and starting to live by, an "inward voice." Readers who recognize an even sharper recall than their own are literally engaged in what Milton liked to call, with its literal meaning intact, "discernment." In this sense, *all* readers of the brief epic are privileged auditors, like the audience of a masque in the Platonic manner— witnesses to heroic deeds that are (almost by their very nature, it seems) "unrecorded" (1:16). During *Paradise Regained*, we too are are given the chance to undergo a similar final phase in our education, as though we were the younger brothers to the Son's Lady at Ludlow Castle. In a particular way, we become the Seventh Prolusion's virtual "contemporaries of time itself," provided only that we are (in Milton's phrase) "members incorporate" of that all-inclusive body spoken for so strikingly at, say, "our Morning Star (1:294). In fact, membership is made a variable matter in this poem; it is perhaps a smaller, more time-bound group that would be drawn to lament that storm / shroud near the end of the poem (4:419ff.). There are moments when it seems all but impossible to segregate truth from error, even on a syntactic level. Worst of all, we are virtually abandoned by our old guide the Miltonic bard. Replaced in his role as the poem's expositor by the impossibly expert divine Son, the narrator seems reduced to neutral scribe—or at least that might be our impression were it clearer that such an abstraction could really be involved in this (or any) poem. However well the Son succeeds in locating an authentic, "inner" voice, in any case, the *poet* does not seem quite up to the challenge of the whole endeavor.

II

Milton did not bother to reiterate within *Paradise Regained* the doctrine which explains so much of the physical world in both his epics: the insistence that spirits are so "soft / And uncompounded"—so 'unmixed'—that

> in what shape they choose
> Dilated or condens't, bright or obscure,
> Can execute their aery purposes,
> And works of love or enmity fulfil. [*PL* 1:425–30]

"Dilated or condens't": the "spirits" are somehow conceived as *gaseous* beings, like the mists and exhalations Satan and others may or may not inhabit during their travels. (Clearly, this is more than a minor instance of folk superstition, as Milton suggests at 9:638) Whatever may be said about the literary suppression of Satan during the poem, *all* the devils both are diminished and "reduce their [own] shapes immense" during the very first book of *Paradise Lost* (1:790). But in *Paradise Regained*, we seem to be dealing with a radical form of narrative dilation, appropriate to that wilderness in which the Son can best descend "into himself." As in the earlier epic, Satan's assistants can disappear; but when they do, their place is taken by darkness, or the wild beasts of night. This may be why the animals of the brief epic seem to become more resistant to the Son's Orphic talents as the work progresses. Even in the first book, where Milton first suggests such a sphere of influence, he uses a disjunctive "But" (310) to exclude from this immediate kind of magic the "aged man in Rural weeds" that is really Satan. As in *Paradise Lost*, we are told (early in the poem) of the all-embracing power of that "will / And high permission of all-ruling Heaven" and somewhat reassured (through an allusion to Ps 114:20) of night's own divine parentage (*PL* 1:211–12; *PR* 1:494–502). As always, Satan is said to be "serviceable to Heaven's king"; and even minor local angels give him "in command / What to the smallest tittle thou shalt say / To thy adorers" (*PR* 1:449–50). But this too is a truth we are allowed to forget in *Paradise Regained*, along with the idea that those dark Chaotic "materials crude" can endow something as awful as the "depopulation" witnessed by Noah—or a "shroud" for the divine Son—with creative potential (*PL* 11:756).

In a sense the increase in divine permissiveness had become evident in the tenth book of *Paradise Lost*, and it is vividly displayed in the visions and narrations of the final two books. Within *Paradise Regained* and *Samson Agonistes* too it is hard to miss its pressures; and in the brief epic as earlier, they involve the poet's presentation of the poem's visible world. Long after we have been told that the particulars of historical setting for this fable "are not revealed," Milton mentions a sunny hill "Back'd on the North and West by a thick wood" (4:448), as though to challenge our memory of this detail's irrelevance. The landscape is populated with "couched" fowls and other "wild beasts"—we are dealing, in this work, with "nature's bounds" (1:13). Althogether there is a more paradoxical sense of heaven's "will and high permission" here, in keeping with the tone of that Sonnet to Cyriack Skinner. Some of the many prospects of the poem seem oddly alive; the city of "fair" Jerusalem "lifted high her towers," and the "glorious" Temple (Satan, who is responsible for these descriptions, will eventually call it "thy Father's house," 4:552) "rear'd / Her pile" (4:547). The structure, like Pandemonium and Jacob's ladder, is conspicuously magnificent.

Not that we are denied the chance to resist these particulars. When we first meet that proto-Wordsworthian "aged man in rural weeds" engaged ("as seem'd") in the "quest of some stray Ewe," Milton's parenthetic formulas remind us that first appearances are misleading here again; the poet encourages our curiosity about the historical particulars of setting and plot only to rebuke it, in this way making the details of his story problematic indeed:

> Full forty days he pass'd, whether on hill
> Sometimes, anon in shady vale, each night
> Under the covert of some ancient Oak,
> Or Cedar, to defend him from the dew,
> Or harbor'd in one Cave, is not reveal'd.   [4:303–07]

Elsewhere, there are hints that Satan is involved with the environment's "dark shades and rocks," just as he seemed to inhabit the mists and exhalations of *Paradise Lost*; and these particulars too are qualified or denied only by the Son. But it is not long before Satan poses the ultimate challenge to such critical resistance, on the part of narrator, Son, or reader, by giving instructions in stage management to "a chosen band / Of Spirits likest to himself in guile / To be at hand, and at his beck appear, / If cause were to unfold some active Scene / Of various persons each to know his part" (2:236–40). Innocuous though it seems at the moment, the incident involves a structural shift almost as fundamental as the unframed response of Apollo in "Lycidas," "But not the praise" (76). At some level, we know that Satan is as tied to heavenly intentions as those bad angels of *Paradise Lost*, *left* at large with Satan to perform their own dark designs (1:213). Differently, but just as inescapably as the earlier epic, the brief epic obtrudes the valuable, perhaps necessary correlative that Satan and his friends indeed "were [and are] at large" (*PL* 1:790). Here, we are allowed to forget all wisdom, so to speak, and to entertain an apparently irreversible attachment of staging to demonic agency; and Milton is at some pains to keep this quasi-authorial supervision in mind as we proceed through the poem. Since the brief epic is an authentic record (once again) of heroic deeds done (in secret) and "unrecorded left through many an Age," the narrator is in some fashion bound to full authenticity in presenting his material. Thus is Satan allowed to benefit from a gradual retirement of the narrator as expository assistant; he has displaced the narrator as the purveyor of the story in its external aspect—the visible world within the brief epic—and has become the poem's own insidious White Devil. If the Miltonic orator can command words to fall "into their own places" in the fashion of "nimble and airy servitors," as Milton wrote in the *Apology against a Pamphlet*, the brief epic extends his verbal powers into the realm of visible, apparently real, events (*CPW* 1:949).

On the face of it, *Paradise Regained* is very differently handled from the more forthright, sager-than-thou approach of *Paradise Lost*, in which the Bard appeared so much more straightforward on doctrinal matters. For our sojourn in Milton's Hell and Bower of Bliss, we were lucky enough to have the company, in effect, of a Spenserian Palmer, Milton's bard—theologically expert and occasionally even clairvoyant—not to mention those numerous assistants (in *Paradise Regained* assigned only to Satan).[4] Ill-digested and less comprehensive than the poem's own realities though they were (and were meant to be), these lectures seemed to put things in perspective; they aroused us abruptly from the complex reveries to be found, for example, in the epic similes. The clarifications reminded us that for all the visual fascination of the first books, it is really the *ear* of that belated peasant which is getting charmed—the reader of the poem who is tricked into thinking he sees things—and so they keep us from the kind of "stupidity" into which Satan falls upon glimpsing Eve all alone on that sultry summer morning.

In *Paradise Regained* as in the earlier epic, Milton begins with all the appearances of segregating history from doctrine all over again, and with subordinating the one to the other: this story too will be a simple illustration of God's "permissive will." Early in the poem (1:127–28), we are offered the fully explicated presentation of just how the Satanic wiles fit with the divine plan; whatever the Adversary's intentions, we will be dealing with a contrary fulfillment of that "purpos'd Counsel pre-ordain'd and fixt / Of the most High." Thus briefly does Milton's initial exposition surround the Satanic perspective with the governing field of the divine prospect. But in *Paradise Regained*, this kind of assistance (if that is what it really is) is rather quickly removed, and with it our grasp of the doctrine in question. And this is the last such interpretive intrusion on the part of the narrator; his subsequent clarifications are both more limited in extent and (for the most part) also more clearly pathetic. They are responses from the fallen human community rather than a theologically expert critic's kind of intervention. The first book concludes with an exchange on the nature of "permissive will," as though it were still a negotiable matter, not (as in that memorable first homily of *Paradise Lost*) a simple business of pouring yet more wrath upon the Satan. From this point on, we are pretty well left to our own devices, allowed to explore this literary wilderness largely by ourselves, with the assistance of rival guides who clearly *are not* the poet. We are given lots of time alone with Satan, as in the preamble to the second book's temptation. The Son's dream of Elijah precedes Satan's mention of the prophet; even if we remember Eve's observation that "dreams advise," who can blame us for thinking the chain of cause less manifest here, the divine ways more attenuated? We have yet to hear about that "chosen band"of spirits destined to supervise the various "active scenes" in *Paradise Regained*. (Even within the Son's dream, we may well notice a loss of individuation between the Son and "the prophet" [Elijah]; the loss of narrative distance begins to seem a kind of principle when the only interpretive frame is "Him thought, he . . . stood / And saw," when what *was* seen follows immediately without clarifying attribution.) As things happen in *Paradise Regained*, what is "known" (in the root sense of the word "narrative") precedes and is displaced by what is given: the mere playing out of the story, that rehearsal of the divine scenario which seems to prove so much more than the merely declared "counsel preordained." Satan appears almost to initiate the action of *Paradise Regained* when his stated intention precedes the narrator's clarifications (as at 1:126) and the Almighty's decree (especially at 142–44). And there are other examples, in which the narrator's facts interrupt a tempting speech as though to buttress it. More clearly than in *Paradise Lost*, the poem's whole "scene"—dramatis personae, setting, and story—appears to have an independence from authorial (and divine) intent, a New Critic-style life of its own. This autonomy is something Milton suggests, for example, when he closes the first book with an echo of the Psalm (104:20) that most explicitly acknowledges the divine authorship of night, that analogue to the "materials dark and crude" of Chaos. And of course, this whole professedly culminating moment—the moment of "verification"—is also quite emphatically a "beginning." It seems clear that even if Satan *has* been denied the eloquence of his predecessor, he might nonetheless prove to be splendid in a different way; certainly it is he who stands to profit from this gradual weakening of the narrator as a kind of built-in exegete. For now, the more talkative of the poem's guides is evidently in charge of scenery, as though Belial and Mammon had managed to join forces in a latter-day reprise of the Council in Hell.

Milton's strategy carries us through remarkably expansive tracts of his poem. In the middle of the second book of *Paradise Regained*, the Son dreams of Elijah while sleeping in a "hospitable covert . . . / Of Trees thick interwoven." Within twenty lines he has awakened and, fully conscious, entered a similarly enclosed area, determined to rest at noon: the shade (we are told) is

> High-rooft, and walks beneath, and alleys brown
> That open'd in the midst a woody Scene,
> Nature's own work it seem'd (Nature taught Art)
> And to a Superstitious eye the haunt
> Of Wood Gods and Wood Nymphs; he view'd it round.   [2:292–97]

Just the kind of place the Son had dreamed of, and just the kind whose details, we thought, "are not revealed." For the time being we share the Son's vision and experience something like the bard's kind of clairvoyance. Whatever our problems with later prospects and panoramas (and these do persist virtually to the end of the poem), the Son's view of these matters at any rate does *not* involve a "superstitious eye." Nevertheless, even so, this active scene continues to unfold:

> As [Satan's] words had end,
> Our Savior lifting up his eyes beheld
> In ample space under the broadest shade
> A Table richly spread, in regal mode,
> With dishes pil'd, and meats of noblest sort
> And savor, Beasts of chase, or Fowl of game,
> In pastry built, or from the spit, or boil'd,
> Grisamber steam'd; all Fish from Sea or Shore,
> Freshet, or purling Brook, of shell or fin,
> And exquisitest name, for which was drain'd
> Pontus and Lucrine Bay, and Afric Coast.
> Alas how simple, to these Cates compar'd,
> Was the crude Apple that diverted Eve!
> And at a stately sideboard by the wine
> That fragrant smell diffus'd, in order stood
> Tall stripling youths rich clad, of fairer hue
> Than Ganymede or Hylas; distant more
> Under the Trees now tripp'd, now solemn stood
> Nymphs of Diana's train, and Naiades
> With fruits and flowers from Amalthea's horn,
> And Ladies of th'Hesperides, that seem'd
> Fairer than feign'd of old, or fabl'd since
> Of Fairy Damsels met in Forest wide
> By Knights of Logres, or of Lyones.
> Lancelot or Pelleas, or Pellenore.   [2:337–61; italics deleted]

The passage recollects and seems to "verify" all previous classical fable and learning from the earlier exchange with Belial, from the similes and especially the catalogue of demons in *Paradise Lost*, and ultimately from the mythographical speculations of Milton's early reading: those "stripling youths" compared to Ganymede and Hylas, then nymphs "of Diana's train," Naiades bringing fruits and flowers brought "from Amalthea's horn, / And ladies of the Hesperides." (Belial may have been snubbed during the council itself, but his suggestions have been heard.) All these pleasant things, Milton suggests (with his usual willingness to strive in literary wealth and luxury), were much fairer than their fictional predecessors or "figures"; and as he does in *Paradise Lost*, the poet extends the references downward historically, even into the relatively recent grail romances cited by the editors. Moreover, the creatures change in perceptual status; until now relatively inert visual objects, they break into movement and controlled activity, a parodic animation of the Nativity's "serviceable angels." And all of this is attended by a mysterious but distinctly "Lydian" music; "And all the while Harmonious Airs were heard / Of chiming strings, or charming pipes and winds / Of gentlest gale *Arabian* odors fann'd / From their soft wings, and *Flora*'s earliest smells." Given the Adversary's instructions in stage management, it is a passage of virtually irresistible collusion between narrative and "Satanic" art. The luxurious and seemingly objectifying description precedes a speech (by the Adversary) which refers to and incorporates it; and in fact that speech itself is singularly bare, concluding with the reminder, again Prospero-like, that Satan's actors were all "creatures of air." In a fascinating and deeply rooted pun, Milton recalls the continuities he had discovered in his early revisionist classical studies by identifying all these classical deities and half-reified allusions as "Thy gentle Ministers" (2:374).

And this collusion continues without the disclaimers, as is clear if we consider the poem's celebrated panorama from Mount Niphates.

> With that (such power was giv'n him then) he took
> The Son of God up to a Mountain high.
> It was a Mountain at whose verdant feet
> A spacious plain outstretcht in circuit wide
> . . .
> With herds the pastures throng'd, with flocks the hills,
> Huge Cities and high-tow'r'd, that well might seem
> The seats of mightiest Monarchs, and so large
> The Prospect was, that here and there was room

For barren desert fountainless and dry.
To this high mountain-top the Tempter brought
Our Savior, and new train of words began.   [3:251–66]

Even if we remember the "chosen band" of masquers, it is difficult not to think of this as a real mountain, not just "nature taught art" or a vision. It is right there before the Son's (and our) eyes, something to point to, an independent, objective phenomenon of the sort to which Milton elsewhere applies a formula like "He spake no dream" (2:377); and Eve had told us, impressively, that "God is also in sleep, and Dreams advise" (*PL* 12:611). The introduction to this long section of the poem, "It was a Mountain," seems to designate the results of a fiat. It has the effect of validating or authorizing the scene to which Satan, in charge (so to speak) of the visible plot, now brings the Son. Narrative here confirms Satan's words; mere description answers (and sometimes even extends) the "ocular" suggestions and constitutes a sort of tacit argumentation by the Adversary. For professional readers of literature, of course, this is something like epic catalogue, dedicated to the reader's susceptibility to fascination. But some of us have become the kind of readers Satan has always been, the kind he would have the Son become: fixated by the dazzle of world geography and even by mere shapes and forms—marching formations in the "mystic" shapes of rhombs, crescents, stars on the sidewalks. All too readily, well-intentioned editors identify the mountain as Niphates and attempt to visualize the actual view from its summit as though we were taking in a celebrated balloon view or reading the space-age *Times Historical Atlas*. It is clear enough that Milton has succeeded admirably in reaching us (not at all the Son, of course) with the kind of particularity that is unique to literature.

III

Like its companion in the 1671 volume, *Paradise Regained* does not end with the verbal act which seals the self-definition and vocational commitment of the divine Son. The narrator is free to carry on when the central struggle is concluded and the Son and Satan have left the stage; along with the briefest of dismissals for the Son ("Home to his Mother's house," 4:639) there is the angel chorus (596–635) and just before that the peculiar banquet for the poem's hero. The meal in particular is much too close for comfort to the kind of writing, the "Office mean," in which Milton had claimed neither skill nor interest (*PL* 9:39).

So Satan fell; and straight a fiery Globe
Of Angels on full sail of wing flew nigh,
Who on their plumy Vans receiv'd him soft
From his uneasy station, and upbore
As on a floating couch through the blithe Air,
Then in a flow'ry valley set him down
On a green bank, and set before him spread
A table of Celestial Food, Divine,
Ambrosial, Fruits fetcht from the tree of life,
And from the fount of life Ambrosial drink,
That soon refresh'd him wearied, and repair'd
What hunger, if aught hunger had impaired,
Or thirst; and as he fed, Angelic Choirs
Sung Heavenly Anthems of his victory
Over temptation, and the Tempter proud.   [4:581–95]

Placed where it is, the aftermath of the Son's heroic deed is full of disturbing features. If we have read well, I think we cannot help worrying about those "plumy Vans," the "blitheness" of the local air, and (most of all, perhaps) the really un-Miltonic ease of that "floating couch." Like all analogy, this one carries us toward ourselves, in the direction of the world and our own creatures comforts; if there is no brandy and slippers, it is still more than a little decadent, the way this "fiery Globe / Of Angels" gets pictured, rather like that "pomp of winning Graces" suddenly attending Eve just as she leaves Adam and Raphael to their astronomical men's talk.

The problem of this scene is compounded by the fact that the Son's victory over Satan has just involved what can only be called a definitive conflation of speech with actual, not just "visible" plot: "He said, and stood." Having vanquished Satan through this radical fusion of speech with metaphysical reality, why should Milton go on? Why, specifically, does he once again put these realms asunder, regressing to an externally based narrative with something suspiciously like flair in that melodramatic turn to the spectacle of Satan's fall "smitten with amazement."⁵ The banquet begins with what certainly *looks* like yet another mininarrative of Satan's fall, presented with the finest of dovetailing: "So Satan fell; and straight . . ."; and because of our adjustment to a plot relocated in metaphysical or spiritual territory just a moment ago, it becomes difficult to accept the banquet as something that happens *only* to the Son. Despite the narrator's severity in forcing personal distinctions (almost gloatingly in "Who durst so proudly tempt the Son of God"), it is not easy to refer the "him" of two lines later to anyone but the original subject of this sentence. Indeed, I claim that we can do this only after the fact, when once again (in 594–95) Milton tells us who did what to whom, both in the passage and in the epic as a whole. Satan may now be safely "debelled," in short, but Milton appears to *linger* on the fate of the Adversary, and not just in those luxurious allusions to Antaeus and the "Theban monster," either. In general, he makes it difficult not to feel, OK, here is that tour de force we all knew Milton was still capable of, here is strength, real epic . . . at last! The more eagerly the poet disposes of his dramatis personae in space onstage, the greater our difficulties in deciding who is where. Because of the Son's own critical pressures in *Paradise Regained*, the narrative disallows any easy or exclusive application to Jesus' experience, for all Milton's efforts at distinguishing. Until now, indeed, it has been hard *not* to read this poem well, thanks to the conflation of Bard with the divine protagonist himself. But in these last moments, the scene is almost completely free from the kind of interpretive aids which Milton has provided earlier: no tell-tale "as seemed," no click of harpies' wings. As interpretive readers—and that is the kind we have become during this work—we seem to be on our own now, working without much help in a sort of literary analogue to the Son's own wilderness, following his and Satan's departure—if Milton's Satan ever can really disappear.

With this in mind, it becomes easier to understand the challenge posed by the later portions of Milton's brief epic: to remember the providential chain of command behind Satan's masque-like spectacle. For whereas Milton and Satan together ask us to spectate, like the confused night wanderers of those epic similes early in *Paradise Lost*—to "behold a wonder" or (in Satan's case) to "look on mee"—we *see* things in *Paradise Regained* only when the Son is not jogging us out of our amazement at Satan's "talk." We are on firm ground only when the Son no longer speaks—when in this way he stops listening. As he consistently reminds us, it is Satan's speech, evidently seconded by the narrator, which actually applies all this ornament, creates the view from Niphates. Far more consistently than any reader, the Son answers the challenge in the poem's extensive appeal to the mind's eye; he arrests Satan's words and *catches* things like "noblest" or "glorious" amid the welter of all those details—and they are famous too, not merely colorful or dazzling. Part of what he recognizes in pointing to the theologically centrifugal nature of Satan's appeals is that all this visual material, like Pandemonium, is itself just verbal spectacle, a "train of words"; it *is* heroic catalogue, but at very close quarters, culminating here (as in *Paradise Lost*) with a concrete and visible "temple," conspicuously magnificent (4:547) and wrongly (or at least very ambiguously) called "Thy Father's house." If we read and in any way respond to this poem, few of us indeed will be sufficiently undistracted to recognize the force and aptness of that incredibly decisive and disarming "I never liked thy talk" (4:171).

That fit audience, perhaps, would not be seriously put off by what has long been considered the brief epic's greatest embarrassment. The Son's notorious "attack on learning" strengthens a distinction long-standing in Milton's work and fundamental to the design of the brief epic. In *Of Education* and even in the Seventh Prolusion, Milton had insisted that in this world "insight" or contemplation must in effect be 'built on something firm' (see 4:292). But the Son's discussion and rejection of "method" in the fourth book of *Paradise Regained* focus on the trappings or "externals" of learning. He is thinking of things "academic" in a ceremonial and ideological sense, of "conferencing" and "schools of thought," of "abstracts." In this context, Socrates is not really differentiated from, say, Phaedrus; he is the source, not exactly of knowledge or even of superior dialectical technology, but of expository communities. Will *these* "ripen" the Son's knowledge? Satan proposes a consideration or "revolving" of all these texts (it has happened already) whether here or at home. There is a mail-order version of this course. And the result, most likely, will be something like a "system" (a "*Janua* or *didactic*," Milton had called this sort of thing in 1644), or perhaps even what Comus had styled the "canon laws of our foundation" (*CPW* 2:364; *A Masque* 808). This brilliant passage is still regarded as a betrayal of all that Milton (or we) hold dear; but it has much in common, on closer inspection, with the the very source of Milton's alleged modernity or liberalism, the *Areopagitica*. The oration too had sought to distinguish kinds of books: vials, repositories of a "master spirit" but also literary texts. frozen, congealed, the faded coal. From the *Areopagitica*'s literary texts, books in *Paradise Regained* have become something like a variorum commentary without one. Where the orator had spoken of "cramming" oneself with material from the "margent"—hardly the same thing as obtaining real nourishment from knowledge—the brief epic seems to regard the book itself as the source of verbal inebriation or, perhaps, a "crudity." (At 4:327, "books" has about the same force as the earlier "margins.") Altogether, Satan has an almost Polonian appreciation for the Son's intellectual precocity; someone who thinks of a successful disputant as a kind of academic Alexander engaged in an "early action" cannot be blamed for confusing "Moses' chair" with an endowed professorship.

We come upon the Son, then, just at the point when he is prepared to speak of readers (like himself prior to this point) as "children gathering pebbles on the shore." Closely related to Bacon's notion of a better learning's vestiges, the idea of "rudiments" is operative in *Paradise Regained*. If we think of the poem's learning, with Satan, as involving fragmentary sayings, bits and pieces, the Son is dealing rather differently, in epitomes or "models." This is the point of the Son's extensive resort to a kind of ideological shorthand, criticized by Howard Schultz (I think mistakenly) as "the labour-saving device of rejecting only the summum bonum of each sect."[6] In fact, the Son's method here is not only humane in its omission of an entire philosophic critique; it is the most fitting proof, in synecdochic fashion, of his familiarity with the whole philosophy in question. The work itself, in fact, displays a growing mastery over the very texts the Son says he (and we) can do without. It is because his fragments are delivered as principles (something solid, if not "systematic") that the narrator associates his very words with the rise of "our Morning Star." In the way Milton extends into the discursive realm the theological notion of "the word made flesh," we can get closer to understanding one of the most troublesome features of *Paradise Regained*, the way the Son puts behind him the "humane" approach to teaching: the work of what Milton had called rational or "positive" wisdom in the 1640s, the work of persuasion that could "do the work of fear." For this "humanism" of persuasion Milton had once substituted "zeal" and "rhetoric" in thinking of what he considered the eventual treachery of the Long Parliament and the nation. (Dalila is treated in similar fashion.) *Paradise Regained* employs instead the seemingly "private" idea of a plenary (and in a way *silent*) embodiment.

If decorum is indeed "the grand masterpiece to observe," then, both the divinely recapitulatory character and the fictional setting—a human, still-private Jesus on the threshold of his public ministry—lend themselves to effects on the very outskirts of Milton's own sphere of artistic influence. As Milton presents it, that "floating couch" is literally a part of the reception of the Son's victory, all the better if it suggests the reader's armchair which now furnishes so many of our most helpful readings of Milton. Eventually in the brief epic, the visual fascination of the poem is so expertly (or is it wholeheartedly?) indulged that we may easily forget whatever it was the Son taught us. To be sure, Milton gives us the means to resist the "floating couch" in the form of the dissociative, necessarily nonreferential words like "Celestial"—the term Milton applies (in *Paradise Lost*) to light, just as we are sorting out fundamental confusions between the "sovran vital Lamp" and the true (or inward) locus of inspiration (*PL* 3:22). And "divine" and the reiterated "Ambrosial" are here too with their world-abandoning pressures, together with the powerful repetition "tree of life . . . fount of life" (4:589–90). To negotiate this successfully, we must have become what Milton would have called "self-suspicious" readers and so remembered the Son's critical teachings. The general effect here *ought* to be close to the way in which the narrator of *Paradise Lost* reorients us so abruptly near the end of Book 1. There, words like "aery" and "incorporeal" (applied to "spirits" and "forms") prevent a literal reading of the fallen angels' size-and-shape-shifting and help to suggest that their "strait'n'd" condition has less to do with numbers, size, or physical confinement than with the constrictions of the Hell within them.

But if the Son has taken the place of a "retired" Bard in *Paradise Regained*, his expertise (or at least his influence) seems just as limited in his new sphere as that of Raphael, say, or the Attendant Spirit, his nearest predecessors in this kind of relocation. With good reason, Milton has decided to arrest his progress toward the Fatherly manners of the Heavenly Council in *Paradise Lost*, emphasizing instead the more immediate future on earth. He was never really willing to help us out, and now, in any case, he has resumed his "private" life offstage. On the other hand, the Satan of *Paradise Regained* is more clearly susceptible to fascination, not merely the practitioner of deceit which Luther had found in the "White Devil." More clearly than in *Paradise Lost*, the project of making others "such as I" is based upon the kind of vulnerability exploited when the dazzling serpent meets a "Circean" Eve among her roses. Indeed, what is almost bound to impress us, paradoxically, is the compulsively reflexive practice of his inexhaustible imagination; the "softness" that Coleridge rightly found to be an essential part of Milton's own idiom is functional *because* it is escapist. This poem's Adversary is undoubtedly a far cry from what Harold Bloom has called the "strong poet" in Milton. Far from commanding an "angels' ken," much less the kind of purview enjoyed on the Almighty's watchtower, Satan is reduced to offering in its place the contrivance that I have called the visible or "external" (the "historical") setting and actions of *Paradise Regained*. But as we have seen, "reduced"is a most misleading word here; precisely because Satan can (almost *must*) still "contemplate and admire," he secures the narrator's own, seemingly uncritical, collusion and so adds an entire dimension to his influence over the audience situated *within* the poem's world. (I except, of course, the single "perfect" member of his onstage audience.) One of Milton's most difficult problems in creating *Paradise Regained* was to disentangle the demonic predicament from the poet's own habitation, the sphere of things "simple, sensuous, and passionate."[7]

The general loss of critical resistance extends to the poet himself and seems bound to affect all but the most heroic readers. Like the appearance of demonic swords drawn from Cherubic thighs in Hell (*PL* 1:663–66), divine history here answers Satan's words, if indeed they are not anticipated by Mammon's own kind of special effects. Unlike Uriel "once warned," we get drawn yet again into the sensuous particulars, feeling that "sharp sleet of arrowy showers (3:324) and forgetting all about the orderly ranks of Milton's own archers. This is the manner in which Milton constructed the concluding books of the earlier epic, the visions of Book 11 and their eventual replacement by Michael's and Adam's collaborative hermeneutics. Given the inherent dazzle of human traditions, his narrator's vigilance flagging even prior to the retirement of the poem's uniquely perfect respondent, Milton had better hope that the divine Son has somehow managed to linger "unobserved." The ending of *Paradise Regained* provides Milton's severest test for his audience by challenging us to distinguish a weary abandonment of the world from a chance to exercise our faith in a context of near-perfect literary freedom—something we can do only by improving upon the poet's own performance. Here, only the fittest of us will remember to apply that very professional admonition of 1642: "The author is ever distinguished from the person he introduces" (*CPW* 1:880).

Chapter Nine

Samson's Jurisdiction: The Pattern of a Christian Hero

Time servs not now, and perhaps I might seem too profuse to give any
certain account of what the mind at home in the spacious circuits of her
musing hath liberty to propose to her self, though of highest hope, and
hardest attempting, whether that Epick form whereof the two poems
of *Homer*, and those other two of *Virgil* and *Tasso* are a diffuse, and the
book of *Job* a brief model: or whether the rules of *Aristotle* herein
are strictly to be kept, or nature to be follow'd, which in them that know
art, and use judgement, is no transgression but an inriching of art, and
lastly, what K. or Knight before the conquest might be chosen in whom
to lay the pattern of a Christian *Heroe*.
The Reason of Church Government

Milton's fascination with the imaginative experience of earliest Christianity
and its forerunners goes back at least as far as the Nativity Ode.[1] But the
most immediate and detailed clarification of the tragedy's peculiar emphasis
and terminology occurs in the concluding book of *Paradise Lost*. Samson is
not mentioned by name in Michael's account of the behavior and public
reception of the Old Testament judges; this is rather the story of the great
"teachers." Adam learns that Israel's sins will disrupt her peace, "Provoking
God to raise them enemies: / From whom, as oft he saves them penitent / By Judges first, then under Kings" (12:317–20). There is no
mistaking the temporary nature of the arrangement, the conditions for
relief, and even the ambiguous experience of citizenship "under" those royal

successors to the judges.[2] In some respects, Milton's portrayal of Samson seems faithful to Michael's account. In the final exchange with the Danites, we may recall that the single word "unrepented" carries crucial weight; and later Manoa too emphasizes the conditional nature of Samson's legacy by suggesting that honor and freedom are available only to those who will "find courage to lay hold on this occasion" (1376; 1716). The work as a whole seems to trace a movement from a national to a larger focus, so that Samson's encounter with a distinctly nationalist (and also zealous) Dalila can invoke the mysterious but recognizably Christian (Pauline?) content of the "ends / For which our country is a name so dear" (893–94).

Considering the traditional role of Samson in exegetical tradition, we may not be surprised that Michael's description of the judges falls short of describing everything Samson represents here. But even Krouse's exhaustive study does not quite prepare us for the particular ways he matches up with another group prominent in the final books of *Paradise Lost*, the modern descendants of those biblical "just men" who spring historically from Noah. As Michael describes them to Adam, these teachers will receive a "Comforter," the divine "Spirit within them" to inscribe "the Law of Faith upon their hearts" and arm them with "spiritual Armor" (12:491). They are bound to "evangelize the Nations" and to this end are given "wondrous gifts . . . To speak all Tongues, and do all Miracles, / As did their Lord before them." Clearly, Milton does not forget the prophecies, like Joel's, which had so preoccupied him during the 1630s. Like their earliest predecessors, the faithful will suffer persecutions; but there will be a compensation which, paradoxically, will be inward and yet sufficiently public to "amaze / Thir proudest persecutors" (496–97). Most impressive of all, in light of the tragedy's hyperextended ending, is Michael's emphasis upon the survival of the teachers' office even among "Wolves," in the double record of "thir doctrine and thir story" (506–07). Like Samson's legacy, this record—in part already veiled in mysterious terms—is accessible only under certain conditions:

> With superstitions and traditions taint,
> Left only in those written Records pure,
> Though not but by the Spirit understood. [512–14]

And it all happens in a recurrent, seemingly cyclical fashion; Milton's syntax makes it difficult to say very positively whether all this is spoken of the Apostles alone, or potentially of any baptized believer. Indeed, we should perhaps hesitate to force an overly historical distinction that may well have been scrupulously obscured in the text, where the whole era under scrutiny—in the manner of the *Apology*'s "times of opposition"—seems to precede almost immediately the day of "respiration to the just" (*CPW* 1:900; *PL* 12:540).[3]

If Michael provides the best clarification of what Samson represented to the later Milton, it is the antiprelatical pamphlets, and particularly the *Apology*, which originated Milton's long-term discussion of the divinely appointed teachers and also suggests a fundamental structure on which the tragedy is based. It was during the early 1640s, and especially through his "vehement" creature the anonymous Apologist, that Milton first explored Samson's kind of jurisdiction. Consolidating and generalizing from the experience and reflection embodied in the familiar letters of the 1630s, Milton developed on his own behalf, then historified and doctrinalized, the appeal to "divine impulsion" that so perplexes Manoa (and several later critics as well) in the speeches of Samson. The Jews, we are told (in Milton's account of the Israelites' return from the Egyptian captivity), did nothing momentous "without divine intimation"; and it seems clear that (as we might well suspect, given the polemic habits of the time) the point is not merely directed historically at Old Testament times (*CPW* 1:757). As Milton put it in the *Animadversions*, "that some men inspir'd from God should have an extraordinary calling to appoint, to order, and dispose, must needs be" (*CPW* 1:714). The antiprelatical pamphlets, furthermore, anticipate the place given in the tragedy to Manoa's and the Danite community's response to Samson's disturbing appeal. For a prime source of confusion in our understanding of the divine plan for humanity springs from the fact that an original and archetypal intention has been forgotten in favor of mere historical fact. The separate and distinct jurisdiction of magistrate and spiritual adviser, mistakenly conjoined in James I's famous remark "No bishop, no king," remains theoretically in effect despite the historical fact that both roles were once united "in each father of family," and notwithstanding the various kinds of specialization subsequent to the Fall. Even though the early heathen assigned "inward" instruction and censure to "the wise men and philosophers of the age," for instance, Milton insists that the arrangement was "a thing voluntary and no set government." And similarly among the Jews, whose "Priests, Levites, Profets, and at last the Scribes and Pharisees took charge of instructing, and overseeing the lives of the people" (*CPW* 1:837), Milton traces the original and persisting model even in the crucial period of the Gospel; as James I had argued in an earlier cause, the model is still the way things were "in the beginning . . . in each father of family," even though (as we might well expect) Milton sets off the congregational polity sharply against the government of the judges: "God [is] now no more a judge after the sentence of the Law, nor as it were a schoolmaister of perishable rites, but a most indulgent father governing his Church as a family of sons in their discreet age" (*CPW* 1:837). The *Apology* too works the familiar distinctions between Old and New Testament eras primarily to emphasize the original and overarching pedagogical intentions; far from insisting that "divine intimation" was limited to the experience of the Israelites, Milton expands the historical jurisdiction of the "extraordinary calling," to the point of supplying his Apologist with Luther's own kind of vehemence and attributing to the Long Parliament the kind of efficacious wisdom that royalist pamphlets had claimed for the kings of Judah. Like its predecessors, in short, the *Apology* is scrupulously vague in the way it defines a historical—or better, extrahistorical—context for Milton's ideal teacher, someone who might well refuse (like Samson) to acknowledge his lay or private status.

Milton's tragedy provides an interesting case in which a biblical author's source and even the exegetical tradition can easily be oversimplified. This work too seems to illustrate Milton's belief about the "uncertain keeping" of some scriptual texts, and we are forced to reconsider the relations between a particular fiction and what we might have thought to be its scriptural or exegetical basis. As Chrysostom and others had noticed, a peculiar feature of the Bible was that a given segment might "speak all things at once" in the manner of Paul's Epistle to the Ephesians. And for Milton it seems that a fictional work too might well treat a history directed to "aftertimes" in the manner of Scripture, written (as Bacon had put it) "to the thoughts of men, and to the succession of all ages."[4] In "Lycidas," the swain's discovery of a diverted angel seems to release the prophetic words of Isaiah and John; it is in voicing them that he becomes the true poet, adumbrating the entire sweep of Christian history, the very span which encloses the poem's reader. But in Miltonic works like these, what scholarly readers (often rather loosely) call Christianity here serves as a kind of window on figures like the uncouth swain and Samson, perspectives through which we observe the thoughts and speeches of a speaker who approaches the porch but never quite arrives.

As a "type," Milton's protagonist would have to demonstrate what an astute observer of Shakespeare's Prince Hal called a "double spirit / Of teaching and of learning instantly," a talent Milton had considered deeply since the later 1620s (*1 Henry IV* 5.2.63–64). And in both works, it is significant that we are dealing with an *emerging* model, a type "in the making." In reading *Samson Agonistes* (as with its partner in the 1671 volume), this means that we are attending the last phase in an educational process when these two activities come together in what Samson calls "presage in the mind," that final preliminary (in Milton's educational and antiprelatical writings) to wisdom in verbal action, knowledge dovetailing with event. All that Milton came to call in 1644 the moment of insight is replicated in equally mysterious references to those "rousing motions." Samson, of course, is also an insistently Old Testament teacher. With Milton's "archetype" in mind, we can better understand the nature and also the limitations of his discovery, as well as what it is he attempts to teach. Samson's final words to the chorus, and for that matter his reference to "my own accord" at the stadium, point to hard-won but nonetheless accessible discovery and decision, not just another inarticulate "motion"; Samson has managed to surmise nothing less than the purpose or "reason" of the Law, an institution whose "end" (as the reliable Michael explains it in Book 12 of *Paradise Lost*) is partly to incite natural depravity against its own jurisdiction, with the following results:

> that when they see
> Law can discover sin, but not remove,
> Save by those shadowy expiations weak,
> The blood of Bulls and Goats, they may conclude
> Some blood more precious must be paid for Man,
> Just for unjust, that in such righteousness
> To them by Faith imputed, they may find
> Justification towards God, and peace
> Of Conscience, which the Law by Ceremonies
> Cannot appease, nor Man the moral part
> Perform, and not performing cannot live.
> So Law appears imperfet, and but giv'n
> With purpose to resign them in full time
> Up to a better Cov'nant, disciplin'd
> From shadowy Types to Truth, from Flesh to Spirit,
> From imposition of strict Laws, to free
> Acceptance of large Grace, from servile fear
> To filial, works of Law to works of Faith.   [12:287–306]

Samson has abandoned the effort to communicate this insight when he refers so mysteriously (so reassuringly too, given the choric character) to those "rousing motions." But these oracular words, which seem to signal a reversion to Samson's earlier "riddling days," in fact take us beyond Samson's (and perhaps our own) era by engaging us in one last exchange on the function of "the law" in divine governance. Much earlier, the Chorus had initiated this discussion with their truism that "with his own Laws [God] can best dispense" (314); and Samson gives the key word new life during his final attempt to suggest that the Danites, and we too, can participate in significant action: "He may dispense with me or thee / Present in Temples at Idolatrous Rites / For some important cause" (1377–79). The grim pun on "dispense" here conveys Samson's despair in the form of something like mental reservation. But it also expresses the work's—or at least Samson's—glimpse of the realm beyond flesh, reason, nations, and time itself, a world he has all but entered, I think, when he assures the Danites, in yet another ambiguous remark, that they will hear nothing about him "unworthy / Our God, our Law, my Nation, or myself" (1425). Samson's double entendre, indeed, bridges the testaments in what seems a fairly clear-cut intimation of the "second covenant," that "accord" available to all faithful "sons of Abraham." If we judge from the manner in which he attempts to deliver his discovery, Milton has staged the end point in a stylistic history as well as the approaching death of the Danite hero. Until the moment when Samson once more becomes a mystery surmounting the "reach" of his onstage observers and recedes into the haze of legend and idolatrous celebrations, he comes close to rehearsing the whole sweep of human history in the traditional pattern modeled by Scripture itself: *vetus testamentum velatum, novum testamentum revelatum.*

Thus does Milton scrutinize the problematic territory of divine history, a world in which time and tradition are part of the sacred record. For the moment, Judges and the rest of that definitive book are to be considered as a remote aftermath of the work we are attending, and perhaps even as its product, in the sense that Genesis may be thought to preserve in cold print the wonders of Raphael's story of creation (*Paradise Lost,* Book 7). Besides the story's forgotten materials, Milton offers us the beginnings of its seemingly inevitable corruption into legend and idolatry. In his own suggestive phrase, he "prevents" the established or conventional encounter with the Danite hero of Judges and exegetical tradition alike, just as his preface functions to remove the work from the stage both practically and imaginatively. If he blinds his audience in his manner, he also obliterates our memory for the purpose of achieving a fresh approach to his difficult, mysterious subject; indeed, a re-velation. The plight of Gaza, in short, seems to image the essential nature of the pre-Christian world—perhaps, for Milton, *the* world—which in *Samson Agonistes* we experience in its closing phase. If the *Apology* and the preceding antiprelatical pamphlets suggest that Milton conceived Samson on the model of the quintessential teacher (in any age)—and even sketched an ideal discursive scene for a person like this—the later, angelic expositor (Michael) adds the specific structure of *Samson Agonistes* in the motives and special predicament peculiar to the teachers of the final days; the entire matter of his reception—including landscape—is implicit in Michael's answer to the difficult question of how the divine "comforter" is to work in the last days, a question clarified (if not quite answered) in Samson's determined isolation, his final "mysteriousness" to his countrymen, and perhaps even that legendary status to be preserved in Manoa's monument and embodied in the Judges narrative itself.[5]

Chapter Ten

The Sense of
Heaven's Desertion

As we saw in chapter 3, Milton had extensively explored the territory of
the divinely appointed teacher and his reception between 1633 and 1645.
The Apology against a Pamphlet records his discovery of an ideal discursive
scene in the collective words of the Long Parliament, expressing (in
Milton's memorable description) "the force of so much united excellence
[met] in one globe of brightness and efficacy": "With such a majesty had
their wisdome begirt it selfe, that whereas others had levied warre to
subdue a nation that sought for peace, they sitting here in peace could so
many miles extend the force of their single words as to overawe the disso-
lute stoutnesse of an armed power secretly stirr'd up and almost hir'd
against them" (*CPW* 1:925–26).

In view of the prominent conjunction of "words" with "force" in this
passage, it may seem incredible that Milton could propose seriously that
the parliamentary success had involved a kind of evolutionary leap beyond
the ancient worthies' employment of mere power, as though a magical
combination of wisdom and that ineffable "vertu" had really killed the
dragon menacing the British Andromeda. But as we have seen, the *Apology*
everywhere relies upon this thought, and perhaps even the texts in which
Milton had first considered the questions of "heroic wisdom" and his own
vocational options back in the early 1630s. His early reluctance to enter
the priesthood as an "unweaponed creature in the world," the survey of
poetry's various powers in the "Ad Patrem"—any number of permutations

on the theme—were eventually collected and concentrated into the *Education*'s recipe for a nation's prophetic pedagogy, including the final preparatives for what Milton calls "insight": those frequent reviews to be undertaken by Milton's scholars to unify "the whole body of their perfected knowledge" (*CPW* 2:406, 407).

The *Apology*'s treatment of public incidents like the death of Strafford shares with *Samson Agonistes* a preoccupation with the shape and structure of discourse that becomes efficacious, that is, with the cultural and literary conditions, we might almost say, for radical divine intervention. In a situation like this, language acquires (or regains) its fullest poetic potential, the kind of virtue which empowers the true poet in more than just an inward way. For Milton in 1642, this was language as it ought to be, the circumstance recalled so vividly by the Bard when he prepares to render the actions of the Omnific Word and somehow engage with the meanings, not the mere names, of things. For the swain of "Lycidas," a similar but collectively possessed Orphic power was an important part of a time when "together both . . . We drove afield" (*Lyc* 25–27). In this situation, language might aspire to the primitive condition of Wisdom's play with her sister even in the presence of the almighty Father, a kind of discursive (and familial) Eden preceding even the creation of the world (*PL* 7:10). It is easy to get the impression that all Milton's fictional speakers or personas—the swain, the brothers of the *Masque*—either aspire to that "universal insight into things" or possess it already, like the Lady, or at least the "Daemon" the children call Thyrsis. The formulations in *Of Education* and *Apology* (and perhaps even the *Reason*'s more traditional commendation of literary powers) are attempts to describe and arrange the dissemination of these literary feats, together with what Milton took to be their reception—a most important matter for a literature of conscience. In theory, much would depend upon the way in which such language behaved. If these words were "lucky," a true poetry could mysteriously entail what Milton persistently called "event." Whether it is in the pulpit or within a poem, moreover, the possession of "insight" is obviously distinct from the kind of discursive technology we find in Dalila or predecessors like Comus. And by the same token, there is an essential difference between the brute subservience of the Comick "herd"—Satan's "military obedience," as Gabriel calls it in *Paradise Lost* (4:955)—and the brothers' more original, "ventrous" kind of youthful responsiveness or the obvious freedom of a "nimble and airy" verbal servitor that finds its *own* place (*A Masque* 609; *CPW* 1:949).

For Milton, language so defined was clearly at the heart of the new, "unpremeditated" decorum, something we may recognize by noticing that its fullest description is presented anonymously by the adventurous, explicitly "vehement" Apologist, not by the more safely conscientious Milton of the earlier *Reason*. Provided that we keep in mind the qualifications noticed in chapter 5, we may take his account of the Long Parliament's "virtuous words" as a convenient epitome of an ideal Miltonic discursive scene and, with it, define Miltonic tragedy as involving one kind of modification in the scene: the removal, specifically, of the kind of correspondence or "answerability" that made Orpheus and Amphion the types of a Reformed poetic efficacy and in some minds brought England to the verge of being an entire nation of prophets. Even within the *Apology*, something like this modification seemed to be at work in the uneasy way Milton insists on his very Lutheran Apologist's spontaneous and irrepressible "vehemence," and at the same time the kind of urbane and "literary" professionalism we commonly associate with the *Areopagitica*. Milton's most passionate defense of the divine "gift of free conceptions"—in effect of the "unpremeditated" poetics that would govern *Paradise Lost*—is part of a scholarly correction of his antagonist Bishop Hall. (For the moment, we are not to mind that the Apologist, like Luther, is incapable of writing in a dull style.) It suggests that a particularly sharp passage of the *Animadversions*, which Hall had found crudely shocking, was specifically designed "to astound and to astonish the guilty Prelats" and was kept well under control. It was not in fact a prayer at all, but a perfectly traditional "hymne in prose frequent both in the Prophets, and in humane authors" and requiring a style "greater then for an ordinary prayer" (*CPW* 1:930).

It is in this context, when public circumstances have so spectacularly caught up with prophetic hymns and prayers, that Milton ambiguously calls for his new decorum, adopting Hall's own privileged term "decency": "Certainly Readers, the worship of God singly in itselfe, the very act of prayer and thanksgiving with those free and unimpos'd expressions which from a sincere heart unbidden come into the outward gesture, is the greatest decency that can be imagin'd" (*CPW* 1:941). In attempting to absorb prayer into the sphere of literary convention or the Apologist's own psychology, Milton necessarily distracts us from the less convenient elements in the acts of the prophetic poet or speaker. At this point in the *Apology*, his theatrical metaphor includes only the performance of the actor, and this is viewed with surprising narrowness as the expressions of a "sincere heart." In effect, Milton isolates the figure of the actor-sage from his scene: the prophet has become a spectacle (as the Chorus find Samson at the outset, and as we experience his final act offstage), the scene or act diminishing to the point of confinement within his "outward gesture." By sharp contrast, what Milton hopes to recover in urging the nation's re-sumption of "zeal" is precisely the rest of the scene as he now imagines it to have been during 1641: a "virtuous wisdom" in the original sense of the words, by which Parliament is said to have extended "so many miles . . . the force of their single words" (*CPW* 1:926). If we borrow from the *Reason*'s way of defining a tragic action, we can see that what Milton remembers in this prose retrospection is the convergence of "the changes of that which is call'd fortune from without, [and] the wily suttleties and refluxes of mans thoughts from within," a convergence no longer in effect at the moment he writes the *Apology* (*CPW* 1:817). Here (as at the outset of Milton's tragedy) those inward motions or "refluxes" seem divorced from fate, the divine narrative; and as he does in the *Apology*, Milton explores the "very act of prayer" turned in upon itself: worship become apparent solilo-quy. There is a world of difference between empowered wisdom—words given the kind of force which the Apologist associates specifically with "majesty"—and the kind of defensiveness about "hindsight" that distin-guishes Samson: the sense of nostalgia for a time when "I knew / From intimate impulse" or for the gift of strategic anticipation which Milton thought Samson possessed at Etham (*CPW* 1:925; *SA* 222–23).[1]

As we noticed in chapter 5, this kind of nostalgia is not entirely missing from the *Apology* itself, though it has commonly been read as a document belonging to his early millennialism. Not long after he wrote the *Apology* (and certainly before he turned his full attention to *Samson Agonistes*) Milton thought he found this kind of shift in the historical record—in the subse-quent history, indeed, of the Long Parliament itself. His description, written perhaps in 1648, was removed from the first published edition of *The History of Britain* (1671), "Struck out for some harshness" as we are told by a later editor ("To the Reader," 1681; *CPW* 5:i:440). The "digres-sion" (as Milton calls it) survives in the 1681 edition of the *History* and also in a manuscript version which Milton's modern editors have found more faithful to what he "may have written in the late 1640's" (*CPW* 5:i:407). Given the procedures of the *Apology* and other works of the antiprelatical period, "harshness" is something we might well expect to encounter in one of Milton's well-signposted excursions. Here, he further clarified what can happen to the ideal discursive action in writing the history of the Long Parliament—a history "ruminated," as Bacon might have put it, to the point of becoming a "character." As Milton tells the story, the failure of the Long Parliament was a relatively simple matter of mistrust in "the Virtue of their own Spiritual weapons." These were weapons given them, Milton goes on, "with full warrant of sufficiency to pull down all thoughts and imaginations that exalt themselves against God."[2] In the place of the Edenic unanimity remembered in the *Apology*—that "incorporate" solidarity in which the Apologist had been engaged—we encounter a dissociative triangulation of speaker, audience, and subject: there are the "Statists," "the People," and "we"—the readers who notice everything. More specifically, "the People" are described now as spectators "looking on" all this, actually seeing the hypocrisy, the ignorance, the "counterfeit zeal of their pulpits." (Uriel's difficulties in recognition of what *Paradise Lost* calls hypocrisy, "invisible, except to God alone," 3:684, are interesting in this context.) The very metaphor of spectatorship expresses nothing like critical perspective but what Milton himself calls the situation's alienation, a fundamental collapse in the very elements of prophetic community. Faced with "rhetoric" and mere spectatorship in counterview, the present, conspicuously single speaker—very much in the vein of *Paradise Lost* 11–12— explores the true basis of liberty:

> Thus they who of late were extoll'd [by Milton himself in the *Apology*] as our greatest Deliverers, and had the People wholly at their Devotion, by so discharging their trust as we see, did not only weaken and unfit themselves to be dispensers of what Liberty they pretended, but unfitted also the People, now grown worse and more disordinate, to receive or to digest any Liberty at all. For Stories teach us, that Liberty sought out of season, in a corrupt and degenerate Age, brought *Rome* itself into a farther Slavery: For Liberty hath a sharp and double edge, fit only to be handled by Just and Vertuous Men; to bad and dissolute, it becomes a mischief unweildy in their own hands: neither is it compleately given, but by them who have the happy skill to know what is grievance, and unjust to a People, and how to remove it wisely; what good Laws are wanting, and how to frame them substantially, that good Men may enjoy the freedom which they merit, and the bad the Curb which they need. [1681 version, *CPW* 5:i:448]

Hand in hand here, we have the notions of the former deliverers, the "bad men"; reduced versions of a driving ideology, now in the hands of rhetorical virtuosi like Comus or Satan. At the same time, we witness the extinction of linear or "messianic" history and its replacement by a kind of national (or almost biological) determinism; the inevitable outcome of the Long Parliament's "errors, mischiefs, & misdemeanors" is a reversion to ancient historical cycles, to "what befel those antient inhabitants [of Britain, but also of storied Rome] whom they so much resembl'd." This experience Milton somewhat oddly calls "confusion in the end." And he speculates that there may be a kind of built-in deficiency in the "temper" of the nation's spiritual weaponry, a national style which has resulted in our being "entangled and opprest with things too hard," a little like Peter's experience in trying to administer the Gospel:

> For *Britain*, to speak a truth not often spoken, as it is a Land fruitful enough of Men stout and courageous in War, so is it naturally not over-fertile of Men able to govern justly and prudently in Peace, trusting only in their Mother-Wit; who consider not justly, that Civility, Prudence, love of the Publick good, more than of Money or vain Honour, are to this Soyl in a manner Outlandish; grow not here, but in minds well implanted with solid and elaborate Breeding, too impolitick else and rude, if not headstrong and intractable to the industry and vertue either of executing or understanding true Civil government. Valiant indeed, and prosperous to win a field; but to know the end and Reason of winning, unjudicious and unwise: in good or bad Success alike unteachable. For the Sun which we want, ripens Wits as well as Fruits; and as Wine and Oyl are Imported to us from abroad; so must ripe Understanding, and many civil Vertues, be imported into our minds from Foreign Writings, and examples of best Ages, we shall else miscarry still, and come short in the attempts of any great Enterprise. [*CPW* 5:i:450]

It is a classic statement of the public circumstances in which Milton's "materialism" was developing in the 1640s, together with all other aspects of his thought. Already, much more clearly than in the *Apology*, heroism is an individual matter, and the idea of militant zeal in particular has undergone a drastic change. "Vehemence" and "zeal" have become superficial things, either simulated or limited to what Milton calls a "private Fancy" (446/47). At the same time, "Heroic wisdom," a term which 1681 italicizes, seems to involve nothing less than an "artist's" kind of knowledge—among other things, the knowledge of "exquisite proportions" (*CPW* 5:i:448).

Chapter Eleven

Samson Agonistes as Lament

So spake, so wish'd much humbl'd *Eve*, but Fate
Subscrib'd not; Nature first gave Signs, imprest
On Bird, Beast, Air, Air suddenly eclips'd
After short blush of Morn.
PL 11:181–84

At the outset of *Samson Agonistes*, certainly, it is hard to imagine a tragic protagonist much farther removed from the sage's powers than Milton's blind, imprisoned Danite. Samson begins by complaining specifically that his self is his "sepulchre." He appears to be suffering from the kind of self-containment (a very different thing from self-sufficiency) that is unique to Satan, at least in the world of *Paradise Lost.* Of course, the first epic took its time getting around to the corrective distinction between the angels' fall ("by thir own suggestion") and the forgivable lapse of our first parents, "deceiv'd / By th'other first" (3:129, 130–31). After the first human disobedience, Adam too suspects for a time that his predicament is "to Satan only like, both crime and doom." It appears that Milton was far from taking lightly Satan's announced purpose to make all others "such as I." In *Samson Agonistes*, thoughts "return" to torment Samson in the manner of Eve's return in Book 10 of *Paradise Lost.* Directed initially to himself, Adam's great lament incorporates the voices of his "Maker" and "Sons"; he is led "to [his] own conviction" through a kind of evasive "reasoning" which involves the multiplication of voices we remember from the soliloquy on Mount Niphates. For the time being history seems suspended, the way it does initially in "Avenge, O Lord, thy slaughter'd Saints," to be resumed only when the lament redoubles. For a time, it seems, Adam *is* "like Satan," until the arrival of Eve allows him to move along in the penitential itinerary by engaging with someone more original than the vocal creatures of soliloquy.

Almost everyone in the tragedy offers Samson's kind of thoughts, self-consciously recommending the kind of disguised Stoicism that Milton thought he had found in the writers on regeneration. Still worse, this consolation is halfheartedly presented as proverbial "sentences" that might or might not work. The Danites consistently find in Samson not so much a Nazarite as another Adam, an epitome but certainly not a pattern for mankind: a "mirror of *our* fickle state" (164; my italics); his strength, which "might have subdu'd the earth" if only it had been attended with "virtue" (173–74), has instead vindicated the common wisdom of the old *de casibus* tragedy. In keeping with the immutable laws, the exceptional Samson just fell farther than other men and from a somewhat different *kind* of high estate, possessed as he was of strength and (for a time, anyway) of virtue, not "long descent of birth" (171) or luck. "In fine, / Just or unjust, alike seem miserable, / For oft alike, both come to evil end" (702–04). Recalling the way in which Satan "must" perceive God's beneficence in *Paradise Lost*, these summary lines strongly suggest the Danites' most characteristic gesture, the accusation or "appointment" of the governing deity. In the choric account as in Manoa's (at times the outlooks seem indistinguishable), God not only permits evil; it is the divine obsession, a predisposition to throw His own elect "lower than thou didst exalt them high" (689). The divine order is essentially tragic in the old-fashioned way, and He has surely dealt *already* with Samson in bringing him to his present depths. The dispensation they consistently assume to this point in the play is champion centered, not really theocentric; their Samson seems almost a Satan of *Paradise Lost* manqué.

Milton is at pains to remind us that this quintessentially Euripidean chorus represents the men of Dan, and even "Israel" in potentia. What is so striking about them, I think, is their spectatorly *distance* on heroic martyrdom; the Danites express not so much the anguish of real oppression as a vulgar audience's wish for another underdog's comeback. We might almost say of the Danites that their willingness to celebrate or otherwise accept only a total and instantaneous delivery—and by such an athletically Messianic deliverer, at that—is a measure of their inability to understand tragedy. Like the Psalmist, they may long for something more than ministers who contain only in part what could be all in a *real* deliverer; they live in a world, theoretically, in which men can be "thy glorious Champion" at one moment and in some single way. But wishing does not help; Milton reduces them to prayer for an exception, for yet another exception, to the old rule: "So deal not with this once thy glorious Champion, / The Image of thy strength, and mighty minister" (705–06). Their brand of patience requires the kind of magic that recalls the promised effects of Stoic resolution in Milton's hell. Here, in hyperbolic fashion it makes "each of his own Deliverer, / And Victor over all / That tyranny or fortune can inflict" (1289–91). Ultimately, with Manoa and Dalila alike, they ask for peace or, more specifically, a "peaceful end" to Samson's labors. Like Manoa, they seek to bring him back "Home to thy country and his sacred house" (518), surely a regression inappropriate to any true descendant of Abraham. As we might expect, they offer a decadent form of the outlook we commonly think of as "classical." Closer to the seeming disillusionment of Ecclesiastes than the prophetic chiliasm of Milton's early pamphlets, with their echoes of the Wisdom books (and for that matter voicing something like the initial outlook of Milton's own eighteenth sonnet), the Chorus offer a view of history that could never be confused with Milton's early intent in quoting the poet's "proverbial close." Small wonder, then, that history seems frozen at the outset of the work—and throughout that seemingly long stretch of time prior to the catastrophe.[1]

In an influential and telling objection, Dr. Johnson wrote that "the intermediate parts [of *Samson Agonistes*] have neither cause nor consequence, neither hasten nor retard the catastrophe." And Johnson further commented on what he thought had taken the place of the missing links in the tragic action: Milton "had never studied the shades of character, nor the combinations of concurring, or the perplexity of contending, passions."[2] In fact, of course, the tragedy begins with something very like the welter of contending passions which afflict Satan on Mount Niphates, and for Milton these had a close connection with real events, much less the parts of a fictional design. I suggest, indeed, that much in the tragedy is clarified if we notice that initially, like the *Apology*, it looks back to a time of "artistic" knowledge, including a misunderstood period of quasi-military "forecasting" (254) and then its pathetic aftermath. The allegedly inconsequential "middle" of the tragedy is concerned with Samson's escape from the vicious circle which (in *Paradise Lost* 10) nearly traps Adam in Satan's kind of dilemma, and specifically with reversing his fall into reason or "thought" or memorial repetition. And here too, an artist's kind of knowledge involves literary matters of a deceptively trivial sort. At the outset, Samson's own speeches move into sententious forms of thought, forms which it is easy to associate too exclusively (and after the fact) with an oversimplified notion of choric "character." (As we shall see, the choric outlook itself is Samson's own creation.) The rational structure which betrayed Samson with Dalila has devolved into schools of thought and further fragmented into proverbial sentences, their constituent words, and the mere sounds of words—a kind of discursive "first matter." The action of Milton's tragedy actually reverses this dynamic, allowing Samson to move through reason's mazes / evasions and toward the "rousing motions" he announces as he leaves the stage. Even his most despairing speech seems to imagine something to build on; and the later phases in Samson's recovery are marked by a renewed conjunction between "fancy" and "accident," to use the misnomers with which Milton presents the renewing (or developing) prophetic psychology and scene. With his remarkable reference to "some rousing motions," Samson all but announces the possession (not quite the recovery) of that ultimate sign of wisdom, "presage in the mind" (*SA* 1387); and the Messenger himself— the nearest thing to a narrator in this poem—arrives to report the catastrophe *without consulting* reason, finding us instead specifically by "instinct of nature." It is not really stretching the point to say that such a catastrophe includes the destruction of the kind of legal or rational system which Milton had associated with the Jewish Temple in Jerusalem, and (before that) with the institutional and discursive "magic structures" of Comus.[3]

As Dr. Johnson's analysis suggests, it is no easy matter to make sense out of Samson's inspired act without adopting the work's own idiom or falling into something like Eliot's appeal to special qualities of sensibility. Few readers really believe that Samson's strength is literal or literally "hung in his hair," any more than we believe that the rind of Eden's "mortal fruit" really concealed what Satan calls a "sciential sap." A steadfast rejection of magic is a central part of Milton's effort to demystify the all-encompassing fable. But by implanting terms like "presage," "rousing motions," and "instinct of nature" in the Messenger's account of his own arrival and at such critical points in the tragedy's various biographies of Samson, Milton does not quite discourage the view that Samson possessed a special kind of talent, lodged with him useless for a time. And those later references to secret matters like "my conscience and internal peace" and the opacity of the champion's final moments (both onstage and at the arena) seem about as close as we are likely to come to the important question of Samson's working credentials and what we may call his "jurisdiction."

Given the private, even cryptic behavior masked by Samson's jocularity as he confronts Harapha and his mass audience at the temple, it is hardly surprising to encounter the frequent suggestion that the drama's "action," if it really exists at all, resides in the inward recovery or even the "regeneration" of the protagonist. Like the later books of *Paradise Lost*, *Samson Agonistes* is remarkably full of references to penitential doctrine, and the tragedy in many ways reflects Milton's challenging and independent treatment of the subject in the *Christian Doctrine*, particularly in its insistence on a suffering that crosses the threshold commonly supposed to separate body from mind, in this way to prey on Samson's apprehensive "tenderest parts" (*SA* 624). In the *Doctrine*, Milton found it necessary to criticize those authorities who had arbitrarily divided the regenerative process into separate subheadings for the flesh and spirit ("mortification" and "quickening," respectively). He diverges from earlier treatments of the subject partly on the basis of something like experience and arguing from his favorite philosophic standpoint, the kind of generation which follows upon corruption. He agreed with his predecessors that, by all rights, "mortification of the flesh" *ought* to precede the process of regeneration (just as corruption precedes generation). But Milton seems to have been convinced that one can experience "mortification" subsequent to the beginnings of regeneration; he argues that the category should be associated with repentance *rather than* regeneration (*CPW* 6:463). The *Doctrine*'s adjustment of traditional categories is embodied in the scrupulous way Samson adds a critical condition ("unrepented") to the Chorus's bold suggestion that a merely "outward" participation in the Dagonalia would surely be pardonable (*SA* 1348–76). And Dalila is made a full-fledged expert in these doctrines, as though she were here partly to embody Manoa's outrageous suggestion that although penitence and contrition are decidedly in order, Samson need not "act . . . in [his] own affliction" (*SA* 502–05). But most telling of all is the way Samson seems to experience the truth of Milton's analysis, to the point of calling his present condition "black mortification," a diagnosis which Milton had explored as early as "L'Allegro" in learned conjunction with various kinds of remedy. To judge from the intricate way in which penitential doctrine informs the final three books of *Paradise Lost* (beginning with Adam's first experience of contrition in Book 10), Milton was interested in the demands exacted even by the most liberating doctrines, by the subtle intertwining of categories as actually sensed by the conscientious believer. And in both works, this includes exploring "evasion": the likelihood of *partial* or perhaps unwitting regeneration, or "false" penance (whether wicked or weak Samson will not distinguish).[4]

It is by squarely facing the self-consciousness with which Samson's tormenting "thoughts" are framed as such that we can best recover the connections between the drama Milton actually allows us to hear and that final offstage act of heroic martyrdom. At the outset of Milton's tragedy, to borrow the *Reason*'s terms, the moral and spiritual "refluxes" seem divorced from fate, that divine narrative; and Milton explores the idea of worship in its rudimentary beginnings. Alienated, turned in upon itself in the manner of the soliloquy on Mount Niphates, "the very act of prayer" has become apparent soliloquy. The substance of Milton's drama fills the gap between, on the one hand, a past repeatedly viewed as an ideal conjunction of word with event (marred throughout, to be sure, by a lack of what Samson himself calls "reception") and an ending, an aftermath laden with misinterpretation and perhaps idolatry. But the great act and tragic catastrophe alike begin as a lament. In keeping with any human "crime and doom," of course, Samson's predicament (like Adam's) admits to the possibility of attenuation and displacement, in the sense that a significant action can preempt Samson's initial purpose, to "sit a while and bemoan his condition." Unlike Adam in the tenth book of *Paradise Lost* who is temporarily enclosed in "gloomiest shade," Samson has emerged to find some ease at the bank, a setting, at least, which has "choice of sun or shade," and a place where he can "feel amends, / The breath of Heav'n fresh-blowing, pure and sweet, / With day-spring born" (9–11). But despite his location, he too is prey to a kind of thought. At the bank, he finds

> Ease to the body some, none to the mind
> From restless thoughts, that like a deadly swarm
> Of Hornets arm'd, no sooner found alone,
> But rush upon me thronging, and present
> Times past, what once I was, and what am now.   [18–22]

In the most immediate way, mind has become body and apparent reprobation a matter of "sense," the very kind of testimony consistently denied by the Satan of *Paradise Lost*—otherwise, a similarly Promethean figure. As Samson puts it later,

> Thoughts my Tormentors arm'd with deadly stings
> Mangle my apprehensive tenderest parts,
> Exasperate, exulcerate, and raise
> Dire inflammation which no cooling herb
> Or med'cinal liquor can assuage,
> Nor breath of Vernal Air from snowy *Alp*.
> Sleep hath forsook and giv'n me o'er

To death's benumbing Opium as my only cure.
Thence faintings, swoonings of despair,
And sense of Heav'n's desertion.   [623–32]⁵

The lines present Milton's most detailed exploration, perhaps, of Satan's
own experience at the moment he "thought himself impair'd"—a moment
which oddly overlaps, we may recall, with the appearance of Sin and the
entirety of the War in Heaven. In this innermost recess of the mind,
Samson's tormentor can "exercise all his fierce accidents, / And on her
purest spirits prey, / As on entrails, joints, and limbs, / With answerable
pains, but more intense, / Though void of corporal sense" (612–16).
Milton seems determined to locate his Nazarite's affliction in the "animal
spirits," just at the level of what Raphael had called "life and sense, / Fancy
and understanding," in that series of zeugmas which so drastically revises
our notion of "mind" by literally demodifying it (*PL* 5:485–86). In his
suffering—and that is what constitutes this work's "true experience"—
Samson can find little meaning in the kind of distinction Milton had drawn
in the *Reason of Church Government* between "inner" and "outward" realms.
The realm of accident—"what is called fortune from without," as the
Reason had termed it—has found its way "within," even to the *inmost*
mind.

Samson reconsiders his past, indeed, very much as Milton had reviewed
his own early career (or its preliminaries) in 1642; and I suggest that
Milton's tragedy recalls with striking clarity the way in which he had
treated the concluding phases of the regenerative process and further
heightens the prominence he gave at the time to the psychology and external conditions of prophecy. Despite the almost notorious late-Miltonic
bareness which *Samson Agonistes* shares with its companion in the 1671
volume, the terms of prophetic psychology, together with their attendant
distinctions, virtually dominate the retrospections and also the critical
moments of decision in the body of Milton's tragedy. In the way they are
deployed, they may even suggest the shape of Milton's fable, the nature of
this tragic action. Near the beginning of the poem, Samson recalls a time
when "What I motion'd was of God" and claims that a special way of
knowing had led him to the Timnite; at that time, he recalls impressively,
his knowledge was based upon a different source:

> I knew
> From intimate impulse, and therefore urged
> The Marriage on; that by occasion hence

> I might begin Israel's Deliverance,
> The work to which I was divinely call'd. [222–26]

Samson goes on to suggest that his downfall with Dalila was rooted in an abandonment of this "impulse" and a reliance instead on a rationalized sense of tradition: he no longer "knew"; he merely "*thought* it lawful from my former act, / And the same end; still watching to oppress / *Israel's* oppressors" (231–33). The basis of this thought, we may notice, was his own past experience, his former "act"; what matters most—even more than the reference, presumably to his first marriage—is a sense of continuity, now seemingly lost, among God, impulse, act, and "thought." He no longer thinks it was lawful, or that his own thinking could somehow *constitute* lawfulness. He was just desperately wrong (a judgment challenged by the work as a whole). In any case, he clearly now lacks that radical integrity of personality and psyche in which Milton was so interested from his early writing onward.[6] It may seem too good to be true for the older historicism, but Samson appears to think, in effect, that he fell into reason.

"Intimate impulse," as against the laws of thought: this is the manner in which Milton remembered his own declaration to Diodati in 1642. It is difficult to think of a terminology better calculated to disarm the critic— or to provoke our agreement, for that matter, with Samson's bitter complaint that his chief endowment is hung in his hair. If anything, the tragedy has given a new prominence to the idiom which so offends Hobbes in *Leviathan*: that radical talk of a new sort of decency, of being "instilled" with a "vehement love of the beautiful."[7] Samson leaves the stage professing to feel "Some rousing motions in me which dispose / To something extraordinary my thoughts" (1381–83); and although his words are nearly as mysterious as Wordsworth's celebrated allusion to "Something far more deeply interfused," Samson does go on, almost, to say that these "motions" just might include "presage in the mind" (1382–83, 1387), as though Samson had reversed himself and recovered at least a measure of "insight."

But it is the Messenger (the nearest thing here to Milton's epic bard) who best clarifies the ways in which the idea of "motions," the rudiments of thought, governs the whole narrative design of this work, including the invisible "event" itself. The Argument anticipates our difficulties with his two-part narration, announced in advance as an interruption: "In the midst of [Manoa's] discourse an Ebrew comes in haste; confusedly at first; and afterward more distinctly relating the Catastrophe, what Samson had done to the Philistins, and by accident to himself; wherewith the Tragedy ends." But Milton carefully links two *kinds* of confusion, the description of his report with the matter of his arrival onstage. The Messenger apologizes for his breathlessness and the other effects of his hasty flight from the temple. Good rationalist that he is (or would be), he trusts that time and a bit of oxygen will clear up his memory and "sense distract." If Milton's wording seems odd here, it is no isolated accident but a matter of the Messenger's understandably "sudden" phrasing and its impressive accuracy: the pressure he feels actually springs from the content, the *life*, of his story. It "would burst forth," he reports, "but I recover breath / And sense distract, to know well what I utter" (1555–56). After all, his initial inkling was close to the mark; for something very like "sense distract" actually got him before our eyes in the first place.

> But providence or instinct of nature seems,
> Or reason though disturb'd, and scarce consulted,
> To have guided me aright, I know not how,
> To thee.   [1545–48]

We seldom encounter a dramatic character worrying the matter of exits and entrances; at this level, only those offstage (and in the classroom or study) would question the author's prerogative, however tyrannically exercised. But here, the Messenger's own lines—and I believe that they are crucial—specifically recall what led Samson to the Timnite, and also to what he *says* got him offstage and to the Dagonalia; they do so because Milton is at this point (rather belatedly) consolidating our sense of how this poem's scene works. The Messenger's indecision as to which of his conductors was in charge points up the fact that in the world of *Samson Agonistes* these are, eventually, replaceable components—that providential "event" itself is once again (or, perhaps, is always) to be found in collusion with the prophet's instinct. He fuses what have until now been presented as radical alternatives in the poem, the rational (and quietistic) "faith" of Manoa and the Chorus with the antinomian part of Samson's outlook, abandoned with his marriage to Dalila but now resumed. The characterization of the Messenger's report also applies to the business of getting him onstage, as though this mundane piece of stage business were somehow an extraordinary event, the dramaturgical fall of a sparrow. His very arrival is presented in a manner that unmistakably recalls the "unpremeditated" inwardness of *Paradise Lost*. Falstaff was right; instinct is a great matter.

Unlike *Adam Unparadised*, *Samson Agonistes* "never was intended" for the stage, at least according to the preface of 1671. Despite the poem's occasional attempts to suggest that the Chorus is here partly to visualize Samson or the beribboned Dalila, it is not until the Messenger arrives that we are likely to feel encouraged to visualize the spectacle of this work, as we certainly do, for example, in the case of the brief epic's view from Mount Niphates. It may even help to consider that—like Samson himself—we never really see any of the poem's speakers except through the eyes that cannot tell the Officer's "quaint staff" from a scepter (1303). In a way that Adam's lament cannot do, the fallen champion's initial soliloquy can be said to originate the entire cast of players. The Danites' entrance provides Samson not only with the first instance of speakers outside himself, but with a significant "hearing" for his own words in this first part of his final day. By asking us to "See how he lies at random" (118), they continue an integral sequence begun in the opening soliloquy, extending (and "extenuating") the viewpoint, the behavior, and several key phrases of their originator. As though in keeping with a rather strict notion of tragic katharsis, Samson's monologue actually creates these attitudes and voices— all but the visible persons—of the drama, including the crucial idea of a divine "dispensation" beyond Samson's "reach" (61–62). It is to awaken Samson's griefs in therapeutic fashion that they subsequently materialize in person, as characters in a story everyone onstage supposes to be concluded already, allowing us to hear Samson's own voice by means of projective attachment to specific, and historically significant ownership. Milton's procedure helps to explain, among other things, the full force of his odd greeting to Dalila ("Out, out, hyaena!"). In a very real sense, then, it is Samson's *own* speech which reaches his ears in "disjointed" form, surviving its journey only as a "sound of words." His distinction, a critic's (or judge's) act, points to much more than the aural blurring of "counsel" and the very different word "consolation"; he has caught the way in which, almost immediately, the Danites seem to comment on the choral function itself. Given the chance to arrest his own words, he can discover the materials of innovation; he can now sort out the intentions—the mere arrival—of these well-meaning friends from the inadvertent sense of what they may say. It is his *own* experience that might teach him, those hornet-thoughts now disguised as a nation's representatives:

> Your, coming, Friends, revives me, for I learn
> Now of my own experience, not by talk,
> How counterfeit a coin they are who friends

Bear in their Superscription (of the most
I would be understood); in prosperous days
They swarm, but in adverse withdraw their head
Not to be found, though sought.   [187–93][8]

For Samson at this point, the Danites' nation has become something like a discursive vehicle, conversation or counsel or consolation in its lowest terms. A "country" has been imaginatively relocated; their identity as members of a specific tribe or nation has become a label or "superscription," something like Luther's "black devil" or the "Apostate Angel" of *Paradise Lost*. They describe their own potential function in the most enthusiastic terms partly, it seems, because they are paralyzed by the case at hand. Even as they voice the extravagant hope to soothe mind and body alike, they advertise the very ingredients of their wisdom as nothing more than "apt words," an abbreviated version of "Lycidas"'s frail thoughts dallying with false surmise.

In this way, Milton marks the nadir of Samson's outlook—it is also the threshold of Samson's insight—as something like Satan's "talk" in the brief epic. The following passage (which occurs just after Samson's prayer for "speedy death, / The close of all my miseries, and the balm") brings to a head the the poem's critique of "vain reasonings":

Many are the sayings of the wise
In ancient and in modern books enrolled;
Extolling Patience as the truest fortitude;
And to the bearing well of all calamities,
All chances incident to man's frail life
Consolatories writ
With studied argument, and much persuasion sought
Lenient of grief and anxious thought,
But with th'afflicted in his pangs thir sound
Little prevails, or rather seems a tune,
Harsh, and of dissonant mood from his complaint,
Unless he feel within
Some source of consolation from above;
Secret refreshings, that repair his strength,
And fainting spirits uphold.   [652–66]

The passage crystallizes what Samson has said (about his own "quarrel" as well as the choral efforts) from the very beginning of the work; and it is remembered later, in Samson's public reference to a secret "accord," disguised as the announcement of gymnastic improvisation. It marks the point of maximum disjunction, not only between the consciousness of the community and its erstwhile champion, but Samson's isolation from his own former mood—from all that the Danites now represent with such enervated self-consciousness.

Chapter Twelve

Unapocryphal Visitors

For books are as meats and viands are—some of good, some of evil
substance, and yet God in that unapocryphal vision said
without exception, "Rise, Peter, kill and eat," leaving the choice
to each man's discretion.
Areopagitica

Like *Paradise Regained*, *Samson Agonistes* seems to be almost without those
occasional raptures that mark the "inspired" moments of Milton's earlier
verse and prose)—the sudden encounter with that cherub Contemplation
or the angel Lycidas, the *Animadversions'* hymn which had so recently been a
"spontaneous" prayer, in *Paradise Lost* the vocal convergence of fallen poet
with angel chorus or earliest Man (*PL* 3:413–15, 5:202). Milton gives
his Danite hero no signs of inspiration that we would call literary in any
ordinary sense, even as he leaves the stage. Of the poem's two sustained
lyric passages, one is prompted not so much by inspiration as memories of
the angel's promise; the other (Samson's ironic praise of his own bootless
abstinence) is a fully controlled, very self-*consciously* literary diversion,
displaying no poetic talent that he does not share with the Chorus. At first
glance, the poet seems to have his Nazarites' inspiration a private affair,
safely confined to the recesses of Samson's "conscience and internal peace,"
or—even more problematic, if that is possible—those "rousing motions"
which Samson announces as he leaves for the Dagonalia. What takes its
place?

For most readers of *Samson Agonistes*, the answer has been the "rousing motions" which Samson claims to feel toward the end of the work; we too, perhaps, are meant to be reassured by the great champion's "Be of good courage." But despite our first impressions of a Miltonic hero fully as mysterious or "secret" as the newly fallen Eve, it makes sense to assume instead that the work permits full access to what Milton thought we could know of the conditions for prophetic insight, and suggests that they remain hidden only to the Danite chorus (a bit like the soul of Harmony at that moment of anxiety in "L'Allegro"). In the fashion of his own "Eternal Father" commissioning the sociable Raphael in order to fulfill all justice, Milton is at pains to prevent the claim of "surprisal" (*PL* 5:245–47). Samson's strange words are not so much the straightforward announcement of Milton's deus ex machina as a bit of outright deception, the deliberately assumed mask for a mind already made up—hardly in the throes of unpremeditated "first motions." There is a considerable difference between these words (just the kind of thing the Chorus thinks we like to hear from God's champions) and the vehement reminiscence "I knew / From intimate impulse" (*SA* 222–23). This is unquestionably one of the tragedy's crucial moments, but it is a different matter altogether from the Messenger's account of arriving onstage, not quite by accident, but through "instinct of nature"—pursued, indeed, by "dire imagination" (1544). The Messenger's words are designed to mark the completion of a cycle, to establish the perfect coincidence between the present moment of poise and potential "event" and Samson's recollection (perhaps flawed) of an older way of knowing. "Intimate impulse"—or the "rousing motions" which Samson claims to feel during his final exchange with the Chorus—has a local habitation within the work, in the way we hear the entire exchange between the protagonist and his onstage spectators (including himself). What takes the place of those earlier "flights" of inspiration, above all, is *listening*, which is Samson's primary activity at the "bank" where all this takes place.[1]

Appropriately enough, Samson seems most "awake"—stylistically speaking—in the moment just prior to the poem's "great event." As in *Paradise Regained*, that moment is (like so much of the choral part) a quotation, the Messenger's performance of Samson's extemporaneous speech before the Philistine lords. The speech is demonstrably in the manner of Samson's most recent discursive works, the ones we have heard firsthand. It is a telescopically reduced autobiography, the epitome of a life. Like his mysterious final exchange with the Chorus, it culminates with the reference to a private "accord" and announces a bit of improvisation to top off the performances merely required up to this point—the school figures, so to speak, "not without wonder or delight beheld." (We shall return to the Horatian banter here.) It is Samson at his most flexible in tone: here, besides the grimly laconic "Threat'ner," is the pliant man of sense who so ironically agreed with the Officer's (and his own countrymen's) reasoning:

> Now of my own accord such other trial
> I mean to show you of my strength, yet greater;
> As with amaze shall strike all who behold.   [1643–45]

Never before in the play have we heard anything quite like the detached, grim humor of that reference to something which might prove so "striking."[2] Odd though it may seem, the passage marks a conjunction between the young Milton's prophetic inspiration and the traditional "alacrity" with which some of the ancient heroes had died. Samson's new tones have a relatively recent antecedent in certain kinds of metaphysical wit, or the profound levity which seems to have fascinated Shakespeare during the middle 1590s: the kind of thing we observe when John of Gaunt plays so nicely with his name, or the climactic scene in the Capulet tomb, when Romeo virtually names the phenomenon, suspecting that the color returning to Juliet's cheeks can be nothing more than a dying man's "lightening" (5:3:88–91). Milton has attached this ancient idea to the "internal peace" traditionally attributed to the conscience of the forerunner.[3]

In practice, it has proved all too easy to mistake Samson's new kind of behavior with a defensive sarcasm, and even a continuing fear of public ridicule. But his departure from the Chorus with the announcement that he now begins to feel some rousing motions is not just carried out in an ironic tone; the work insists that the exit defines and expresses a new, authentically unconfessional, personality or self, an identity effectively in place by the conclusion of the Dalila episode and practiced from there on to the end of the poem. Milton allows Samson to recognize "wonted arts," including his own, from another perspective, and so to continue the play-long activity of careful listening that begins with his notice of the Chorus's "sound of words." To judge from the patterns and tone of Samson's valedictory— among other things, it moves neatly from past to a projected future— Milton's sudden allusion to a private "accord" (like the announcement of those "rousing motions") marks the access of what Milton had called "insight" in 1644, something involving (as we have seen) a "presage in the mind," as Samson calls it at 1387. By making the "rousing motions" accessible within the work, Milton seems to be insisting that this new dramatic flexibility is not so much a function of "character" in any narrow sense as an actual constituent of dramatic action. That is, it marks Samson's arrival as an "artist," or (better) as a full-fledged Miltonic "author."

I

In a moment of demure introspection just after completing her share of the Fall, Eve thanks "Experience" for opening "Wisdom's way . . . though secret she retire"; in a pointed afterthought she adds that "I perhaps am secret" (*PL* 9:809–10). At the moment we have just considered (the virtual midpoint of *Samson Agonistes*), it is most interesting that Dalila should now appear in conspicuous affiliation both with the state-sponsored "zeal," and (more important) with the idol Dagon ("this thing of sea or land"), at times the notorious object of the Danites' own worship. In the despairing medial exchange with the Chorus, it is the hero who has become what could be called a secret text, confronting the garrulous collective "margin" upon which Milton had so often poured his contempt during the 1640s; when disappointed, as we have seen, he had been quick to associate the Long Parliament (if not all England) with the mercenary rhetoricians of antiquity. Samson's Nazaritic authority will ultimately depend upon his triumph over his own "effeminate garrulity"—something Milton makes it all too easy to explain in psychological terms. Among other things, though, Dalila represents a complex past intimately related to the "nation" that has just fallen silent. By bringing her on at this juncture, in effect, Milton allows or forces Samson to confront the Danites' discursive nationalism in its nascent form. That is, Samson can come to terms with his "effeminate garrulity" only by coming to terms with his authorship of Dalila herself, "my accomplished snare." What better moment could there be to introduce the first of his two apocryphal visitors in this authentic, "unapocryphal" account?

Milton's account of Dalila's visit certainly seems to call for a feminist criticism that can recognize the way in which she brings us to the linguistic roots of such matters as revolutionary (and reactionary) theory. Attempts to explain her motives or purposes seem perfectly natural, but they are also virtually doomed to misrepresent her. By her own account, she arrives with "doubtful feet and wavering resolution" (732); but this phrase, however accurate it may be in describing the rhythms of her evasive rationalizing, seems to turn the choral announcement of her arrival in the direction of pathos and encourage us to probe for the deeper, psychological causes.[4]

Dalila's suspiciously Gallic word for what she wishes to accomplish in her visit is "parley":

Let weakness then with weakness come to parle
So near related, or the same of kind,
Thine forgive mine; that men may censure thine
The gentler, if severely thou exact not
More strength from me, than in thyself was found.   [785–89]

"*was* found"; Dalila is clearly writing Samson's own *kind* of history here, all of it built on the assumption that the story has ended. The definitive biography may now be safely written. The "authentic" Samson, like the cause of "what [Dalila] did," is already out there somewhere—a comforting idea, entertained from the beginning of the poem but certainly not a rooted Miltonic principle behind it, even in this work. She *seems* to be proposing a kind of informal (not to say aimless) collaboration, the choral kind of sociability. But as she speaks, it is hard to tell what she thinks. Does that final "was found" refer to some fixed, determinate reality, to historical fact? Or is she thinking of her own logical construction—a judicial sort of "finding," completed much more recently in an artificial, discursive sort of past?

In fact, like Sidney's poet, she affirms nothing. She may not know whether tears may expiate; but she is prepared to say that *if* they do, then "my penance hath not slack'n'd" (738). She will not confirm that love caused what she did; whatever it was will in any case be misconstrued by Samson, who would no doubt say (with Satan) that love or hate are "to me alike."[5] Superficially, she seems to have been involved in the kind of circumstantial experience that the *Areopagitica* calls morally neutral or "indifferent." However others may judge her actions, she acted (she says, in effect) on the basis of how she saw things, "sought by all means *therefore* / How to endear, and hold thee to me firmest" (795–96). My italics here are meant to point to what we (not necessarily Samson) hear in this. Samson seems unquestionably alert to metaphoric gesture, to the suggestion of a physical stifling that makes Dalila a "bosom serpent" who would, like Comus, hug him into snares. At the same time, however, there is the patently constructed quality of the argument here, the way it moves from remembered experience into pragmatic inference and deduction. Thence it develops (as we shall see) into at least a pretense of victimization by laws, maxims, priests with their "schools of thought"—the kind of thing the very "original" Samson dismisses at the outset of the play as "talk."[6] Everyone notices the extraordinary sensibility involved in such a gesture: at once casuistical and histrionic, it finds cause for satisfaction (and even for a reprieve) in a highly self-conscious, managed performance. And it is a performance which, paradoxically, denies its own freedom, to judge from the astonishing suggestion that she has been led here by what amounts to conflicting abstractions: "conjugal affection / Prevailing over fear, and timorous doubt." As she describes it, the situation bears a striking resemblance to Satan's evident victimization, claimed by the narrator (in a moment of naiveté) by Guile, itself, in turn, the pawn of Envy and Revenge (*PL* 1:34–35). And other features of Dalila's whole manner, from the plosive character of her delivery to her facile command of penitential doctrine, suggests that she *stands* for "thought," and for the kind of community to which Samson has been in bondage for some time. She would bring back that sociable world so easily subjugated by Comus's charms and "wily trains," a realm in which language becomes what we naively call communication. For both Dalila and the "juggler" of the *Masque at Ludlow*, Milton describes language thus conceived as serpentine: involved, subtle, insinuating, producing finally an adder's wisdom, very likely in the form of that "moroseness" which Calvin thought might reject all manner of doctrine.

We can best describe what happens during this pivotal scene using an analogy from art and the necessarily "uncontrollable intent" involved in all language, especially, perhaps, in a revolutionary period. While Dalila is onstage there is a sense of language's beginning to be "on its own" again, a sense of words at play, and so beyond the control of all but the least premeditated intentions. It is during the Dalila episode that name-calling itself becomes an explicit issue. Samson revises the Chorus's introductory term for Dalila ("my wife, my traitress") as well as her motives for coming (it was "malice, not repentance"). Indeed, roles and names, including the sounds of words, seem to proliferate here, as though the text itself were at this point made subject to Milton's own materialism. For the purpose of confronting the problem of Samson's "effeminate" garrulity, Milton introduces a lower common denominator that is gender connected: just as "Friends" became a "superscription," terms (like "Woman," "man," "God") become detachable and interchangeable, subject to striking revisions by the vigilant Samson. Here, for instance, is Samson's welcome for Dalila:

> Out, out Hyaena; these are thy wonted arts,
> And arts of every woman false like thee,
> To break all faith, all vows, deceive betray,

Then as repentant to submit, beseech,
And reconcilement move with feign'd remorse,
Confess, and promise wonders in her change,
Not truly penitent, but chief to try
Her husband, how far urg'd his patience bears,
His virtue or weakness which way to assail:
Then with more cautious and instructed skill
Again transgresses, and again submits;
That wisest and best men full oft beguil'd
With goodness principl'd not to reject
The penitent, but ever to forgive,
Are drawn to wear out miserable days,
Entangl'd with a pois'nous bosom snake,
If not by quick destruction soon cut off
As I by thee, to Ages an example.   [748–65]

Samson is clearly starting to hear the sounds and sense of words in a deeper way, and his almost instantaneous recognition of "wonted arts" is a measure of his ability to resist her varied discursive "train," which Milton describes throughout with reference to mimicry, and in language recalling the encounter of Eve and that very articulate serpent. Samson's "Hyaena" deprives Dalila of an authentic or original voice—or sex, for that matter; she is reduced to a mimic, a puppet or "motion." "Out, out!" (with another variation on the great predecessor in English tragedy) somehow recognizes that the "parle" she says she has come for has long since begun, that she has been sent, perhaps to extenuate or exhaust parley and "thought" itself. In fact, the scene effects a fundamental partitioning among the various audiences for Samson's words. The whole passage quoted above displays all the signs of an emerging "narrator," of exposition rather than personal reaction. This kind of personal history seems to crystallize into principles, dark and timeless laws of what "must be," including enduring tyranny and death.[7]

In Samson's mind, the terms "wife" and "traitress" are as far apart in meaning as he wishes Dalila to remain from him physically. With "my wife, my traitress," he moves much closer to a self that is "my conscience and internal peace"; even as he declares his ownership of that "wife," he conveys Milton's suggestion that in these four words a husband becomes a nation or "country"—a place to be found (in the deceptively pacific words of *Doctrine*) "wherever it is well with one." This is, of course, a different kind of identity from the self his countrymen (and he himself) sing and proverb him for earlier. Faced with these later references to a new kind of selfhood, we may forget the particulars of his earlier imprisonment within a sepulcher / self, or the precise way in which, during Dalila's visit, he twice converts his surroundings—the "bank" where all this occurs is something the preface insists *we* cannot see to verify—as in "This Gaol I count the house of Liberty / To thine whose doors my feet shall never enter" (949–50).[8]

The question of what's. in a name (or a misnomer like "fate") clearly has an unusual importance here, as in Milton's earlier works. Here as in "Lycidas," the decision to call someone an angel or "Messenger" (as Samson does with the Philistine Officer) indicates an entirely new way of viewing the world of "accidents," including his own more or less responsible place in that world. And there are related forms of innovation. Having accepted a term already in circulation previously in the work, Samson anchors it in original and striking fashion to a particular use, as in "Weakness is thy excuse, / and I believe it, weakness to resist / *Philistian* gold" (829–31). He enters easily into his antagonist's next argumentative step, with an effect not so much of bitter sarcasm as distanced analysis: this talk is precise, revisionary, densely self-quoting:

> But Love constrain'd thee; call it furious rage
> To satisfy thy lust: Love seeks to have Love;
> My love how couldst thou hope, who took'st the way
> To raise in me inexpiable hate,
> Knowing, as needs I must, by thee betray'd?
> In vain thou striv'st to cover shame with shame,
> Or by evasions thy crime uncover'st more.   [835–42]

And this innovative precision persists, in this and other forms, like Samson's "Or peace or not, alike to me he comes (1074), and the careful "prediction": "If there be aught of presage in the mind, / This day will be remarkable in my life / By some great act, or of my days the last" (1387–89), where future realities require complementary vocabularies.

At this point in the poem, many readers have yielded to the temptation just to sit back and enjoy the hero's momentary advantages (or for that matter the eventual ruin of the Philistines) and so to accept them—to agree, in some measure, with Samson's own description of what he is doing in these scenes, or to celebrate those "rousing motions" that have enabled him to do it. After all, it is just a straightforward business of stripping away the varnished appearances, is it not? A matter of getting to the bottom of things both human and divine. Here is the pre-Restoration pamphleteer—or the Son of *Paradise Regained* again—calling things by their right names at last. In falling into the kind of appreciation that asks us to "Think about it!" though, we join the Chorus in their nationalistic and almost barbaric celebration, and give an added point to the way in which the Danites are discriminated from the Philistines themselves with increasing difficulty as the work progresses. We become something other than that interested bystander in the *Apology* and forget that the tragedy explores, among other things, the ambiguities of standing, safely, "aloof" (*SA* 1621). If we "go along," we may not catch the development of Samson's skills in recognition, and we run the risk of forgetting Milton's virtually lifelong discussion of these skills, a discussion this work continues.[9]

For here, Samson has moved beyond autobiography and history in the naive sense; no longer concerned with questions involving the simple matter of reference—the accuracy of memory or records—he seems to *practice* history in a more familiar, modern sense of the word. At the center of it all is Samson's new relation to his own (and others') language—the discovery, perhaps, of language as an artistic and potentially prophetic medium, and the correlative sense (equally strong) of all inauthentic language (including his own "garrulous" phase) as either the abstract or "systematic" studies of the *Areopagitica* or *Of Education*—as the "wonted" rhetorical arts of Belial and Comus—or the nonsensical "*sound* of words," the mere buzzing of those tormenting thoughts which are so clearly the descendants of *Paradise Lost*'s "bees in springtime." "Coming to parle" with Dalila is precisely what would involve Samson once more in the "toils" that victimize that early juggler's "easy hearted man," the arts recognized by the Lady of the *Masque* (in very similar terms) as "magic structures."

Milton has designed the encounter with Dalila as something like a competition between rival historians, would-be expositors of what is perennially real or true. And by displacing his rival in this sense, Samson acquires something like the authority of the Pauline orator responsible for the *Areopagitica*'s moments of eloquence. More clearly than the earlier arrivals, her visit involves the kind of encapsulation which (Milton had urged in *Of Education*) seals the acquisition of "insight." By endowing his protagonist with what Milton had termed "the life of teaching," Milton marks the emergence of Samson as a lawgiver, the kind of judge he was supposed to be. Needless to say, it could not have occurred without the sense of contending passions Dr. Johnson thought Milton had "never studied." It happens here by allowing him to gain a hard-won *onstage* ascendancy, something like the more entertaining (and easily managed) dramaturgical revolutions accomplished, say, by Richard of Gloucester or Prince Hal.

In this way, Samson comes to recognize the true object of his name-calling even as it becomes part of a more complex development in his behavior; he discovers his own "effeminate garrulity" in a very different kind of Dalila, a built-in "traitress." There is a public dimension to this discovery as well. By giving his Nazarite such a fine ear, Milton provides a kind of minimal standard for our own listening. Samson can be said to initiate our own talents in hearing the unintended rhymes and virtual nonsense that point to the Danites' continuing "deafness," their resistance even to stylistic change. Without the slightest sign of recognizing the way in which Samson's names now patently "redound" on his own head, they continue the abuse of a more literal Dalila and widen the generality to include the whole tribe of "his [man's] female"; the results are manifestly farcical because their target has become irrelevant:

> Is it for that such outward ornament
> Was lavish't on thir Sex, that inward gifts
> Were left for haste unfinish't, judgment scant
> Capacity not rais'd to apprehend
> Or value what is best
> In choice, but oftest to affect the wrong?
> Or was too much of self-love mixt,
> Of constancy no root infixt,
> That either they love nothing or not long.   [1025–33]

To the Chorus, Dalila will always be the archetypal serpent or scorpion; their names, their way of knowing seems always to be a function of hind-sight, their Dalila "a manifest Serpent by her sting / Discover'd in the end, till now conceal'd" (997–98). Nothing ever changes, they tell us to the very end. But their declaration is met with a significant revision: Samson, who begins the episode by calling her his "accomplished snare," disagrees with their final misnomer, wittily and without bitterness:

> So let her go, God sent her to debase me,
> And aggravate my folly who committed
> To such a viper his most sacred trust
> Of secrecy, my safety, and my life.   [999–1002]

This is to answer the Chorus's name with the observation that a responsible speaker had chosen his audience poorly. But the meaning of the passage is more complex; and it depends on the way in which a name (or term of abuse) gets absorbed into a historifying syntax. Early in the work, the word "fool" seems to point to an external entity in something like the manner of Dalila's (or, in *Paradise Lost*, Satan's) personifications; the outburst interrupts one of Samson's efforts at telling his story in such a way that he actually joins what he takes to be the vulgar derision:

> for a word, a tear,
> Fool, have divulg'd the secret gift of God
> To a deceitful Woman. [200–02][10]

Now there is a new and different sense of agency from the time when Samson virtually claimed sole authorship for Dagon's run of good luck. As a term, "my folly" becomes a new syntactic venue; hovering between the status of victim and perpetrator, the authorial folly absorbs the pride of Samson's earlier claim without the whining of "my folly *made* me do it." In calling her a "viper" now, Samson actually modifies the Chorus's "manifest serpent" and so claims a larger measure of responsibility in "publishing" the divine secret. The proverbially deaf reptile has taken the place of an entangling constrictor-of-prophets; in this locution, Samson, who had such a beast "as audience," has become the speaker, controlling as though in Eve's "Circean" fashion the now domesticated adder, once his "sorceress."

Increasingly during the episode, we must be impressed by Samson's growing control over his verbal medium, a kind of control which enacts the strenuous self-subjection reported by the Messenger later on. Even the initial "Hyaena" marks a midpoint between the tendency to inarticulate rage ("fool!") and the laconic detachment of his later question to the "Messenger" / Officer: Are the pious Philistines not already well enough stocked with "Jugglers, and Dancers, Antics, Mummers, Mimics" (1325)? To characterize the kind of threshold represented by Dalila's visit, we may borrow a distinction from Milton's own characterization of a younger self as "all serious to learn and know," and say that the present incident provides the moment, belated in the extreme, at which Samson's "learning" becomes—in the young Milton's almost magical sense of the words— knowledge, wisdom, *virtue*.

II

Samson's new way of hearing his visitor's speeches is projected in a new dramatic flexibility, a histrionic talent, the ability to project his antagonist's probable next move. In *Samson Agonistes*, the hero's new (and very different) eloquence—the grim mock-heroics with Harapha, the pseudo-compliance with the Chorus, the oddly patterned agreeability in the arena—spring from the linguistic ruins of the Dalila incident. Few readers would deny that Samson is affected by this encounter; each incident adds to his affliction in a way that is consistent with Milton's analysis of "mortification" in the *Doctrine*. The "new" Samson is the creature, in effect, of his own garrulous, "effeminate," sensuous shadow. But it is also true, I believe, that the dialogue which so creates him is largely of his own making. Just as Samson has projected, not merely recalled his own past, he imaginatively anticipates Dalila's pretexts and even *creates* her part. The would-be objective unmasker of others turns out to be an author instead, applying the varnish to his "accomplished snare."

This is evident from the way Milton presents the next "apocryphal" visitor, the giant Harapha. Rather than reciprocate in anger when he is accused of being a "Revolter," Samson actually fills in the substance behind the epithet:

> My Nation was subjected to your Lords.
> It was the force of Conquest; force with force
> Is well ejected when the Conquer'd can.
> But I a private person, whom my Country
> As a league-breaker gave up bound, presum'd
> Single Rebellion and did Hostile Acts.
> I was no private but a person raised
> With strength sufficient and command from Heav'n
> To free my Country. [1205–13]

His Giantship is hardly capable of understanding the distinction anticipated in lines 1208–10; but the abrupt reversal can be achieved only when "Revolter" is provisionally accepted and explained by the offender himself—when it is understood by being entertained, in something like the way Samson plays with the loaded seventeenth-century term "Friend," turning it into what he calls a "Superscription" (190).

And the same is true in the tragedy's hyperextended *"exit auctor,"* accomplished in the exchanges that follow. After Harapha's angry departure, the Chorus worries that Samson will now suffer further at the hands of the offended lords. Samson's response indicates a very clear sense of the challenge he has just met, but without ignoring his continuing pain. Harapha would be unlikely to get too specific about the visit since the lords might raise the wrong questions. Still, men do act perversely in their own affliction. Samson now anticipates first a possible coincidence between ordinary Philistine self-interest and his own survival—undesired on his part, to say the least. But he goes beyond this to imagine a darker irrationality, a Philistine hate that might prove both self-destructive and at the same time paradoxically "friendly" to himself:

> Much more affliction than already felt
> They cannot well impose, nor I sustain;
> If they intend advantage of my labors,
> The work of many hands, which earns my keeping
> With no small profit daily to my owners.
> But come what will, my deadliest foe will prove
> My speediest friend, by death to rid me hence,
> The worst that he can give, to me the best.
> Yet so it may fall out, because their end
> Is hate, not help to me, it may with mine
> Draw thir own ruin who attempt the deed.   [1257–67]

The movement here, signaled with some care, is from imaginatively entertained economic pragmatism—why the Philistines need to ignore Harapha's wounded pride—to an acceptance of paradoxical values; and thence to a discovery barely beginning to crystallize. This too is practical in its way. Samson has triumphed over the Chorus specifically in his knowledge of the world—presumably the Danites' own specialty.

What the Chorus understands of all this is, naturally, another matter altogether; the Danites seem to mistake the correction for mere vengefulness, a canonical motive which Milton took pains to remove from this rendition of the ancient story. To judge from the way the Danites now recommend patience as "more oft the exercise / Of Saints," at least (1287–88), they cannot understand—or will not recognize—the notion of a delivery that is partial and involves social responsibility and cost. To be sure, it is comely and reviving when God works through "plain Heroic magnitude of mind," whatever *that* involves. But in any case, the Chorus puts this simply as one of those interesting alternatives in the never-ending course of history, as part of a well-balanced common-sensicalness that we have just seen Samson surmount in a well-charted, dialectic fashion precisely by imagining, once again, the antagonistic (in this case, the Philistines' own) point of view.

All this constitutes the kind of "listening" and "hearing" that Milton associated with the process of regeneration but modifies here to suit his own outlook and the fictional world he develops to project it. Just as Manoa discovers a variety of motives during his attempt to secure his son's ransom, we may well feel that once there was more to Milton's Danites than the silliness they display, for example, on the departure of Dalila. Like the Long Parliament, or the fallen angels awakening on the burning lake, they are a study in collective evasion. The many scholarly attacks on the Danites may be as aptly directed at the old Samson, someone who has just reappeared in the person of Harapha. But the criticism hardly applies to the way in which Samson dramatizes and extenuates the choral part in these later moments, especially in the dismissal of the Philistine Officer and the long, brilliant struggle with the Chorus which precedes his own exit. Strangely enough, when we next hear the national voice, it has become detached from their collective person. Here we can easily recognize the Danites' tones as an ironic overlay of Samson's own coalescing attitudes. In view of Milton's early exploration of Reformation commentaries, it is fascinating that Samson's topic of the moment is the text of "subjection," the issue deliberately omitted, we may recall, from Paul's all-important Letter to the Ephesians.[11] With the signal exception of the identity Samson attaches to the initial word of the following passage, we have a perfect rendition of the choric outlook, accurate even to the detail of the parenthetic truism:

> Masters' commands come with a power resistless
> To such as owe them absolute subjection;
> And for a life who will not change his purpose?
> (So mutable are all the ways of men).   [1404–07]

Addressed as it is to more than his onstage audience, this is indeed a duplicitous speech, a remarkably vivid continuation of Samson's "act." In fact, it is part of a fundamental revision in the work's social alignments, a combination of the nations we had thought to be simple opposites. While Samson so playfully adopts the Danites' position, the Chorus continues the arguments of the departing Officer, quite unself-consciously playing the "Philistine" to Samson's ironically assumed Danite. If we consider Samson's dramatic flexibility as a constituent of emerging discovery—or even if we just notice the logically debilitating "Besides" of the following passage—it becomes clear that we are engaged once again with a process of review. In a considerably more engaging fashion than the brief epic's divine Son, Samson consolidates a new, revolutionary position even as he revisits his own past and specifically the tragedy's opening soliloquy. In so doing he reawakens our memories of this work's scriptural source and the predestined "event":

> Shall I abuse this Consecrated gift
> Of strength, again returning with my hair
> After my great transgression, so requite
> Favor renew'd, and add a greater sin
> By prostituting holy things to Idols;
> A *Nazarite* in place abominable
> Vaunting my strength in honor to thir *Dagon*?
> Besides, how vile, contemptible, ridiculous,
> What act more execrably unclean, profane?   [1354–62][12]

The articulation of the choric wisdom by a more conscious (or "awakened") Samson takes on the stichomythic form of rhetorical combat in the final exchange, in which the Chorus attains the utmost extent of collective reason's reach. These thrusts and parries too develop points already gained; they sharpen the familiar Miltonic distinction (for example) between religious and civil spheres, clarified during the exchange with Harapha but not quite grasped by the Chorus at 1363–64. The lack of evident progress here may well be a function of flagging choric reason or will; and we have seen that until reason (and the Law) can be fully deployed in *all* its impossible rigor, there can be no understanding of its governing purpose. It is thus Samson who provides the collective, "rational" response requisite to this very difficult stage of the argument and thus replaces the Danites' evasive suggestion that he resort to a Dalilan mental reservation:

> *Chor.* Yet with this strength thou serv'st the *Philistines*,
>   Idolatrous, uncircumcis'd, unclean.
> *Sam.* Not in their Idol-Worship, but by labor
>   Honest and lawful to deserve my food
>   Of those who have me in their civil power.
> *Chor.* Where the heart joins not, outward acts defile not.
> *Sam.* Where outward force constrains, the sentence holds;
>   But who constrains me to the temple of *Dagon*,
>   Not dragging?   [1363–71]

Here again, the idea of discovery entails something beyond mimicry or merely imitative play. Samson has quite self-consciously *completed* the choric position. And Milton may well have considered this extenuation to be an integral part of the repentance to which the work refers so frequently: he has somehow heard what the Chorus cannot bring themselves to say—

however fallaciously. The tone of the exchange is extraordinarily difficult to capture, for Milton's purpose is not so much to humiliate the Danites with their evasiveness as it is to articulate, perhaps for the first time, a nation's position—the true source of their embarrassment here.

Adopting their own terms, Samson provides the embarrassing principle actually governing this situation: in fact—or at least theoretically—he may *not* obey the Philistine strictures except "where outward force constrains." Only by voicing this position can Samson discover the "reason" of the Law and thereby the necessary paradox of a special "dispensation."[13] The rhetorical turn which follows is dramatically devastating but essentially explanatory in its purpose: what Samson has voiced is an open and general possibility, heroic indeed but available to "thee":

> The *Philistian* Lords command.
> Commands are no constraints. If I obey them,
> I do it freely; venturing to displease
> God for the fear of Man, and Man prefer,
> Set God behind: which in his jealousy
> Shall never, unrepented, find forgiveness.
> Yet that he may dispense with me or thee
> Present in Temples at Idolatrous Rites
> For some important cause, thou needst not doubt. [1371–79]

In a very different kind of speech which provides the key to so many readings of this work, Samson will shortly announce that he feels "some rousing motions, . . . which dispose / To something extraordinary my thoughts," something very close to constituting, among other things "presage in the mind." In fact, the passage above (with much that precedes it) records Samson's extraordinary thoughts. The passage requires a careful reading. We can find the fullest contents of a phrase like "my conscience and internal peace" (1334) in Samson's idea of "dispense": the word conflates the speaker's own sense of uselessness (or even reprobation) with the glimpse of an instrumental purpose in his own death. (It helps here to recall how prominently the meditative sonnets employ "use," as in "All is, if I have grace to use it so, / As ever in my great task-Master's eye"; and especially the way in which, in Sonnet 19, "use" becomes "expend," as in the syntactically buried assertion that "my light is spent.") At the same time, it is the imagination of a *completed* choral position that accomplishes the new "disposition." Samson is thinking generously as well as adventurously here: in terms of ordinary (not just special or "heroic") possibilities.

In effect, he is replacing the Chorus—something he has fashioned during the work—with a more fully conscious and potentially heroic audience, something like the one Manoa mentions at line 1715. It is a most fragile moment, this instant of a recovered historical crisis that is easily mystified, as in Milton's own sources. What Samson has recovered, I suggest, is the moment of responsibility, or practical "uses." In the sonnet, we begin by focusing on a talent lodged "useless" within the helpless speaker and move toward the strenuous reminder of faithful service. In the early prose, the attack on the clergy became (in retrospect) a matter of prescience. Here, it seems, we have an act of mystification following the crucial discovery, fast on the heels of "insight." Samson appears to reassure the Danites in straightforward Hollywood-tough fashion to "Be of good courage." He does not mention the rousing motions until he has given up the effort to extend the heroic "call." His mysterious words suggest the idea of an isolated, implanted talent primarily because only this kind makes sense to the nation which at this crucial moment has "persisted deaf" and continues "to love Bondage more than Liberty, / Bondage with ease than strenuous liberty" (270–71). What they have just rejected, essentially, is "knowledge in the making," opinion in a good man—nothing so special or unsharable as the gift of foreconceit. In the face of their champion's discovery about self-sacrifice—in effect, about how the divine ways are best "found"—the Chorus wonders how their unfortunate rascal will get out of *this* scrape.

At the conclusion to the second book of *Paradise Lost*, Milton presents a Chaos which comes close to advertising his own methods in the early portion of the epic: "stunning sounds and voices all confused." Rather differently, *Samson Agonistes* marks the preliminary to a known "great event" as the *disappearance* of a highly individual "Herculean" style, or rather its getting mingled with the idiom of "the world." In this context, it is most interesting to notice how the persistent Miltonic metaphor of mixture is applied here. Mixture is at the heart of things here as in the *Areopagitica* or the *Masque*: earth with sky, Samson with the Philistine victims, Dagon or Dalila themselves ("things of sea or land"), "promiscuous" tribes as well as voices. Virtually every inhabitant of the drama tries to sort things out: the Chorus deciding which prison is the "real" one or which misfortune to lament first, Manoa asking the Messenger to "tell us the sum, the circumstance defer," or even his later hope to extricate and cleanse his son's body. In these interpretive and ritual attempts, we are forced to confront the "tragic" confusion at the heart of the poem's world. We may recall that at the very point when the Messenger reports most directly as an eyewitness, Samson is seen "immixed" with the Philistine lords and priests, and that the Messenger stresses (for the second time) the inevitability of his fate. The Messenger's horror reminds us of Samson's own contempt for Dalila's excesses of sociability and also recalls a long-term motif, displayed in Comus's announced methods (winding / hugging), in the poet's brief sally at "mixt dance" and (perhaps most striking of all) in the disgust Satan feels at the prospect of a serpent disguise:

> O foul descent! That I who erst contended
> With Gods to sit the highest, am now constrain'd
> Into a Beast, and mixed with bestial slime,
> This essence to incarnate and imbrute,
> That to the highth of Deity aspir'd;
> But what will not Ambition and Revenge
> Descend to? Who aspires must down as low
> As high he soar'd, obnoxious first or last
> To basest things. Revenge, at first though sweet,
> Bitter ere long back on itself recoils:
> Let it.   [PL 9:163–73]

Whether or not the serpent mask actually involves the constraint to which Satan refers, this is recognizably the temporary mixture of evil with good in advance of its ultimate "redundance": that eventual segregation (in a post-Samson world) when evil "on itself shall back recoil, / And mix no more with goodness, when at last / Gather'd like scum, and settl'd to itself, / It shall be in eternal restless change / Self-fed and self-consum'd" (*A Masque*, 593–97). In the meantime, of course, there is the *Areopagitica*'s profound truth (quite definitely at work in the tragedy) that "the matter of them both is the same" (*CPW* 2:527). At the play's center, too, is the recognition that Samson's apparent compliance involves a knowing kind of mimicry. There is a world of difference between an "inevitable" or "accidental" immixture with his own Philistine victims and an instance of venturing freely (1373).

On Samson's part, Milton's fiction requires a struggle as difficult as Psyche's task, nothing less than the extrication of a new, "Nazaritic" self from the old garrulity represented by the various visitors to the bank where all this takes place. As we have seen, Samson's visitors are not quite the truly other characters of Milton's source; these "unapocryphal" visitors materialize from the voices of the initial monologue, eventually appearing "in person" but with the sharpened focus provided by a true surrogate. Encountering such shadows, Samson can venture into the next dispensation by separating himself from his own former behavior; he cannot be identified with the swaggering Harapha or the "effeminate" Dalila if he quite knowingly mimics them. Given the literal meaning of "Nazarite" and the obvious need to distinguish a seemingly private authentic self from the old garrulous one, it is a fascinating irony that Milton marks the moment of success as a seeming stylistic convergence with the world surrounding his hero. We are not far from those conjunctions of idiom explored so finely by George Herbert in poems similarly dedicated to the matter of extricating oneself from the "sense" of literary language ("Jordan II").

Addressing the Officer (who returns with some of Milton's weakest iambics), Samson speaks for the Hebrew Community, but with what is, for us, recognizable duplicity. With a wonderful mock-passion he recoils at the imagined indignity of being dragged through the streets (the very circumstance which would prevent a voluntary decision to comply, on Samson's part), at the notion of doing anything "Scandalous or forbidden in our Law" (the scruple he has just examined so critically with reference to the unknowable "important cause" [1379]). The ambiguity he now finds in his countrymen's truisms is clear in the wholesale reassurance he offers them just after the Officer's departure:

> Happ'n what may, of me expect to hear
> Nothing dishonourable, impure, unworthy
> Our God, our Law, my nation, or myself,
> The last of me or no I cannot warrant.   [1423–26]

In our minds by now there is a world of difference between the various jurisdictions mentioned, between "our Law" and "my nation," for example. We sense here that the latter part of 1425 proposes not so much a continuing series of alternatives as a new center of value; here as in the *Doctrine*, "my self" has *become* "my nation," even if (as the passage clearly suggests) it may be Samson's alone. It is as though "our country" has diminished in extent *during the work*, from an entire nation to a marriage to a single, quite isolated self.

For us, again, there is a crucial distinction between the new tones we hear and the confident, jocund Samson so welcome to the Chorus; what is "comely and reviving" to the men of Dan is something like an athlete's comeback, Samson the petty-god once again. Surely, there is no illusion in Samson's mind that he could manage the kind of unblemished victory which they have fondly projected in their recommendation of Patience as "more oft the exercise / Of Saints, the trial of thir fortitude, / Making them each his own Deliverer, / And Victor over all / That tyranny or fortune can inflict" (1287–91). In the vein of Puritan reprimand, Samson here "speaks home" to the Danites, speaks with partly concealed irony, from the standpoint of an "insight" evidently beyond their reach. This, perhaps, is to speak "from within," from the standpoint of a fitter audience offstage, and perhaps also located in one of those "aftertimes" (*CPW* 1:810). In the way the "apocryphal" and succeeding visits involve Samson's simultaneous invention and response to his antagonists' positions, it seems that the tragedy effects a progressive vocal disjunction between Samson and the various audiences attending his words. Because of the way in which we are given to hear the extinction of the choric part of Samson's personality, we can now start to take Samson at his word, as though he were a poet or a judge. At the same time, though, it is not hard to guess what the Chorus hears in these same words: "don't worry about a thing, everything will turn out fine, there'll be no dirty work, all very honorable and worthy—no matter what happens, no matter what happens to me." There will be a good *report*. And in two ways at least, this is true, or at least it works out as Samson here predicts. He is addressing the authors (or at least the editors) of the report in question. But we hear the reassurance quite differently, of course, and know that from the standpoint of the Law's "ends," the considerable naughtiness Samson proposes—including his own death—displaces (and so *cannot* sully or "dishonour") the Law.

It is important not to evade the full implications of the fictional scene which Milton chose for the concluding work in his final volume of poetry. Confronting a world presumably possessed of what Michael calls the "Comforter" (*PL* 12:486), Milton offers his composite Samson: a passionate, decorously limited, Old Testament version of the brief epic's Son, a partial version of the Pauline virtuoso we have noticed in certain moments of the *Areopagitica*. It helps to view him as a kind of "uncouth swain" with an elaborate, previously furnished set of familiar associations. Upon this familiar or known figure, Milton superimposes his own pattern. Until now, words have proved to be a curse for Samson; once redeemed they can acquire (or recover) the status—at once "literary" and efficacious—of the Apologist's "nimble and airy servitors," can engage with the divine program and its mysterious "ends." Milton spends his hero's passion in this work by marking the whole incident (in the vulgar view all preliminary matter) as a threshold moment from words as autobiographical or confessional thought—from language as communication—to a world of "mute deeds." And even here, Milton does not quite forget the *Reason*'s way of describing tragic mimesis. It is at the moment he leaves the stage for the known, obligatory outcome that Samson acknowledges most formally that radical split between the world of accidents and willed action, precisely the gap to be filled by heroic faith. "Happen what may" and "I cannot warrant" surround and frame the most sweeping of all possible reassurances.[14]

Chapter Thirteen

Tasting the Great Event

Let them beware an old and perfet enemy, who though he hope by sowing
discord to make them his instruments, yet cannot forbeare a minute the op'n
threatning of his destind revenge upon them, when they have servd his
purposes. Let them feare therefore, if they be wise,
rather what they have don already, than what remaines to doe, and
be warn'd in time they put no confidence in Princes whom they have provok'd,
lest they be added to the examples of those that miserably have tasted the event.
The Tenure of Kings and Magistrates

A number of valuable recent studies have considered the various ways in
which doctrinal points—sometimes including the central mysteries of
Christian faith—are illustrated in the major poems. Less attention has been
paid lately to the form and texture of Milton's poetry, and to the ways in
which Milton stresses the difficulty or mysteriousness of his subject in
Samson Agonistes and, more specifically, the difficulty of remembering or
retrieving it. In a significant development, the focus of what is made
mysterious has shifted from a traditional mystery like the Incarnation of the
Nativity Ode to something *differently* canonical.[1] Quite effectively, the
poem resists our attempts to define what "really happened" offstage following the departure of the resolved Samson; and there is a real question
whether, or how, the facts are ever revealed in their true light, "at nearer
view" (723). The reader in search of those hard facts—at least if he
assumes that these might be something different from a secret presage in
the mind or a cataclysmic "noise"—might well concur with Manoa's

complaint to the Messenger that "the accident was loud, and here before thee / With rueful cry, yet *what it was* we hear not" (1552–53; italics added).

In the final books of *Paradise Lost*, as we have seen, Michael sketches the specific structure of *Samson Agonistes* in the motives and special predicament peculiar to the teachers of the final days. The entire matter of his reception is implicit in Michael's answer to the difficult question of how the divine "Comforter" is to work in the last days. In an age of superstitions and traditions, Michael tells us, the success of the latter-day teachers will depend upon their "story" as well as their doctrine, and the further contingency of a reading and understanding "by the Spirit" (PL 12:507, 514). Consistent with Milton's belief about the "uncertain keeping" of Scripture, *Samson Agonistes* provides such a reading and understanding. This is especially clear in the close attention Milton has given to the poem's ending, which we may regard as a kind of external validation of the struggle which culminates in the victory accomplished onstage in Samson's resolution to join the festival of Dagon. The actual destruction of the Philistine temple is our final glimpse of an ideal Miltonic discourse in its entirety, and the sort of thing Samson had thought possible only in the early phases of his own career. Like the particulars of where the divine Son spent each night in the wilderness, though, Milton shrouds the great act in mystery. Even the sole Danite eyewitness cannot remember what happened. And then, as so often in the brief epic, his story is met with an almost bewildering miscomprehension. Here, it seems, the question about the operation of the divine "Comforter" is clarified—but not quite answered—in Samson's determined isolation and what may be a deliberately staged "mysteriousness" to his countrymen. And on the other hand, there is his instantaneously legendary status, destined to be preserved in Manoa's monument and embodied in the Judges narrative itself. Altogether, it seems that the true nature of this action has been buried in memorial and recognizably literary debris, as though the rubble of tradition and even idolatry were actually built into the work.

The mysteriousness I have mentioned extends to the presentation of the "great act" itself. Arnold Stein has called the destruction of the Philistine temple "the poem's big scene," and readers commonly feel invited to visualize or to reconstruct its floor plan, as though the poem enclosed a vestigial blueprint, an encoded counterculture Plan of St. Gall.[2] *Another* Miltonic edifice modeled, like Pandemonium, after St. Peter's in Rome? In any case, Milton surely found pleasure, unlike the God he described in *The*

Reason of Church Government, "in measuring out the pillars, arches, and doores of [the first epic's] material Temple" (*CPW* 1:757). And there is a similar interest, as we have seen, in the "externals" of whatever scale in *Paradise Regained*. When this curiosity is finally, belatedly indulged in *Samson Agonistes*, this is what we "see":

> The building was a spacious Theatre,
> Half round on two main Pillars vaulted high,
> With seats where all the Lords and each degree
> Of sort, might sit in order to behold,
> The other side was op'n, where the throng
> On banks and scaffolds under Sky might stand;
> I among these aloof obscurely stood.
> The Feast and noon grew high, and Sacrifice
> Had fill'd thir hearts with mirth, high cheer, and wine,
> When to their sports they turned. Immediately
> Was *Samson* as a public servant brought,
> In their state Livery clad; before him Pipes
> And Timbrels, on each side went armed guards,
> Both horse and foot before him and behind,
> Archers, and Slingers, Cataphracts and Spears.
> At sight of him the people with a shout
> Rifted the Air clamoring thir god with praise,
> Who had made thir dreadful enemy thir thrall.
> He patient but undaunted where they led him,
> Came to the place, and what was set before him
> Which without help of eye might be assay'd,
> To heave, pull, draw, or break, he still perform'd
> All with incredible, stupendious force,
> None daring to appear Antagonist.
> At length for intermission sake they led him
> Between the pillars.   [1605–30]

Altogether, it is not easy to remember, in reading this, that the work "never was intended" for the stage, or that we were not meant to *see* the great man at last, as he bides his time, and basks his hairy strength. In fact, of course, the scene is full of reminders as to its mediation, from the belaboring of the conventional "Messenger's" entrance to the suggestion that certain parts of this eyewitness report are second-hand. (Samson's request to his guide to be allowed to "lean a while" against the pillars, we are told, was heard "from such as nearer stood" [1631]). Even in the clearest memories of the Messenger there are curiosities and suggestions of vehement phrasing: the gratuitous balance of "Archers and Slingers, Cataphracts and Spears," the thought of a popular shout "rifting" the air, the activity of the verb "clamoring." Certainly, the particulars seem just right in view of Samson's recent behavior: the guise of a "public servant" in the state "Livery," and the moving detail that he appeared "patient but undaunted."

Then there is the matter of the act itself. The Messenger conveys a sense of almost methodical precision in the preliminary assays, "To heave, pull, draw, or break." Finally, we arrive at an "intermission," an inset correlative to Milton's own fictional setting:

> At length for intermission sake they led him
> Between the pillars; he his guide requested
> (For so from such as nearer stood we heard)
> As overtir'd to let him lean a while
> With both his arms on those two massy Pillars
> That to the arched roof gave main support.
> He unsuspicious led him; which when *Samson*
> Felt in his arms, with head a while inclin'd,
> And eyes fast fixt he stood, as one who pray'd,
> Or some great matter in his mind revolv'd.
> At last with head erect thus cried aloud,
>   "Hitherto, Lords, what your commands impos'd
> I have perform'd, as reason was, obeying,
> Not without wonder or delight beheld.
> Now of my own accord such other trial
> I mean to show you of my strength, yet greater;
> As with amaze shall strike all who behold."   [1629–45]

As many readers have noticed, the passage is brilliantly faithful to the work thus far. It refuses to inform us as to whether Samson was fatigued; it reminds us that prayer can be offered while standing and cannot easily be distinguished from thought itself. The posture of the head seems especially important here, as elsewhere (for example, 197, recalling *PL* 1:211). Considering Samson's recent tones, we may be in some doubt as to who leads whom here; but the "unsuspicious" recollects Milton's own lifelong interest in the problems of "implicit" faith.

Presumably, Samson's final speech "comes down" to us in an accurate rendition, even though we are familiar enough by now with the various distortions to which speech is liable even when "cried aloud" (1639). For all this, however, we may be surprised by the scrupulous precision in the eyewitness account of this speech's aftermath, if that is what it is:

> This utter'd, straining all his nerves he bow'd;
> As with the force of winds and waters pent
> When Mountains tremble, those two massy Pillars
> With horrible convulsion to and fro
> He tugg'd, he shook, till down they came, and drew
> The whole roof after them with burst of thunder
> Upon the heads of all who sat beneath,
> Lords, Ladies, Captains, Counselors, or Priests
> Thir choice nobility and flower.   [1646–54]

After all the buildup, what really *happened* was a "bow" which perfectly enacts the great difficulty of self-submission. And as a reporter, the Messenger too is struggling here. For his words are literature in the making: from the syntactic isolation of "This utter'd" (the two massy pillars for the entire passage) to the gratuitous "or Priests" and the satiric filigree that follows, the Messenger's account captures the strain of memory yielding to rudimentary epic. The heroic simile, grammatically as uprooted as its subject, points to a space somewhere between the difficulty of Samson's self-subjection (recognizable to us) and the slick-magazine version of this whole story, the physical, pictorial wonder of Samson's last bit of carnage. Given all this, who can doubt the Messenger's accuracy in his having called what he saw "dire imagination"?

It is significant, I believe, that the prefatory Argument to Milton's tragedy dwells upon the placement and style of the Messenger's narration, while it notes Dalila and Harapha only as "other persons" and fails altogether to mention the final choruses. In fact, the way in which Milton establishes the Messenger's veracity is instrumental for any correct understanding of the work's conclusion. The Messenger's story "enters" almost in the manner of the actual characters who precede him, for this too is a sound of words, a "noise" like the catastrophe. The report provides not so much a culminating, separate incident for the work as a surrogate action, a narrative equivalent for the heroic wisdom gradually discovered earlier, onstage. In this respect, it resembles the elegy's final view of the uncouth swain against the sky, giving a final hitch to the "Mantle blue." But "Lycidas," of course, ends on a note of succession and historical continuity, posited if not quite guaranteed. Borrowing from Milton's early sketches for Old Testament and other tragedies, we might say that the monody truly presents the word of the Lord, brought in "after all arguments [are] drivn home."[3] The Messenger's account, on the other hand, becomes the basis for a very different kind of ending. Much more clearly than in the brief epic, the final assessment of Samson amounts to little more than a combination of memory and fame, the constructions, respectively, of the Messenger and the Chorus of Danites. And unlike the Messenger (who *knows* he is confused) and the young Milton (who admitted, for instance, that the mystery of the Passion was a subject beyond his years), the Danites seem totally unaware that the true subject of this work—indeed, the very nature of the world they inhabit—is beyond their reach.

Like Manoa, the Danites seek to define the nature of Samson's final act and its relation to "this great event" (1756). In their explication of the Messenger's account—so frugal and precise with respect to Samson's experience—they perform an action that is appropriate to tragedy but at the same time a distortion due to human "thought." As in the final choruses of Euripides, the moral drawn seems vague enough to cover almost any conceivable phenomena; it represents a lowest common denominator of tragic wisdom, not at all the inspiring recognition, also Euripidean, that had initially attracted Milton to literature in all its primitive variety in the first place: the various accesses to the divine, the abundance of beauty's "shapes and forms" in this world.[4] In fact, the final choruses seem to represent a systematic and national effort to evade the paradoxical truth of evil's temporary mixture with good. They may be viewed as the ambivalent appreciation of Dalila's double-faced "fame."

The misunderstandings of the semichoruses can be tested against our memories of the work as a whole, and the recent experience of Manoa and the Messenger. Their accounts seem conspicuously prone to a dualism (of the kind long resisted by Milton and rejected by this work) between Philistine and Danite, body and spirit. In his farewell speech to the "brethren," we may recall that Samson had satirically foretold the ruin of the Philistines by describing a caricature of the "lordly" enemy: "Lords are lordliest in thir wine; / And the well-feasted Priest then soonest fir'd / With zeal, if aught Religion seem concern'd" (1418–20). This is the vein of the Bard's presentation of Belial, always on hand "when the Priest / Turns Atheist" (*PL* 1:494–95). But Manoa has recently described a variety of motives among the Philistines he has visited in his efforts to procure ransom for his son; his conclusions seem both more understandable and more complicated:

Some much averse I found and wondrous harsh,
Contemptuous, proud, set on revenge and spite;
That part most reverenc'd *Dagon* and his Priests,
Others more moderate seeming, but thir aim
Private reward, for which both God and State
They easily would set to sale: a third
More generous far and civil, who confess'd
They had enough reveng'd, having reduc't
Thir foe to misery beneath thir fears,
The rest was magnanimity to remit,
If some convenient ransom were propos'd.   [1461–71]

When we consider what the Danites say in the first semichorus, it is hard to believe that they ever heard this speech. Instead, they echo and substantially extend Samson's uninformed projection about the inevitable fate of zealous lords and priests. They are guilty of almost everything they say about the gloating Philistines, and so (for that matter) is Samson. The woodenness of their signposting almost seems designed to call attention to connections and parallels which we cannot have missed and which include what their champion *shares* with those Philistines, blinded as they are with unconscious suicidal impulses. The perversely welcome destroyer of the Philistines was the deliverer repeatedly rejected by the Danites. The choral rhetoric itself seems designed to extricate a conqueror from the victims with whom he is inescapably "immixed." Indeed Samson's "recapitulation" of *both* sides seems almost inevitable in the final words of this semichorus, which paint a picture of unjustified clarity, ascribing a suicide exclusively and evasively not to Samson but to mortal man's being "insensate left, or to sense reprobate, / And with blindness internal struck" (1685–86)—just what Samson is not. The Philistines can be seen here as a collective, and perhaps less conscious, version of the "suicidal" Samson; the attempt to make pat and pious distinctions serves only to telescope more clearly the victors and the vanquished. No less than Samson, the Philistines who "Unwittingly importun'd / Thir own destruction to come speedy upon them" (1680–81) are entangled in the fold of dire necessity. Earlier, we may recall, the Danites had hailed Samson's resolve to participate in the Dagonalia without quite hearing all that he was saying about scandal and the Law. In doing so, they join the Philistine officer in praising a compliance we know is dissembled, an "outward act." Indeed, they had continued this Philistine representative's arguments in their attempts to free their former champion. At the conclusion too, Milton seems to encourage the view of nations converging, or banding together in a collective "deafness," a reprobation "to sense"—something the men of Dan embody together with at least *some* of the Philistines, and something from which the work's own echoes of itself seem specifically designed to release us.

The second semichorus too reveals a community unaware of its authorial potential, much less its own involvement in dispensing "fame." (This is in fact the target of their initial denunciation.) The Danites now proceed to spiritualize events they so recently admitted were beyond their grasp, and they do so by abstracting Samson the bodily man from his "virtue" in a way that removes themselves from responsibility—and the instrumentality of "dispensation" to which Samson alone in this work seems open. In this passage, the hero's virtual extinction becomes an elementary, almost comic mistake—the Philistine's mistake—and Samson's exemplary victory, which they seem to consider a historically final thing, is an act of "fiery virtue." But based as it is on simple oppositions between body and soul, appearance and reality, their picture of this self-enclosed heroism offers a vulgarized, indeed, almost Satanic revision of the two most powerful invocations in *Paradise Lost*:

> But he, though blind of sight,
> Despis'd and thought extinguish't quite,
> With inward eyes illuminated
> His fiery virtue rous'd
> From under ashes into sudden flame,
> And as an ev'ning *Dragon* came,
> Assailant on the perched roosts,
> And nests in order rang'd
> Of tame villatic Fowl; but as an Eagle
> His cloudless, thunder bolted on thir heads.
> So virtue giv'n for lost,
> Deprest, and overthrown, as seem'd. [1687–98]

Given for lost by whom? "Deprest, and overthrown, as seem'd" to whom? This, surely, is the kind of false exposition Milton indulged so effectively in the early books of *Paradise Lost*, where our knowledge of the epic "cause" is prematurely, prejudicially answered by the scapegoating of "Th'infernal Serpent, hee it was," and where we can so easily form the impression that the final purpose of the Fall itself was the emptying of divine "wrath and vengeance" upon Satan (1:34, 220). The choral (or semichoral) Samson does not match up well with the jocular assurance we have so recently heard in the Messenger's quotation, and even less well with the blind poet of the invocation to the third book, in need of eyes inwardly "planted" (3:53). He is much more the vengeful figure of *Judges* or the plaintiff of the same invocation, whose virtuous "orbs" are "quencht." Before we nod our assent to these rhythms, we need to ask whether Samson's revival could have occurred without those "outward" conditions. We are told that Samson was illuminated "with inward eyes," that he roused this fiery virtue "from under ashes into sudden flame." But it is reasonable to object that Samson's virtue, as a matter of "intimate impulse," *is* a "mixed" and partly corporeal thing, that the semichorus's initial concessive clause "though blind of sight" involves the very taproot of Samson's special *kind* of power. Whereas the first semichorus had voiced Milton's own critique, that the inner blindness of most men is a matter of being reprobate "to sense" (1685), the second never mentions our own best guide in this work, the complex functioning of Samson's "ear."

Like its predecessor, the second semichorus makes some difficult and suggestive distinctions in defining what Samson did, how he "came." We are told that he did so "as an ev'ning Dragon . . . / Assailant on the perched roosts, / And nests in order rang'd / Of tame villatic Fowl." There are significant parallels here with history's "first grand Thief," arrived in Eden and intending "to unhoard the cash / Of some rich Burgher" (*PL* 4:188–89); the dragon's target is orderly and suburban, a satiric version of "L'Allegro"'s poultry (49–52). But this was "cloudless thunder," and they compare it to an eagle (the national bird of the *Areopagitica*) before turning to the emphatically feminine phoenix, that self-begotten bird "embost" in the Arabian woods. Milton cannot easily eliminate conventional "typological" associations from this final extended flight in a poem which is (like its companion in the 1671 volume) remarkably free of lyric indulgences. But he is free to present them in a distorted, enthusiastic manner appropriate to the Danites. Like the idea of "lordship" entertained in Milton's rendition of the Eighth Psalm, what makes the phoenix unique here is partly the isolation that comes with heroic virtue:

> Like that self-begotten bird
> In the *Arabian* woods embost,
> That no second knows nor third,
> And lay erewhile a Holocaust,
> From out her ashy womb now teem'd,
> Revives, reflourishes, then vigorous most
> When most unactive deem'd,

> And though her body die, her fame survives,
> A secular bird, ages of lives.   [1687–1707; see *PL* 9:40–47]

There are certainly recollections here of the great apostrophe to the divine Spirit of *Paradise Lost* 1, present "from the first," brooding on the vast abyss and also making it "pregnant" (1:19–22). But the Danites' Samson is conspicuously unaffiliated. Milton may wish to insinuate the metaphysical fate of an evil that is "self-fed and self-consumed," but the phoenix, their final figure for depression or "virtue giv'n for lost" is also uncomfortably reminiscent of the Satanic predicament (at least as he describes it to Abdiel): "Self-begot, self-rais'd / By our own quick'ning power" (*Masque* 597; *PL* 5:860–61). The Danites' words isolate heroic virtue, circumscribe it almost physically. This phoenix does not know it will "reflourish"; the bird itself has disappeared from the final summary lines. If she has not perished outright (like the mortalist's soul), she seems destined to endure only as fame. In the Danites' view, heroic virtue is still self-enclosed, imprisoned; if it lives at all, it survives only temporarily and only here, "A secular bird ages of lives"—not much of an improvement over the plant that grows on mortal soil (*Lyc* 78). Far from being the reader/warriors sprung from "those Dragon's teeth" mentioned in the *Areopagitica*, they are part of a very different legend, the kind preserved only "So long as men can breathe, or eyes can see" (*CPW* 2:492).[5] As yet, they have not done much to disprove Dalila's allegation that

> Fame if not double-fac'd is double-mouth'd,
> And with contrary blast proclaims most deeds,
> On both his wings, one black, the other white,
> Bears greatest names in his wild aery flight.   [971–74]

Reading the poem's concluding stanza, we find ourselves face to face once again with the Miltonic Euripides, and (very likely) in the sway of some very impressive rhythms. Like Milton's theology and so much of his poetry, the stanza emphasizes the problem of knowing and worshiping God, whether in the specific pre-Christian context of the Jewish Captivity or that latter-day equivalent immediately prior to the end of time. (Near the end of *Paradise Lost*, Adam had emphasized a similar sense of reversion in adding that beyond time is "all abyss, / Eternity, whose end no eye can reach" [*PL* 12:555–56].) In such circumstances it seems natural and comforting to dwell on the disparity between human doubt and the "unsearchable dispose / Of highest wisdom." In this setting—or in human affairs at any time when viewed tragically, Milton implies—we may well experience the peculiar mixture of historical progression and cyclic recurrence that is revealed in the verbs of these lines. Uncharacteristically for the Danites, the passage seems to project something fuller than a tribal or national response to all we have been through together. More complexly than Manoa's response to the semichoruses, for example, their words accommodate truth in complementary rather than antithetic fashion. With recollections of the tragic theory discussed in the preface, this quintessential choric act presents the ingredients of heroic experience and tragic affect. And the "just measure" to which the tragic passions of "pity and fear, or terror" have now been reduced is displayed as the kind of normative frame that can be related to what Joseph Summers has called "hieroglyphic form."[6] If we leave aside the particulars of Manoa's proposed shrine, here is the work's own monument to the "great event":

> All is best, though we oft doubt,
> What th'unsearchable dispose
> Of highest wisdom brings about,
> And ever best found in the close.
> Oft he seems to hide his face,
> But unexpectedly returns
> And to his faithful Champion hath in place
> Bore witness gloriously; whence Gaza mourns
> And all that band them to resist
> His uncontrollable intent;
> His servants he with new acquist
> Of true experience from this great event
> With peace and consolation hath dismist,
> And calm of mind, all passion spent.   [1745-58]

The questions raised here can be clarified only if we recognize at once the fundamental differences between these thoughts and what Milton supposed he had found in the poet's proverbial close during the later 1630s. As soon as we think of these as "Danite" thoughts once again, we can more easily notice the facile way, for example, in which they move from what the very inscrutable highest wisdom "brings about" to how it is "found" in human affairs. Found by whom, we must ask, and by what means? The "true experience" they mention seems to be truly a private matter; this sentence removes the true "servants" from all present company by delaying the predicate "hath dismist." Their "in place"—this is how God has borne witness "gloriously" to their truth about his mysterious returns—sounds too much like "in its *own* place." As we listen to the Danites gloss over these problems and blithely connect heroic with "our" experience of God's unexpected returns, there is the nagging thought that the Danites have somehow identified "calm of mind" with their hero's *death*—that the tragic catharsis they seem to be discussing (virtually throughout the play) is impossible, at least for all onstage observers/survivors. The "close" which ought to amalgamate the experience of Samson and the audience entails the loss of Samson himself; "Gaza mourns," to be sure, but their "*Whence* Gaza mourns" points to costs they seem to have forgotten. In general, the Danites segregate "true experience" from the knowledge of "what is best" in a most disturbing fashion. For them, "in the close" does not seem to mean anything much different from "at the end," or "in the event." They seem quite unaware of the musical sense of "close" even though they are *speaking* one: the sense of "cadence" to which Samson has alerted us, perhaps, in his reference (1643) to "my own accord." Like the epic poet in the later invocations of *Paradise Lost*, their classically sponsored generic theory seems rooted in the experience of depression, or "evil days" (*PL* 7:26). By contrast, Manoa's conclusion shows an admirable grasp of the divine "permissiveness" in all its dark possibilities; God was "not parted from [Samson], as was feared [by Manoa himself, as well as the Chorus], / But favouring and assisting *to* the end." Given the ostensibly ancient scene of *Samson Agonistes* (relative to its predecessor in the 1671 volume), who are they to inform us that divine truths are best discovered "in the close"? As "closes" go, this is a minor historical juncture, and in any case the phrase is too close for comfort to an endorsement of mere hindsight. In short, the Chorus has struck a false note, of the kind some readers notice in the endings of Dickens's "dark" novels. They have patently forgotten the hidden form or purpose presumably at work in the history they have witnessed. Like Luther, they "often wonder about the example of Samson" (*Table Talk, LW* 54:79); but they differ in being made responsible, one might almost say, for the shape (or lack of it) we notice in the chronicles of Judges. We may think of them as willing enough participants in that final, vast panorama of the first epic's concluding books, the desert world eventually to be crossed, inhabited in the meantime by most of us, including those who would "polish Life" (*PL* 11:610). Can we say with much confidence that this kindly, spectatorly chitchat is unrelated to the nation's cowardice in refusing to "receive" Samson—that the Danites are not among the mourners who have "band[ed] them to resist / His uncontrollable intent" (1753–54)?

In the seventh sonnet, a phrase very similar to the Chorus's (All is . . .

as ever) encloses a double contingency, "if I have grace to use it so"; and the enclosure does as much as anything else in the sonnet to prove Milton's own suspicion of himself to his critical correspondent. At the conclusion of *Samson Agonistes*, the contingency is so completely removed that the knowledge of "what is best" is altogether divorced from the practice (or art) of "doubt." In this context, what "we" might or might not doubt would be the connection between the divine wisdom and what it "brings about" —what Milton had long called "event"—what is called, mistakenly, "fortune from without," as he had put it in 1642. Their conclusion that the disposition of highest wisdom is "unsearchable" may be a step ahead of Dalila's complaint about a "perverse event" (737). But it is hardly in keeping with the earlier Miltonic resolve to search throughout the various shapes and forms of things divine, as though in deference to the Pauline admonition to "Prove all things." To defer to the chorus at this (admittedly impressive) moment, we must forget Donne's advice to "doubt wisely." Instead, let them speak again: "All is best *if* we oft doubt."[7]

In a sense, they do speak again (or they speak better than they know) with an "uncontrollable intent" well within Milton's ken and also our own. For here and elsewhere in the work, in commenting the way Euripidean countrymen do so often, the Danites serve to prove Samson's point at the very moment the "rousing motions" are clearly discernible (and perhaps not very mystifying) to us: the point, namely, that "their servile minds / Me thir Deliverer sent would not receive" (1213–14). Even within this work, of course, Milton makes sharper memories available. Virtually alone among the Danites, Manoa seems open to new possibilities. It is true that the shrine he proposes to build (as though to match Dalila's) is not much more encouraging than the separate gold statues to be erected in Verona's marketplace at the conclusion to *Romeo and Juliet*. But Manoa suspects that Samson's legacy is not yet extant even at his death, but contingent even now upon his public's opportunism. Whatever we or the Danites may make of all this, *Israel* will have honor and freedom only if they can find "courage to lay hold on this occasion" (1716). Only we know, of course, that Manoa's "yet"—like Samson's final exchange with the Chorus—points beyond the immediate future in Gaza to a different dispensation, and perhaps even beyond the "world" altogether. The plight of Gaza seems to image the essential nature of the pre-Christian world, which in *Samson Agonistes* we experience in its closing phase; it may glance beyond that to the sense of a more definitive ending to *this* world. In his affecting assumption that the pieces will eventually fit—or when he thinks, later, that

Samson's legacy will depend upon the engagement of the Danites (or Israel)—we are exploring Milton's not-quite-resolved distinctions between "political" (even military) action and the more pacific or quietist claims of the "paradise within." We are dealing, that is, with the essential and "tragic" confusion at the heart of the poem's world.

Our own best guide to this confusion is perhaps the Messenger. It is important, I think, that we first glimpse him—the nearest thing in *Samson Agonistes* to a narrator—in the breathless moments prior to "exposition" or straightforward reportage. His scrupulous disclaimers about his luck in finding us convey Milton's thematically central suggestion that *what he saw* somehow partook of fantasy, "instinct of nature," and there is the further acknowledgment that he cannot shake it—he is still pursued by a memory he calls a "dire imagination" (1544). And the Messenger is an excellent scribe as well. His quotation provides the fullest embodiment of the notorious "rousing motions" ever made available in this work; it carries us a step beyond Samson's aptly hypothetical reference to a "presage in the mind," something we can even better verify. By offering us a fairly precise echo of Michael's references to those later teachers' "inward consolations . . . oft supported so as shall amaze / Thir proudest persecutors" (12:495–97), the Messenger puts us back in touch with the integral constituents (in Milton's mind) of significant "action," even as he acknowledges the considerable pressures within his own mind to abstract, to rationalize, to turn away.

Here Milton's analysis of the surviving community's response is most illuminating. Part of Manoa's function, indeed, is to put such pressures into bolder relief, to dramatize the ordinary, "unheroic" inclination to domesticate Samson and his final "deed." Unlike the other survivors, Manoa seems genuinely impressed with the excessive, chaotic nature of the Messenger's narrative materials: "More than enough we know; but while things yet / Are in confusion, give us . . . / Relation more particular and distinct" (1592–95). He knows "more than enough" precisely because "things yet / Are in confusion," and they remain so (for onstage observers, at any rate) up to the final ambivalence of his own "*Samson* hath quit himself / Like *Samson*" and the choric "All is best, though we oft doubt" (1709–10; 1745). Still, like the Messenger, Manoa supposes it will all eventually clear up; his next request reveals assumptions which are significantly at odds with Milton's long-standing suspicion of abstracts and other kinds of argumentative redaction. In asking for the "sum" and only *then* a detailed account, Manoa takes for granted a correspondence between an "argument" and what in *Paradise Lost* is called "process of speech"; and his comments can be taken as an effort to read these assumptions into an account that is confused—and by Milton meant to be confused—almost to the core. In its lack of an orthodox moral, the "sum" he receives is unsatisfying, to say the least. To the familiar and complex Miltonic question about the "cause" for such an embarrassing act of self-violence among his foes, Manoa receives the answer "Inevitable cause, / At once both to destroy and be destroy'd" (1586–87). In this, Manoa can find only an ignominious death, according to the patly expressed principle "death to life is crown or shame" (1578); and his concluding apostrophe is "lastly over-strong against thyself!" (1590). However this vestigial lament may work for readers familiar with the Reformers' recommendations of "self-suspicion," it seems clear that the very nature of the Messenger's materials precludes easy determinations as to "cause" or the common critical distinctions between form and matter, "sum" and "circumstances." It is a mistake to suppose that a "relation more particular and distinct" will also be more comfortable.

In "Lycidas," the corrective intrusion of Phoebus punctuates the swain's bitter attack on the illusory attractions of earthly fame, the "fair guerdon" so often snatched away when we "think to burst out into sudden blaze" (74). In its nationalistic form, this is Dalila's ambition, to be "nam'd among the famousest / Of Women" (982–83); like the swain, Samson will instead refer mysteriously to an "other" land, or at least to "the ends / For which our country is a name so dear" (894–95).

Among the work's few fit hearers, Samson is the least inclined to exposition, at least toward the end of the work. This is precisely the tendency he has given up once the Danites declare their unwillingness to extend their understanding of his predicament—their "reach." Situated as he is, Samson is the kind of Miltonic character we can take "at his word," at least on an occasion like this. Consider again, for example, the passage (surprising to the Danites, who would just as soon go on complaining about women's innate treachery), in which he releases his "traitress":

> So let her go, God sent her to debase me,
> And aggravate my folly who committed
> To such a viper his most sacred trust
> Of secrecy, my safety, and my life.   [999–1002]

We resist translating or paraphrasing "my folly who" (or we *should*) because of the way it makes a new kind of history, accepts responsibility without making folly a dead issue. Samson further proves he is not guilty of Dalila's charge of deafness by applying her own word "aggravate" in boldly claiming providential supervision of this, a previously unrecorded, incident in the work. He does so in order to reject the view that anything could be objectively "weigh'd, by itself, with aggravations not surcharg'd." Samson's "my folly who" somehow brings his past to life, reopens the story just as Dalila seems most confident that the definitive biography may now be safely written: his folly lives, it may be in some sense "fruitful of golden deeds." We are well on the way in this seemingly innocuous moment to the extraordinary claim that the Philistine Officer too is a "messenger" (1384).

Milton's Nazarite is a prime offender against the kind of critic or editor represented here by the Chorus. To any such Miltonic author, thus set off (by Dalila or an equivalent), we must listen most intently since it is such a figure's destiny literally to define the world in which we are moving, to *become* the expositor or legislator of meaning, however unacknowledged within the confines of his own fictional "country." Let us turn to what Samson is saying as he describes the results of Dalila's—and perhaps, as I have suggested, of his own—kind of art:

> That wisest and best men full oft beguil'd
> With goodness principl'd not to reject
> The penitent, but ever to forgive,
> Are drawn to wear out miserable days,
> Entangl'd with a pois'nous bosom snake,
> If not by quick destruction soon cut off
> As I by thee, to Ages an example.   [759–64]

Our task in reading such passages is partly to resist what a zealous reader once called "the heresy of paraphrase," a mistake decidedly akin to Milton's own notion of religion-by-deputy.[8] Instead, we may follow Samson's effort to encounter what such lines say literally, no matter how strange: to accept the adventurous thought (in "Lycidas") that "Now the Sun had stretcht out all the hills" (190), or, in Sonnet 18, the daring ellipsis of "Their moans / The Vales redoubl'd to the Hills, And they / To Heav'n" (8–10). As for Samson's "wisest and best men" in the attack on Dalila above: it is not merely that they are so *often* fooled. They are "drawn to wear out miserable days." Condemned to *survive* those days? That diurnal fabric is worn thin or "fretted"? What is *happening* to the wisest and best men in this passage is not at all clear: they are racked, or trapped in a web, "entangled," or cut to pieces, drawn-and-quartered? Samson seems perilously close to putting his selfhood back into his hair again in that "As I by thee." And what about those wisest and best men in the first place? Are they not "drawn" even before their downfall, burdened with unstable modifiers pointing to attributes we always thought were virtues? They are "beguil'd with goodness." As though it were hyphenated throughout, the modification clings to those wisest and best men like freshly spun spiderweb: what entangles and traps them, we gather in some discomfort, is their very inclination to forgive the penitent.

In these meditations on a new and mysterious "dispose," as in *Paradise Lost*'s introduction of a kind of "fortitude" (and the seemingly attendant "heroic martyrdom") previously unheard of, we are involved in an idea clearly close to the core of the work's (and poet's) vision, so integral that goodness can never mean quite the same again once we close the book. This happens largely thanks to our predecessors onstage, so to speak, the kind of *inadvertent* listening performed much earlier, say, by Manoa when he introduces the same paradox, in slightly more explicated form:

> O ever failing trust
> In mortal strength! and oh, what not in man
> Deceivable and vain! Nay, what thing good
> Pray'd for, but often proves our woe, our bane?   [348–51]

And it is a play-long meditation. In their bare and (we must insist) purely "factual" announcement of the play's final arrival, the Chorus voices the same paradox in more compressed fashion but with the help of an equally unintended pun: "Evil news rides post, while good news baits" (1537), they sing, wishing (it seems) for the worst: "And to our wish I see one hither speeding" (1538). And the moment is significantly punctuated; Milton exercises his frequent practice of grafting such a central idea to a crucial "event," as though to suggest that words alone can mediate between fortune's external realm and "the wily suttleties and refluxes of mans thoughts from within" (*CPW* 1:817). Manoa unconsciously testifies to this when he remarks to the Messenger that "the accident was loud, and here before thee" (1552). It is to criticize debased notions of "action" (ours and perhaps also the poet's own) that Milton permits Abdiel to wish for a military victory, supposing for the moment that this could be a correlative to "the braver fortitude." One of the errors of a relatively enlightened Adam is curiousity about a "duel" between Satan and the Son (*PL* 12:375–85); it corresponds to the common reader's appetite for epic battles, scolded in the invocation to Book 9. What replaces such tilting furniture in *Samson Agonistes* is the confused and explicitly *imagined* recollection of the analogous event; denied the final victory itself, we are presented instead with a memory following hard upon "dire imagination," and then with increasingly comfortable celebrations of that "unsearchable dispose" and "uncontrollable intent"—celebrations that are anything *but* "searching."

It is tempting but only partly accurate to identify developments like these as features of "the later Milton." Certainly, it is true that in Milton's mature work, the management of external circumstance becomes a kind of radical form or type-scene *within the work*, the very nature of his fictional worlds nowhere more clearly revealed than in their vestiges of narrative —those moments when he pushes his actors onstage willy-nilly. Many memorable passages are focused on the dovetailing (and also the failure) of this scene, from the flaming swords which "confirm" Satan's words in masquelike fashion to the astonishing beauty of a postlapsarian dawn "All unconcerned with our unrest," or the general way in which (we are told) "Fate / Subscrib'd not" to the wishes and speech of Adam and Eve (*PL* 1:663–64; 11:174, 181–82). We can regard such details as mature orchestrations of the kind of impulse which, when frustrated, had been called dalliance with "false surmise." In fact, though, it was in the period of the prolusions that Milton had speculated playfully about the ideal collusion of "wisdom" with mere incident, with what in tragedy is supposed merely to *happen*. It is true that the *Reason*'s theorizing hardly prepares us for the subtlety with which Milton manages the coincidence of insight and "event" in the tragedy. "I know your friendly minds and—O what noise!" (1508) cries Manoa, interrupted by the dismal accident. But as we have seen, even the *Apology* testifies to an early Miltonic capacity for nostalgia, premised upon a pervasive tension in his formative years between the term "poet" and "priest," the shifting relations between that single speaker and his milieu, including the choral community, whether angelic or all too human. More than any other, this text celebrates the great event Milton thought he himself had anticipated "occasionally" even as he wrote and revised the seemingly rough-hewn elegy: "the Fall of our corrupted Clergy then in their height." If the fall of the Bishops diminished in significance over the years, given the perspective provided in 1649, it was also an event much less susceptible than the regicide to radically disturbing afterthoughts for a disappointed poet-reformer; in various permutations it is the "speech-act" of 1642 and *its* aftermath that seem to turn up in the later poetry, together with the situations and cast of characters. Joseph Brodsky has recently suggested that writers in exile share a retrospective "machinery" which functions to delay "the arrival of the present." "Whether or not he is of elegiac disposition by nature," Brodsky goes on, such an author "will stick in his writing to the familiar material of his past, producing, as it were, sequels to his previous works. Approached on this subject, an exiled writer will most likely evoke Ovid's Rome, Dante's Florence, and—after a small pause—Joyce's Dublin."[9]

Only three months and the mask of anonymity separate the *Apology* from the earlier *Reason*. Those who would preserve a "stronger" Milton have reason to be troubled by the belletristic way in which the *Reason* phrases its theory—a manner aggravated further by the *Second Defence* of 1654. But I would suggest that a closer look at the *Apology* shows how subtly a belletrist idiom can mask an authentically Miltonic sense of heroic virtue's *isolation*. And this is true even within "Lycidas," the poem for which the final two antiprelatical pamphlets provides a poetics after-the-fact. As it turns out, we have managed to overhear this poem, and we alone; even as it finally establishes an objective landscape, the ottava rima conclusion serves to cancel the poem's internal audiences in the process of redirecting the swain's "eager thoughts" retroactively to "th'Oaks and rills." The external landscape—it is not altogether different from the bleak Alpine setting which introduces "Avenge, O Lord, thy slaughter'd Saints"—suddenly replaces the ritual visit of various rustic and divine mourners (obligatory in pastoral elegy) which had materialized with the response of Phoebus. Milton constructed this poem, of course, in such a way that the swain's eager attempts upon those "tender stops" seemed to generate a dramatic narrative, including a kind of built-in "event" in the form of a sunset and a concurrent impulse of faith ("Tomorrow to fresh Woods and Pastures new"). These elements are very different from the connections which eventually linked this poem with what we call political or ecclesiastical history, and made it "occasional" in another very specific and "special" sense. Well before he enters his "millennialist" phase, Milton demonstrates a precocious sense of faith's distinctness from hope—and the abuse of special talents.

It is useful to distinguish such perceptions from the kind of wholesale ideological disappointment which William Empson describes in *Milton's God* and which is such a common feature of attempts to explain Milton's presumed betrayal of early intellectual or political ideals. And a similar embarrassment is discernible among the poet's most zealous defenders. Too often, the effect of the remedy is a drastic undervaluing of literary indeterminacy in the name of historical scholarship. But as Georgia Christopher has shown so brilliantly, there is far more leeway within the doctrines available to the reforming poets, and (to say the least) more than the simplest doctrinal norms are at work in this writing. Nor was Empson entirely wrong in the way he read the pathos that is such an essential ingredient in the continuing power of Milton's verse and prose. The fact is that Milton's theory and practice alike make it difficult to separate the author from "the person he introduces," something we can do partly by studying more carefully the way he *situates* his speakers. As we noticed in discussing the *Areopagitica*, the recovery of a pristine language (in the guise, say, of Pauline "mastery") might seem to happen within a text, as when (in the *Areopagitica*) the "ingenious" Truth herself snatches the argument, making obsolete, at least momentarily, any speaker bound to the "pace of method and discourse" like the Isocratic orator or even Raphael, a spirit sociable enough to choose reason discursive this time. As readers, we are being consolidated (or, in Milton's word "incorporated") at a moment like "[the argument itself] hath prevented me by being clear already while thus much hath in explaining" (*CPW* 2:521). Someone who talks like this is the creature of a man writing "to the world," and to an ingenious world at that. But again, it is easy to misconstrue this kind of "Baroque" engagement; at a moment like this, an ingenious reader may have "prevented" the speaker, but probably not the author. On the other hand, Milton also stages a rather different author, a man who writes, as we say "for the record"—in Milton's phrase, "to aftertimes." This is the predicament of the swain, specifically denied his old community at the very moment of "insight"; so this second situation is not a monopoly of the later Milton. Even within the Isocratic oration (and elsewhere more often than not), the *staged* recovery of such a pristine language (or "insight") requires not the figure of truth, or even a "member incorporate" of that Chorus envisioned in the conclusion to *Of Reformation*, but a more solitary figure of the kind described with such delicacy in the *Reason* as the "interpreter and relater of the best and sagest things."

All this is to insist, once again, that the "intimate impulse" and "rousing motions" are given a local residence within the work for readers of *Samson Agonistes*, in the palpable form of Samson's behavior when brought to the verge of Miltonic "insight." The knowing reference to "rousing motions" involves not something new or just now beginning (as Samson says) but an accommodation to the Danites' kind of thinking, perhaps even their expectations. Far from removing the critical link from our view, Milton provides it in the form of a mysterious, well-worn old label—like "insight." For Milton in 1644, as we have seen, this word designed the end point to a well-charted educational process, a "method." By no means did it refer to anything so isolated as a special talent or kind of sensibility. Samson's "rousing motions" is an ironically assumed pretense of special powers in the form of a mind suddenly disposed "to something extraordinary." However ignorant he may be of the divine intent or his own (for Milton, a faithful hero *must* be "ignorant" in this sense almost by definition), Samson now gives up the attempt to extend the "call," pretending instead that there is a kind of vocational wall separating him from the reach of the onstage community. We may well have the sense of a certain compliance on Samson's part, an ironic obliquity or "muteness." But what sounds for all the world like an inexplicable return to his "riddling days" is in fact a posture perfectly in keeping with his public's lethargy. It is in several different senses that Milton makes Samson an "author" during this scene. By viewing his behavior up to this point as the kind of recapitulation which was to serve Milton's students in the manner of the last embattelling, we can understand something of that catalytic "middle" which Dr. Johnson thought was missing from Milton's tragedy. Samson's reference to the "rousing motions" pretends to join the Chorus in their (and once Milton's own) more magical view of divine championship. Thus does Milton displace the "great event" itself, disguising the critical moment in history in a way that makes it all too liable to misconstruction. We thought we knew what must happen next; now, we may well be unsure.

It is perhaps the extent of dramatized misconstruction that sets apart Milton's 1671 volume from all but the most recent predecessors and makes it "later" Milton. Early and persistently, it seems, Milton's doctrinally sanctioned "self-suspicion" encouraged a profound and energetic exploration of faith's territory, and especially the sometimes undetermined borderland separating it from millennial and other, worldlier forms of hope. For various and good reasons, the *Masque at Ludlow* offers a conspicuous example, not only of displaced apocalypse but also of abortive "reformation." There is the early display, by the aspiring poet in all his evangelical fervor, of a swain in near despair (to judge, at least from the concluding stanza's "at last") and isolated both socially and within an indifferent and perhaps even hostile landscape. In one sense anyway, the "late" Milton's seeming bitterness, which the poet himself recognized very early as a threat to generic (and especially epic) decorum, is in fact a sign of a profound and enduring generosity. For our purposes, it is important to recognize that even the "later" (and presumably most reactionary) Milton seldom treats those to whom he writes as he does the Chorus of Danites or other of the less-than-fit audiences he so frequently builds into his fictions. Milton was fond of Psyche's predicament, the difficult task of sorting out apparently identical seeds; and he seems to have found an easy analogy in vocal differentiation, to judge from the way he plunges the lady and her brothers into a double darkness, making their ear their best guide. Offered special access to Samson's crucial decision taking shape in those exchanges with the visitors and onstage "friends," have we not been given an easier task? No one really misses the semblance of communication between Samson and the "world's" various representatives in his final scenes with us and with the Philistines; as we say so easily, they are all "speaking the same language." But few of us would finally believe that Samson *meant what he said* in his reference to that special instinctual talent. Samson's final mysteriousness to his onstage audience is Milton's incorrigible way of attempting to reach a fitter (that is, less spectatorly) group offstage. Anyone who has heard the crucial decision taking shape in Samson's exchanges with the visitors and "friends," has, in effect, participated in Miltonic knowledge "in the making"—in part by witnessing the various attempts to institutionalize, ritualize, enshrine, or otherwise unmake it.

Notes

CHAPTER ONE: PROLOGUE

1 Sonnet 11; except where noted otherwise, Milton's poetry is quoted from the text of *John Milton: Complete Poems and Major Prose*, ed. Merritt Y. Hughes (Indianapolis: Odyssey/Bobbs Merrill, 1973).

2 Christopher Grose, *Milton's Epic Process: Paradise Lost and Its Miltonic Background* (New Haven: Yale University Press, 1973), pp. 258–63.

3 William R. Parker, *Milton: A Biography* (Oxford. Clarendon Press, 1968), 2:1142; hereafter cited as Parker.

4 "The Printer to the Reader," *Ignatius His Conclave*.

5 J. B. Leishman, *Milton's Minor Poems* (Pittsburgh: University of Pittsburgh Press, 1969); Rosemond Tuve, *Images and Themes in Five Poems by John Milton* (Cambridge: Harvard University Press, 1957).

6 "Universal insight into things" marks a halfway point between the consensus inherent in all things (*conspiratio omnium rerum*") of the Seventh Prolusion and the much discussed "rousing motions" evidently involved in Samson's recovery.

CHAPTER TWO: PROSE AND THE "LITERARY" MILTON

1 Merritt Y. Hughes, ed., *John Milton: Complete Poems and Major Prose* (Indianapolis: Bobbs-Merrill, 1957), p. 828. For the sake of convenience, translations from the *Second Defence* are quoted from *John Milton: Selected Prose*, ed. C. A. Patrides (Columbia: University of Missouri Press, 1985), except where noted; for comparative purposes, references to the Yale *Complete Prose Works* follow.

2 "J. M. was, and is, a man of great learning and sharpness of wit as any man. It was his misfortune, living in a tumultuous time, to be toss'd on the wrong side, and he writ *flagrante bello* certain dangerous treatises. . . . At his Majestie's happy return, J. M. did partake . . . of his regal clemency, and has ever since expiated himself in a retired silence." *The Complete Works of Andrew Marvell*, ed. Alexander B. Grosart, 3 (rpt. New York: AMS Press, 1966), pp. 499–500.

3 Mary Ann Radzinowicz, *Toward Samson Agonistes: The Growth of Milton's Mind* (Princeton, 1978), p. xvi.

4 Arthur E. Barker, *Milton and the Puritan Dilemma* (Toronto: University of Toronto

Press, 1942), p. 9. See also A. S. P. Woodhouse, *The Heavenly Muse* (Toronto: University of Toronto Press, 1972), p. 103; David Masson, *The Life of John Milton: Narrated in Connexion with the Political, Ecclesiastical, and Literary History of His Time* (Cambridge and London: Macmillan, 1859–94); and Michael Fixler, *Milton and the Kingdoms of God* (London: Faber, 1964), p. 101. Like others, Woodhouse thinks of the Seventh Prolusion as crucial; it explains the humanism apparent in the second group of pamphlets by providing a firm conviction: "For it is Milton's conviction that nothing can be described as for man's good unless it conduces to his benefit at once as an eternal and a temporal being" (p. 110).

5 See also Fixler, p. 101.

6 John Spencer Hill, *John Milton: Poet, Priest, and Prophet* (London: MacMillan, 1979), p. 78.

7 For a shrewd discussion of how the display of Reformed learning relates to millennial thought, see Janet E. Halley, "Sir Thomas Browne's *The Garden of Cyrus* and the Real Character," *ELR* 15 (1985), 100–21, esp. 108–11.

8 Cf. "The deeds themselves, though mute, spoke loud the doer" (*SA* 248).

9 See Hill, p. 78.

10 In *The Ready and Easy Way*, there has been a wholesale revaluation of such terms; the "new fanatics" are the "new royaliz'd presbyterians," otherwise known as "our zealous backsliders" (Patrides 350–51).

11 Since the *Areopagitica* stresses the preservative notion of books and so carries on the *Reason*'s references to authors who write "to aftertimes" (*CPW* 1:810), it is necessary to remember that in *Paradise Lost* he gives great importance to Enoch, Moses, David, and Joshua as "carriers of God's verbal message to their *own* generation," as well as for traditional typological functions. See *Science* 186.

12 Ernest Sirluck, "Milton's Idle Right Hand," *JEGP* 60 (1961), 769.

13 See Barker, pp. 95–96.

14 The protracted "turn" of the 18th sonnet is similarly focused on what really happened on those Alpine mountains cold: "Their moans / The vales redoubl'd to the Hills, / And they to Heav'n." And Abdiel's strikingly similar predicament—that double status of moral participant/military combatant—is placed at the center of the 1667 *PL*. The delicate vantage point of 1654 is beautifully captured in the fine sonnet to Cyriack Skinner, in which the poet recalls (with considerable edge in his voice) his work in "liberty's defence, my noble task, / Of which all Europe talks from side to side." In the version which Edward Phillips printed in his edition of 1694, Milton's nephew emended to "all Europe *rings*" (see Parker 474–75, 1044).

15 Georgia Christopher has recently underscored the literary importance of St. Paul's "humanism" in the Reformation for Milton's purposes "as early as the *Areopagitica* and as late as the preface to *Samson Agonistes*" (*Science* 77). It now seems clear that the Pauline sanction for humanistic studies is evident much earlier, at least in veiled form, in texts deeply rooted in millenarian thought. See H. G. Reventlow's useful account of the Reformation's left wing in *The Authority of the Bible and the Rise of the Modern World* (Philadelphia: Fortress Press, 1985), pt. I, chap. 3. I agree with Reventlow that in general Barker has overstressed "the reactive element" in Milton's pamphlets (p. 156). Reventlow cites Barker's comment that there were contemporary precedents for the oration's apparent confidence in human reason, and he has collected some anticipations

of the *Areopagitica* within the antiprelatical group (pp. 159, 160), including the promise of "an extraordinary effusion of Gods Spirit upon every age, and sexe, attributing to all men, and requiring from them the ability of searching, trying, examining all things" (*CPW* 1:566; italics deleted). He does not offer significant comment on the *Apology*, which (I believe) all but articulates the "new hermeneutical criterion" he finds suggested in the *The Reason of Church Government*.

16 A passage from the *Reason* with likely connections to the Bower of Bliss clarifies the nature of Milton's theoretic shift during the early part of 1642:

> For Truth . . . hath this unhappiness fatal to her, ere she can come to the trial and inspection of the understanding: being to pass through many little wards and limits of the several affections and desires, she cannot shift it but must put on such colours and attires as those pathetic handmaids of the soul please to lead her in to their queen; and if she find so much favour with them, they let her pass in her own likeness; if not, they bring her into the presence habited and coloured like a falsehood. And contrary, when any falsehood comes that way, if they like the error she brings, they are so artful to counterfeit the very shape and visage of truth that, the understanding not being able to discern the fucus which these enchantresses with such cunning have laid upon the features sometimes of truth, sometimes of falsehood interchangeably, sentences for the most part one for the other at the first blush, according to the subtle imposture of these sensual mistresses that keep the ports and passages between her and the object. [*CPW* 1:830–31, quoted Barker, pp. 50–51]

This passage takes on a new color if we remember Joel's handmaids and Milton's fondness for the parable of the wise and foolish virgins. Enchantresses though they are, these "pathetic handmaids" could become serviceable in the cause of a poetry conceived in the *Apology*'s fashion, or as *Of Education* viewed it pragmatically as the "sensuous" vehicle of a reconstituted Truth. Milton is remembering this discussion quite specifically in *Paradise Lost* 4, when Ithuriel and Zephon discover Satan and he returns "to his own likeness" (813; and see also 1:792–97).

17 For a similar allusion to Christ's new covenant (Heb. xii:24), see Vaughan, "Abel's Blood"). We shall encounter the Miltonic ancestor of these presbyterian ministers in the would-be adviser to the scrupulous Dionysius of the *AR*. See below, chap. 6.

18 In Livy's story, the lustful decemvir Appius takes the part of Milton's "king," and his sympathizers (resisting the pleas of Verginius and Lucius Icilius) are the former opponents the "presbyterian ministers." Milton's denunciation might well be taken from the speech of Verginius, newly returned from his military camp and requesting the support of the people not only from sympathy but as his due. Philemon Holland translates the passage as follows: "But what booteth or availeth all this (quoth he) to save the cittie from enemies, in case our children be forced to abide the utmost extremities that befall unto cities taken by the enemies? thus went he about preaching as it were from one man to another" (p. 119). Holland's *plebs* are "the Commons" and his tyrant Appius is interested in suppressing seditious "meetings and conventicles in the cittie" (p. 119); as though guessing the worst, he sees treason in the objections of Verginia's fiancé Lucius Icilius, "even alreadie breathing forth a Tribune's spirit" (p. 118) (*The Romane Historie Written by T. Livius of Padua* [London, Adam Islip, 1600]). The story joined the themes of chastity and political liberty (in Livy, the themes of the

women and men, respectively); if Milton thought of Verginia in using the rare
concionabundus here, she would have had a number of interesting predecessors, notably
the dismembered Truth of the *AR* and, before her, Proserpina, that figure for beauty's
many "shapes" carried from the field of Enna by Dis and sought by her mother Ceres.
The laws designed to protect the tribunes, aediles, and decemviral judges after the
downfall of Appius were to be enforced "at the Church of *Ceres, Liber* and *Libera*" (or
"Proserpina," as Holland glossed the last, following Arnobius and Cicero). The stories
of Lucretia and Verginia were among those to which Milton returned in arguing for a
perpetual "Grand Council" on the eve of the Restoration. See *The Ready and Easy Way*
(ed. Patrides), pp. 343–45.

19 E. M. W. Tillyard, *Milton* (London: Chatto & Windus, 1930), p. 110.

20 See Christopher Hill, *The Experience of Defeat: Milton and Some Contemporaries* (New York:
Viking, 1984).

CHAPTER THREE: VESTIGES OF AUTOBIOGRAPHY

1 It is sometimes assumed that in his later years Milton shared the Son's opinion of
dreams, expressed at PR 4:291–92. But the poet takes no pains to deny Eve's contention that "God is also in sleep, and Dreams advise" (*PL* 12:611); and in *1671*, both
protagonists are conspicuously guided by "motions."

2 Karl K. Hulley and Stanley T. Vandersall, eds., *Ovid's Metamorphosis Englished, Myth-
ologized, and Represented in Figures by George Sandys* (Lincoln: University of Nebraska
Press, 1970), p. 218.

3 *An Exposition Upon the Epistle of S. Paule the Apostle to the Ephesians: By S. Iohn
Chrysostome, Archbishop of Constantinople* (London: Henry Binneman and Ralph Newberie,
1581), p. 147. In an interesting qualification, John added that it is difficult "to gather
out of this place subjection, & preheminence, but by some other Epistle" (p. 145).

4 John Calvin, *Commentaries on the Epistles of Paul to the Galatians and Ephesians*, trans.
William Pringle (Edinburgh: Calvin Translation Society, 1854), 19:280.

5 Milton here paraphrases Jeremiah 20:8–10. See also "Wo is me my mother, that thou
hast borne me a man of strife and . . . contention," Jeremiah 15:10. Milton reviews
this kind of decision in Samson's "Commands are no constraints" (1372); there is an
intentionally deceptive ambiguity (a "concealment"?) in the subsequent "Masters' commands come with a power resistless / To such as owe them absolute subjection" (1404–
05).

Describing John Donne's grief following the death of his wife, Walton records a like
sense of compulsion in the way Donne's "consideration of his new engagements to God
and St. Paul's 'Woe is me, if I preach not the Gospel' . . . forced him to behold the
light" (*The Lives of Doctor John Donne, Sir Henry Wotton, Mr. Richard Hooker, Mr. George
Herbert, and Doctor Robert Sanderson* [London: Methuen, 1895], p. 26).

6 The Yale editor notes that this reference to an "inward prompting" is the first allusion
in Milton's prose to the divine inspiration of poetry. But in the passage (as in "Il
Penseroso,"), poetic achievement is a future possibility, the hypothetical product of a
union which—by the sound of Milton's prose—seems most unlikely: the marriage of
"labour and intent study (which I take to be my portion in this life) joyn'd with the
strong propensity of nature" (*CPW* 1:810).

7 The *Second Defence*'s formulation is otherwise virtually a translation of *Reason*: Pater me puerulum humaniorum literarum studiis destinavit (CE 8:118). Masson appears to accept this later assessment of the period in question and rationalizes it as follows: "Leaving it for his brother Christopher to become the lawyer of the family, he voluntarily chose for himself, or passively and gradually accepted as forced on him by circumstances, a life of less definite character and prospects, hardly recognized by any precise designation in the social or professional nomenclature of those days, though we can describe it now as the life of a scholar and man of letters" (Masson 1:327).

8 Barker, p. 84.

9 *Plato and Milton* (Ithaca: Cornell University Press, 1947), pp. 10–12. For Masson, the letter to the unknown friend implies the same outlook expressed "more boldly" in the *Reason* (1:325); he offers virtually no comment on the letter to Diodati. Parker is similarly brief on the second letter; his general position on the matter is that "there was nothing incompatible in a dedicated ministry joined to dedicated art. . . . There was no essential conflict in the two careers, such as posterity might imagine" (p. 121).

10 Gasparo Stiblini, in *Euripidis Tragoediae Quae Extant* (Geneva, 1602), sig. Yiiir, p. 173. A passage from Plutarch's "Isis and Osiris," mentioned by Sirluck as a gloss on the *Areopagitica*'s use of the fable, points forcefully to the continuities I have been tracing between 1637 and the early 1640s. Isis' enemy Typhon is devoted to "dissipating, defacing, and blotting out the sacred word and doctrine, which this divine goddesse collecteth, composeth, and delivereth unto those who are initiated and professed in this divine religion." This religion, Plutarch writes, requires the "precise observance of a sober and holy life," including abstinence from certain foods and "all fleshly pleasures, for to represse lust and intemperance"; the discipline leads ultimately to "the knowledge of that first prince and lord, who is apprehended onely by intelligence and understanding, whom the goddesse exhorteth to search and seeke after, as conversing and companying with her." Like Ceres' quest for Proserpina, the story of Isis thus involves the familiar Neoplatonic longing for the divine; it is, indeed, "a profession and entrance into religion." Moreover, the search for "such science," as Philemon Holland translates this compendium of "the Aeguyptians doctrine"), is "a work more holy than is the vow or obligation of all the chastity & purity in the world, or than the cloister or sanctuarie of any temple whatsoever." Quotations are from the translation of Philemon Holland (London, 1603), pp. 1286, 1288. If Sirluck is right in his conjecture that Milton took a vow of celibacy in 1637, the passage would have provided encouragement for his double departure from marital and ecclesiastical "temples" alike, not to mention a professional rededication. See "Milton's Idle Right Hand," *JEGP*, 60 (1961), 749–85.

11 In its sense of audience and the way it discriminates among literary methods, the Epistle to the Hebrews is a particularly interesting text for the beginning and end of Milton's literary career. The "manifold" and "fragmentary" method of the older times (1:1) provides a legitimate counterpart to Samson's "riddling days" and, as an allusion, spans Milton's career from the 1637 letter to the choral sonnet concluding *Samson Agonistes*. But there are additional connections. The Paulinist author is specifically addressing the issue of Christ's high priesthood and the way it replaces the Levitical conception of access or "approach"; the treatment of Christ's sacrifice — indeed what one could call its historical Platonism — is close to Milton's own views. The Christians of

Hebrews, moreover, are in danger of indifference (not so much idolatry) and need not just elementary doctrines, but the "solid food" (or "strong meat") that belongs to maturity. And in its list of Old Testament heroes, the just men sometimes called "worthies" in the seventeenth century, *Hebrews* provides just the kind of Christian model appropriate to these hard times. The *Areopagitica* indulges heavily in the ancient parabolic method and explicitly draws the connection between books and "meats and viands," while *Of Education*'s method, similarly "humanistic," recommends "solidity" in an even more particularized alimentary language. *Hebrews* was clearly a prime text for a belated (and book-weary) Reformation public.

CHAPTER FOUR: THE TRUE POEM *IN POTENTIA*

1 I quote Pico from the translation of Elizabeth L. Forbes in *The Renaissance Philosophy of Man*, ed. Ernst Cassirer, Paul Oskar Kristellar, and John Herman Randall, Jr. (1948: rpt. Chicago: University of Chicago Press, 1956), p. 228. Dürer is quoted in Erwin Panofsky, *The Life and Art of Albrecht Dürer* (Princeton: Princeton University Press, 1955), p. 171.

2 H. J. Todd, ed., *The Poetical Works of John Milton, with Notes of Various Authors*, 3d ed. (London, 1826), 5:148–49. Subsequent references to this edition will be indicated by page numbers in the text.

3 For a full account of this influence, see Raymond D. Havens, *The Influence of Milton on English Poetry* (Cambridge, Mass.: Harvard University Press, 1922), pp. 439–77.

4 Samuel Johnson, *Lives of the Poets*, ed. L. Archer Hind (London: J. M. Dent, 1925), 1:97–98.

5 *Romeo and Juliet* 1.4.51–94.

6 For a discussion of Shakespearean echoes, see J. B. Leishman, *Milton's Minor Poems*, pp. 149–51; the larger implications have been recently discussed by Paul Stevens in *Imagination and the Presence of Shakespeare in Paradise Lost* (Madison: University of Wisconsin Press, 1986). The entire passage of "L'Allegro" is heavily allusive; see Todd, pp. 99–100 (where Spenser, Sylvester, and a Puck song are mentioned in addition to Shakespeare), and the discussion of Woodhouse in *A Variorum Commentary on the Poems of John Milton* (New York: Columbia University Press, 1972), vol. 2, pt. i, p. 294.

7 See, e.g., Merritt Y. Hughes, "Lydian Airs," *MLN*, 40 (1925), 129–37; James Hutton, "Some English Poems in Praise of Music," *English Miscellany*, 2 (1951), 1–63; Harris Fletcher, *The Intellectual Development of John Milton* (Urbana: University of Illinois Press, 1956), 1:349–52; and Norman Council, "'L'Allegro, Il Penseroso* and 'The Cycle of Universal Knowledge,'" *Milton Studies*, 9 (1976), 203–19. For the more traditional view of Lydian music see Nan Cooke Carpenter, "The Place of Music in *L'Allegro* and *Il Penseroso*," *University of Toronto Quarterly*, 22 (1953), 354–67; David Miller, "From Delusion to Illumination: A Larger Structure for *L'Allegro* and *Il Penseroso*," *PMLA*, 86 (1972), 32–39; and Thomas J. Embry, "Sensuality and Chastity in *L'Allegro* and *Il Penseroso*," *JEGP*, 77 (1978), 504–29.

8 *Of Reformation*, in *CPW* 1:588. In addition to passages from *Masque at Ludlow Castle* and *Paradise Lost*, cited below, the "soft Pipes that charm'd / Thir painful steps o'er the burnt soil" (*PL* 1:561–62) and the "charming pipes" of *Paradise Regained*, 2:363, might be added as possible allusions to this mode.

9 I quote the translation of F. M. Cornford, *The Republic of Plato* (New York: Oxford University Press, 1945), p. 86.

10 Woodhouse believes that this transition reinforces "the suggestion of a steady temporal progression of particular happenings"; but he also finds "a counter-suggestion of the typical but generally intermittent" (*Variorum*, p. 304). The case against progressive sequence here has been effectively argued by Rosemond Tuve in *Images and Themes in Five Poems by John Milton* (Cambridge, Mass.: Harvard University Press [1957], pp. 23–24) and still more stringently by Stanley E. Fish in "What It's Like to Read *L'Allegro* and *Il Penseroso*," *Milton Studies*, 7 (1975), 79–99. The "And ever" is rather different in effect from "Some time" (l. 57), "Sometimes" (l. 91), and "oft" (l. 125) —with which Woodhouse groups them—if, as I am arguing, it means something like "And for always, forever"; it is more strenuous, more *solicitous* than many synonyms might suggest. Milton steadily resists the variations upon, say, "at all times" until this point in the poem.

11 The Latin phrase already had the sanction of Lucan (2.681) and Horace (1.18.4, 2.11.17–18); Woodhouse suggests that in the *Epitaphium Damonis* Milton combined the Horatian *mordaces . . . sollicitudines* and *edaces curas* (*Variorum*, p. 304), and he proposes Horace (4.15.30–32) as a precedent for later dissent from the traditional condemnation of Lydian music. In the *Epitaphium*, the singer's "eating cares" have been dispelled by the dead shepherd's "delightful conversation" (*Dulcibus alloquiis*), not by Horace's wine. The latter is more in evidence, together with "Tuscan airs," in the sonnet to Edward Lawrence (Sonnet 20 [1655]). For Cassiodorus, see *Variae* II in Migne, *Patrologia Latina* 69:571. To Warton's quotation from Edward Phillips ("The *Lydian* mood is now most in request"), Todd adds Phillips designation, the "mild Lydian" (p. 107; Phillips' italics deleted). It is the Ionic and not the Lydian, which Phillips called "carelessly delighting" (Henry Lawes, *Ayres and Dialogues For One, Two, and Three Voyces* [London, 1653], Sig. A.).

12 Leishman observes that "meeting" translates the Latin *obvius* (*Milton's Minor Poems*, p. 157).

13 The organization of the poem, or of this segment of the poem, is reinforced at ll. 69, 77, and 129–30, with the subtle but important difference that in each of these subsequent moments, we lose track of the conditionality in the original announcement. The suggestion that the poet's eye has in fact "caught new pleasures," really *sees* those "Towers and Battlements," involves an emphasis different from ll. 37–40, where the pleasures yet to come are made contingent upon whether "I give thee honor due." The shift in the way the original program is reannounced points, once again, to the kind of strategic "forgetfulness" I am trying to describe.

14 Hugh Blair, *Lectures on Rhetoric and Belles Lettres* (Philadelphia, 1784), pp. 379–80.

15 In "What It's Like to Read *L'Allegro* and *Il Penseroso*," Fish has claimed to find in the twin poems a "one-to-one correspondence between the activities in the poem and the activity of reading" (p. 94). For example, the long dispute concerning who comes to the window in l. 46, much worried in the pages of the *Times Literary Supplement* (1934) and still reverberating in the *Variorum*, involves a difficulty we do not feel, Fish urges, because it is a function of our freedom, and specifically of a "syntax that is not so much ambiguous as it is loose" (p. 82). For Fish, the poem's lack of syntactic pressures "protects us from meaning by protecting us from working. . . . Anything fits with

anything else, so that it is never necessary to go back and retrace one's effortless steps"
(p. 82). In Fish's view, the mode of the poem is thus single and unpastoral in the sense
that it "excludes from its landscape the concerns of the real world" (p. 85). "What
unifies *L'Allegro* is the consistency of the demand it makes, or rather declines to make,
on the reader, who is thus permitted the freedom from care ('secure delight') which is
the poem's subject" (p. 87). For this reason, Fish agrees with earlier readers that
L'Allegro is the easier of the two poems to read.

16 See Joseph H. Summers, *The Muse's Method* (London: Chatto & Windus, 1962), pp.
11–31. In this context, the notion of a "rising poet" can be extended to include local
and momentary effects, in some respects illusory. I am thinking of passages like the
Seventh Prolusion's fantasy of the wise man's home becoming a "shrine" (Hughes 625),
or the Elder Brother's precocious gravity. See Louis Martz's discussion of the arrangement of materials in *1645*, "to convey a sense of the predestined bard's rising powers"
(*Poet of Exile* [New Haven: Yale University Press, 1980], p. 38 and chap. 2 passim).

17 See p. 55 and n. 19.

18 In Sonnet 13 ("To My Friend, Mr. Henry Lawes, on His Airs" [1646]) Fame is given
leave to set Lawes higher than Dante's "Casella, whom he wooed to sing, / Met in the
milder shades of Purgatory."

19 The two poems share a profound agreement on this matter; in "L'Allegro" the speaker
wishes for a music that might reduce Orpheus to spectator and hence accomplish the
rescue of Eurydice—herself the surrogate, in each poem, for the nymph being summoned. Both poems insist on the historical pastness of the Orphic music (as Sonnet 23
does for the rescue of Alcestis), and "Il Penseroso" is specific (at l. 101) about the
unlikelihood of any recurrence.

20 See esp. ll. 784–86.

21 The belated peasant is discussed in my *Milton's Epic Process: Paradise Lost and Its Miltonic
Background* (New Haven: Yale University Press, 1973), pp. 224–28. Thomas
Warton's confusion on this passage is characteristically illuminating. He begins by
asking, incredulously, "Is the Dream to wave at Sleep's wings?" (Todd quotes the
emendation of Warton's reviewer in the *Critical Review*, "Wave at his wings *an* aery
stream" [p. 139].) And his conclusion sounds distinctly evasive: "On the whole, we
must not here seek for precise meaning of parts, but acquiesce in a general idea resulting from the whole, which I think is sufficiently seen" (Todd, p. 138). Warton's
paraphrase redirects our attention from the rather odd locus of the dream to the strength
of its effect; "an airy stream of rich pictures so *strongly* displayed in vision as to resemble
real Life." (Here the richness of Warton's "pictures" comes close to Todd's church
details, and "vision" seems to give Milton the benefit of Warton's own doubt.) Warton
seems alert to the possibility of deception in this context, in the observation (for
example) that line 150 derives from the flower-juice business in *A Midsummer Night's
Dream*. In *Paradise Lost*, Bk. 7, Milton dwells at some length on the insects' "limber
fans / For wings," and the phenomenon of irridescence (ll. 476–79).

22 *CPW* 1:326.

23 Gerard Winstanley's *A New Yeer's Gift* (1649) clarifies the analogical potential of
domestic relations in exploiting the standpoint of the Younger Brother for purposes
very different from the *Masque*'s: "The Commons are as truly ours by the last excellent

two Acts of Parliament, the Foundation of Englands new righteous Government aimed at, as the Elder brothers can say the Inclosures are theirs." See *Revolutionary Prose of the English Civil War*, ed. Howard Erskine-Hill and Grahame Storey (Cambridge University Press, 1983), p. 174. In the following discussion, I find much to agree with in Cedric Brown's fine *John Milton's Aristocratic Entertainments* (Cambridge University Press, 1985). As Louis Martz has observed in making a different point, the brothers relate somewhat in the fashion of L'Allegro and Il Penseroso (see *Poet of Exile*, p. 46). As I see it, there is a consolidation under way in the hierarchy of this masque allowing the brothers to join their sister as a "national" figure reflecting what Georgia Christopher has called "Milton's youthful confidence in the goodness and staunchness of his countrymen" (*Milton and the Science of the Saints*, p. 56). For a more general discussion of social elements in Milton's poetry, see David Norbrook, *Poetry and Politics in the Early Renaissance* (Boston and London: Routledge & Kegan Paul, 1984), pp. 235–85.

24 In the published version of 1637, but not at Ludlow, the Elder Brother's speech here was anticipated by the Lady's welcome to a hovering angel with golden wings (perhaps borrowed from the Cherub of *IP*): an event provoking (or confirming, as suggested by "I now believe") her belief in what has of course already happened—the arrival of a "glistering guardian," albeit one dressed in the "weeds and likeness" of Thyrsis.

25 For the argument that a "censor" (and not Milton) is responsible for the brothers' part in summoning Sabrina, see Brown, pp. 115–19. In the Bridgewater text, the Elder Brother also addressed the Lady after her liberation and spoke the masque's closing couplet. In Brown's view this was a deflection of Milton's intention, both originally and as repeated in 1637.

26 Thus does Milton in fact incorporate a "trial" with what has often been too severely distinguished from an ascent to spiritual power or "divinity." See Woodhouse, and especially Fixler, pp. 52, 220. It is interesting that the early essay on the congenial Miltonic theme of an eventual separation of good and evil is given to the grandiloquent Elder Brother, a character seemingly vulnerable to the charge of seeking fame "on the basis of a forced and immature style" (Prolusion 7; Hughes 622). See Donald Bouchard, *Milton: A Structural Reading* (Montreal: McGill-Queen's University Press, 1974), p. 26.

27 Carey 250; in the Trinity MS, "To strew" immediately followed line 141, "And purple all the ground with vernal flowers."

28 *Spiritual and Anabaptist Writers*, ed. G. H. Williams and A. Mergal (Philadelphia: Westminster Press, 1957), p. 62.

29 My hasting days fly on with full career
   But my late spring no bud or blossom show'th.   [Sonnet 7, ll. 3–4]

30 See above, chap. 2, n. 15. For a perceptive discussion of botanical metaphor as a basic idiom in Milton's prose and verse, see Constance A. Woo, "Floralism in Milton's Poetry and Prose," Ph.D. dissertation (UCLA, 1970).

31 Northrop Frye, "Literature as Context: Milton's *Lycidas*," in *Milton's "Lycidas": The Tradition and the Poem*, ed. C. A. Patrides (rev. ed. Columbia: University of Missouri Press, 1983), pp. 207–08.

CHAPTER FIVE: MONODY HISTORIFIED

1 Michael Lieb, "Milton's *Of Reformation* and the Dynamics of Controversy," in *Achievements of the Left Hand: Essays on the Prose of John Milton*, ed. Michael Lieb and John T. Shawcross (Amherst: University of Massachusetts Press, 1974), p. 55.

2 Milton's portrait of Luther is borrowed directly from the Lutheran historian Johannes Phillipson (or "Sleidanus"). At some time between 1639 and 1641, Milton had observed in *CPB* that "Luther refrained neither from harshness nor from jests that were now and then even a little shameful. Sleiden. Book. 16. p. 261" (*CPW* 1:390). This is Milton's first reference to Luther and to the source of Milton's expanded portrait in *An Apology*. For the dating, see James H. Hanford, "The Chronology of Milton's Private Studies," *PMLA*, 36 (1921), 251–314, and the dissenting view of Parker, who argues for an earlier date of 1634–35 (pp. 801–02). Sleidan was an author likely to be among those Milton mentioned to Charles Diodati in November 1637; he is considered by Milton an authoritative historian of the reform movement. For Milton's use of Sleidan elsewhere, see Merritt Y. Hughes, "Milton's Treatment of Reformation History in *The Tenure of Kings and Magistrates*," *Ten Perspectives on Milton* (New Haven: Yale University Press, 1965), pp. 220–39.

3 The commonplace of the *recapitulator generis humanae* is mentioned in C. A. Patrides, *Milton and the Christian Tradition* (Oxford: Clarendon Press, 1966). For a discussion which emphasizes the agreement of Jesus' versatility with classical theories of rhetorical decorum, see Thomas Kranidas, "'Decorum' and the Style of Milton's Antiprelatical Tracts," *Studies in Philology*, 62 (1965), 176–87.

4 See, however, the entry in *CPB* to similar effect, dated by Hanford 1635–38?, in *CPW* 1:405. These passages illustrate Milton's personal readiness for the parliamentary apologetics which Sirluck considers to be the chief, if not exclusive, source of the improvements in Milton's arguments for divorce (*CPW* 2:145–47). In a sense, the way in which Luther appears in *An Apology* can be said to initiate that expansion in what Milton thought of as the realm of "things indifferent" which has long been associated with the divorce pamphlets. As Sirluck observes in his notes for *Of Education* (*CPW* 2:413), few writers had paid heed to individual aptitudes, something Milton proposes to correct in his own curriculum.

5 The more standard kinds of literary theory too are here closer to their philosophic origins, as in the remarks (later recollected in the preface to *Samson Agonistes*) on tragedy's cathartic removal of various harmful humors. Milton's interest in the daimonic implications of physiology, so evident, for example, in *Of Education*, dates from at least as early as the Seventh Prolusion.

6 For the view that Milton is usually reluctant to cite divine testimony, see Arthur E. Barker, *Milton and the Puritan Dilemma* (Toronto: University of Toronto Press, 1942), p. 74.

7 Masson finds a purely literary exercise in this hypothetical praise, an example of "how an eulogium on Parliament *should* be written" (2:405; Masson's italics). For Parker its sincerity is essential (p. 222). Neither biographer relates the eulogy to the rhetorical aims, however complex or ambiguous, of the present pamphlets.

8 Fixler, p. 161. See also p. 61 and the quite different emphasis of Barker (pp. xvii, xix) and Woodhouse, for whom Milton's "shift[s] of ground" were "dictated by the course of

the Revolution" (pp. 100–01). In departing from this view, I begin with Milton's adamant refusal (in the *Reason*) to admit the force of "necessity and constraint" (*CPW* 1:823) and the relative candor with which he introduces pragmatic arguments in the *Apology*.

9 "Vehemens" is a name for the grand style in Cicero (*Orator* xxi.69. For a recent study of the orator's place in Milton's prose works, see Joseph A. Wittreich, Jr., "'The Crown of Eloquence': The Figure of the Orator in Milton's Prose Works," in *Achievements of the Left Hand: Essays on the Prose of John Milton*, ed. Michael Lieb and John T. Shawcross (Amherst: University of Massachusetts Press, 1974), pp. 3–54.

10 See Lowry Nelson, *Baroque Lyric Poetry* (New Haven: Yale University Press, 1962), pp. 41–52.

11 Milton pretends that the entire performance is made available almost incidentally for our edification as interested spectators. As Milton puts it, "If I am forc't to be unpleasing to him whose fault it is, I shall not forget at the same time to be usefull in some thing to the stander by" (*CPW* 1:878–79). For discussions of *An Apology*, see Masson, 2:398–409, and Parker, pp. 220–24.

12 It would lack the "sevenfold Chorus of hallelujahs and harping symphonies" of Revelations (as read by David Paraeus), perhaps reverting to the more ironic vehicle of Euripides.

13 See Raymond Williams, *Culture and Society* (Garden City: Doubleday, 1960), chap. 2.

CHAPTER SIX: TRYING ALL THINGS IN THE *AREOPAGITICA*

1 Milton's own scholarly memory in the *Areopagitica* is uncharacteristically flawed, and not all the mistakes can be assigned to his sources. There are two unlikely errors concerning the chronology and the provisions of the Licensing Order itself (*CPW* 2:519, n. 120; 569, n. 303); Milton conflates two stories about Archilochus of Paros, taken from Valerius Maximus and Plutarch (*CPW* 2:496, n. 37); he seems to contradict Jerome on the question of Cicero's editorship of Lucretius (*CPW* 2:498, n. 37; and he makes an egregious error in recalling a recent text in English literature by providing Guyon, in the Cave of Mammon, with a guide which Spenser clearly meant to deny him. (See Ernest Sirluck, "Milton Revises *The Faerie Queene*," *Modern Philology* 48 [1950], 90–96.) Milton's "revision" can be distinguished from the scholarly mistakes; but there are important disagreements with—and even a silent correction of—one scholarly source whom he virtually quotes at some length, Paolo Sarpi's *History of the Council of Trent*. See *CPW* 2:502, n. 59, and (for a fuller account) Sirluck, "Milton's Critical Use of Historical Sources," *Modern Philology* 50 (1953), 226–31.

2 This phrase is taken from a closely related passage in the 1644 edition of *The Doctrine and Discipline of Divorce*, referring to "our ancient *Druides*, by whom this Island was the Cathedrall of Philosophy to France" (*CPW* 2:231). For the implications of "cathedral," see above, chap. 3, pp. 38–39.

3 This community can be related to the "general apocalyptic reaffirmation" in which Milton "treats the nation and the Lord's people as synonymous quantities," according to Fixler (p. 127). But I would claim that rhetorical reaffirmation in the *Areopagitica* is hedged with contingencies, and even helps to clarify "the very real fact . . . that the nation at large appeared to be unregenerate" (ibid.).

4 For this reason, Milton worries the commonplace distinction between "public" and "private" throughout the oration, claiming that "writing is more public then preaching," something Christ had done in the open and not "privily from house to house, which is more dangerous" (*CPW* 2:548). There is a similar blurring of distinctions as early as the Seventh Prolusion (1632). Milton remembers the distinction in Samson's heartfelt denial, "I was no private" (1211); and his brief epic concludes with the Son's "private" return to his mother's house (*PR* 4:639). The latter action, of course, punctuates the Son's definitive victory over the Tempter, an action which Milton considered the "verification" of the divine "oracle" in Genesis 3:15. See *PL* 10:182–90.

5 For the time being, I retain the reading of the first printed edition, "wayfaring."

6 Barker, p. 85.

7 Even the quotation of 1 Thessalonians 5:21 involves a departure from Milton's clearly acknowledged source; as Sirluck observes (*CPW* 2:512, n. 90), it is a "remarkable substitution for what he found" in Dionysius and Eusebius alike. The actual text in both sources, "Approve yourselves bankers of repute," was no longer to be found in Scripture. This "silent correction" of the ecclesiastical record—in the interest of things "unapocryphall," indeed—may well have derived from the digression of Socrates Scholasticus (3:16), from which Milton borrowed material elsewhere in the *Areopagitica*; see *CPW* 2:512, n. 90.

8 Compare the wish to become "an interpreter & relater of the best and sagest things among mine own Citizens throughout this Iland in the mother dialect" (*Reason of Church Government*, *CPW* 1:811–12). As described in the *Reason*, Milton's purpose seems more exclusively literary than two months later in the somewhat different account of the *Apology*; the *Reason's* kind of "interpretation," furthermore, has been significantly postponed by the decision to enter the pamphlet controversy.

9 *CPW* 2:164–78.

10 For the learning of Moses, see Dan. 1:3ff. and Acts 7:22; Sirluck suggests a more immediate source in Basil's "Address to Young Men on the Right Use of Greek Literature" (*CPW* 2:508, n. 75).

11 John Calvin, *Commentary Upon the Acts of the Apostles*, ed. Henry Beveridge (Edinburgh, 1844), 1:420.

12 John Lightfoot, *A Commentary Upon the Acts of the Apostles, Chronicall and Criticall* (London, 1645), p. 236.

13 Foxe renders Luther's "absolute answer" to Charles V as follows: My conscience is so bound and captived in these Scriptures and the word of God which I have alleged, that I will not, nor may not revoke any manner of thing; considering that it is not godly or lawful to do anything against conscience. God have mercy upon me! (*The Acts and Monuments of John Foxe*, ed. Townsend [London, 1896], 4:286). In light of Milton's mockery of Jerome's "lenten dream" (discussed above, pp. 88–90), it is fascinating to find Luther conjoining Galatians 1:8, "Though an angel should descend from heaven, if he preach any other doctrine, let him be accursed."

14 Calvin, *Commentaries On the Epistles to the Philippians, Colossians, and Thessalonians*, tr. John Pringle (Edinburgh, 1851), p. 300.

15 *The Ancient Bounds, or Liberty of Conscience, Tenderly Stated, Modestly Asserted, and Mildly Vindicated* (London, 1645), chap. 6: rpt. in A. S. P. Woodhouse, *Puritanism and Liberty* (Chicago: University of Chicago Press, 1965), pp. 258–59.

16 "The Rime of the Ancient Mariner," ll. 236–91.

17 Discussing Milton's views on establishing the City of God on Earth, Arnold Stein relates Milton's "unzealous awareness of difficulties" (1) to a "stubborn unwillingness to despise the body," (2) to his belief in the impracticality of passing laws for virtue, and (3) to "his belief in the Second Coming." Stein's prime instance of Milton's "good sense" in this last case is the use of the Osiris myth in the *Areopagitica* (*Heroic Knowledge* [Minneapolis: University of Minnesota Press, 1957], p. 67).

18 And himself, to judge from his reference (in the *Reason*) to that "troubled sea of noises and hoarse disputes" which is the pamphlet controversy. In the *Areopagitica*, such fragmentation becomes the "materials dark and crude" for a new kind of verbal and dialectical ordering; the metaphor is close to the tenor of Chaos in *Paradise Lost*, a noisy as well as "illimitable Ocean," producing "a universal hubbub wild / Of stunning sounds and voices all confus'd" (2:892, 951–54) assaulting Satan's ear "with loudest vehemence."

19 See n. 23 below for a brief discussion of the way in which Milton's celebration of the "special times" focuses persistently upon the word "matter"; a related feature of his argument involves a fascinating and bold application of Melanchthon's doctrine of *adiaphora*: "all that rank of things indifferent" (*CPW* 2:563).

20 The *Areopagitica* was written, Milton claimed in the *Second Defense*, "after the model of a regular speech" (*ad justae orationis modum, Works* 8:134). In his prefatory letter to Ralegh, Spenser similarly stresses the miraculous effects of the Lady's armor upon the "clownish person" in search of adventure: "That is the armor of a Christian man specified by Saint Paul v. Ephesians." Thus furnished, "he seemed the goodliest man in all that company, and was well liked of the Lady."

21 In the first edition of *The Doctrine and Discipline of Divorce*; in the second edition Milton followed his disparaging reference to "that sort of men who follow *Anabaptism, Famelism, Antinomianism*, and other *fanatick* dreams" with a parenthetical "if we understand them not amisse" (*CPW* 2:278, and Sirluck's note, p. 568).

22 See also the brief account of Urania and "Wisdom [her] Sister" in *PL* 7:11–12. Sirluck notes that Plutarch's "On Isis and Osiris" had proposed something very like Milton's allegorical significance—a different treatment altogether from the Nativity Ode (ll. 211–13) or *PL* 1:475–82 (*CPW* 2:549, n. 222).

23 The *Areopagitica* can be taken as an experimental early text in the history of Milton's lifelong fascination with the power of matter, a philosophical preoccupation which may have sprung from his speculative consideration of marriage and procreation in the divorce pamphlets. It is this reading and speculation which provides the root metaphor for the discussion of good and evil, as well as for the famous discussion of books, which are not "absolutely dead things, but doe contain a potencie of life in them to be as active as that soule was whose progeny they are" (*CPW* 2:492). For an expert discussion of Milton's philosophic materialism, see William B. Hunter, "Milton and the Power of Matter," *Journal of the History of Ideas*, 13 (1952), 551–62.

24 The phrase is John Crowe Ransom's in "A Poem Nearly Anonymous"; see C. A. Patrides, ed., *Milton's Lycidas: The Tradition and the Poem*, rev. ed. (Columbia: University of Missouri Press, 1983), p. 77.

25 Milton's most interesting exploration of the connections between written texts and actual speech occurs in the *Apology*, a pamphlet prompted by his antagonist's intent

"not so much to smite at me, as through me to render odious the truth which I had written. . . . I conceav'd my selfe to be now not as mine own person, but as a member incorporate into that truth whereof I was perswaded, and whereof I had declar'd openly to be a partaker" (*CPW* 1:871). As for the sense of social relations within the work, the following reveals something of Milton's self-consciousness: "Although I tell [my opponent] keen truth, yet he may beare with me, since I am like to chase him into some good knowledge, and others, I trust, shall not misspend their leasure. For this my aime is, if I am forc't to be unpleasing to him whose fault it is, I shall not forget at the same time to be usefull in some thing to the stander by" (*CPW* 1:878–79.

26 See *CPW* 2:515 and n. 102. For two recent discussions, see Ruth M. Kivette, "The Ways and Wars of Truth," *Milton Quarterly*, 6 (1972), 81–86, and Juanita J. Whitaker, "'The Wars of Truth': Wisdom and Strength in *Areopagitica*," *Milton Studies*, 9 (1976), 185–201.

27 For the implications of "Isocrates," see J. A. Wittreich, Jr., "Milton's *Areopagitica*: Its Isocratean and Ironic Contexts," *Milton Studies*, 4 (1972), 101–15, and Paul M. Dowling, "*Areopagitica* and *Areopagiticus*: The Significance of the Isocratic Precedent," *Milton Studies*, 21 (1986), 49–69. Rhetorical innovation is the focus of fine discussions by G. K. Hunter ("The Structure of Milton's *Areopagitica*," *English Studies*, 39 [1958], 117–119); Balachandra Rajan, "*Areopagitica* and the Images of Truth," in his *The Form of the Unfinished: English Poetics from Spenser to Pound* (Princeton: Princeton University Press, 1985), pp. 85–103; and Harry R. Smallenburg ("Contiguities and Moving Limbs: Style as Argument in *Areopagitica*," *Milton Studies*, 9 [1976], 169–84).

CHAPTER SEVEN: *PARADISE REGAINED* AND MILTON'S "OTHER" SATAN

1 The abandonment of mere historical narrative or "story" is a primary implication of Luther's well-known preference for John's Gospel. Commenting on 16:13, Luther observes that, especially in the last days, we are tempted by miracles (or rather, "artifices") and "the pilgrimages in the name of Mary, also with apparitions and ghosts of the dead" (*LW* 24:369–71). Luther does not mention Jerome of Milton's "Lenten dream" in this context; but "sleeping and snoring people" are especially vulnerable, including St. Gregory and several followers of St. Martin (370). For two recent accounts of the importance of this Gospel in *Paradise Regained*, see Ira Clark, "*Paradise Regained* and the Gospel According to John," *MP* 71 (1973), 1–15, and Stella P. Revard, "The Gospel of John and *Paradise Regained*: Jesus as a 'True Light,'" in *Milton and Scriptural Tradition: The Bible Into Poetry*, ed. James H. Sims and Leland Ryken (Columbia: University of Missouri Press, 1984), pp. 142–59.

2 The problem is well summarized by D. C. Allen, *The Harmonious Vision: Studies in Milton's Poetry* (Baltimore: Johns Hopkins University Press, 1954), pp. 110–13. Woodhouse found Satan "shorn of his grandeur" but essentially the same as his predecessor ("The Theme and Pattern of *Paradise Regained*, *UTQ* 25 [1955–56], 171–73). Satan's strategies are shrewdly traced in recent studies by Stanley E. Fish ("Inaction and Silence: The Reader in *Paradise Regained*," in *Calm of Mind: Tercentenary Essays on*

Paradise Regained and Samson Agonistes in Honor of John S. Dieckhoff [Cleveland: Case Western Reserve Press, 1971], pp. 25–47; "Things and Actions Indifferent: the Temptation of Plot in *Paradise Regained*," in *Milton Studies*, 17 [1983], 163–85) and Georgia Christopher (*Science* 199–224). Arnold Stein seems to me quite right in saying that in *Paradise Regained* Satan is "more nearly domestic. . . . He is fascinatingly wrong, essentially inept" (*Heroic Knowledge*, p. 16); Stein's way of putting it allows us to focus at once upon the human and the sinister, *influential* sides of Satan. Annabel Patterson has recently suggested that Satan is "driven by the need to know the truth and . . . tormented by ambiguity . . . in the divine Word itself" ("*Paradise Regained*: A Last Chance at True Romance," *Milton Studies*, 17 [1983], 202). See also Lawrence Hyman, *The Quarrel Within: Art and Morality in Milton's Poetry* (Port Washington, N.Y.: Kennikat Press, 1972), pp. 83–89.

3 Barker's remark on the origin of the controversialist in Milton applies to the first epic's conception of Satan: "The poet seemed to see in the embattled forces in the church and state the public counterparts of the powers contending in his own mind" (6).

4 Helen Gardner, *A Reading of "Paradise Lost"* (Oxford: Clarendon Press, 1965), p. 54.

5 Whether or not Milton is finally (in R. A. Shoaf's words) a "poet of duality," there are certainly moments (as at *PL* 1:201) when Satan seems to have been reabsorbed into the great structure of God's works and so recovered his original, "serviceable" status in the book of Job as "a lawyer in good standing in the heavenly court of God" (G. Ernest Wright and Reginald H. Fuller, *The Book of the Acts of God* [Garden City: Doubleday, rpt. 1960], p. 196). See R. A. Shoaf, *Milton: Poet of Duality: A Study of Semiosis in the Poetry and the Prose* (New Haven: Yale University Press, 1985). As God's lawyer/ rhetorician, especially in *Paradise Lost*, Milton's Satan has much in common with Luther's Satan, who occasionally functions as a kind of foster parent. See *LW* 24:331.

6 Georgia Christopher relates Michael's shift from "spectacle" to "a purely 'literary' presentation" in *Paradise Lost* 12 to Adam's spiritual growth during Books 10–11 (177–78). And Adam's share of the corrective interpretation increases and is modified in 12, in something like the way the brothers progress during the *Masque*. An important difference in *Paradise Regained* is the evident reversion to spectacle, its association with Satan's "gentle ministers," and the apparent susceptibility to this reversal on the part of the narrator.

7 See Walter Mackellar, *A Variorum Commentary on the Poems of John Milton* (New York: Columbia University Press, 1975), 4:11–16.

8 *The Autobiography of Malcolm X* (New York: Grove Press, 1965), p. 187.

9 For a brief but penetrating discussion of how Gospel history worked in Milton's post-millennialist thought, see Barker, p. 115 and n. 93.

10 This association carries over into *Samson Agonistes*, where similar motives align Danite with Philistine, in the spirit of the Psalms that Milton translated just as he was beginning *Paradise Lost*; Samson may be disaffiliating himself from the Chorus in similar fashion, for that matter, when he refers so mysteriously to the "rousing motions" that will make unnecessary any further thought or action by the Chorus. The biographical connections are not entirely inappropriate, either, if we recall how easily the Reformers linked their era with the "dawn" and imminent "high noon" of the Gospel itself.

11 *Luther's Works*, ed. Jaroslav Pelikan (St. Louis: Concordia, 1963), 40:262. Subsequent references to this edition will appear following quotations in the text.

12 Luther remarks: "This is a passionate zeal, that he has the courage to curse so boldly not only himself and his brethren but even an angel from heaven" (*Luther's Works*, 26:55).

13 Northrop Frye omits mention of a double Scripture in his discussion of this passage and so leaves the misleading impression of a piously bewildered Milton. See *The Great Code: The Bible and Literature* (New York: Harcourt Brace Jovanovich, 1982), p. 228.

14 *The Advancement of Learning* [World's Classics ed. Thomas Case, Oxford 1956], pp. 249–50). It has become a commonplace in twentieth-century criticism of *1671* that the book somehow divides between theology and literature and, further, that the brief epic is "an interpretation" of the "literary product" that is *Samson Agonistes* (Bouchard, pp. 10–11). In a complex variation on this argument, William Kerrigan argues that like the *Masque, Paradise Regained* is a preliminary to the greater work, an "abstract formula" of a Miltonic itinerary which issues not in the tragedy but *Paradise Lost* (*The Sacred Complex: On the Psychogenesis of Paradise Lost* [Cambridge: Harvard University Press, 1983], p. viii, and esp. chap. 3). The approach frequently involves very limiting assumptions about what each work in a canon withholds (or suppresses) and can easily result in an uncritical generosity to the poet: the assumption that *Paradise Lost*, or between them *Paradise Regained* and *Samson Agonistes*, somehow "speak all things," in the fashion of the Reformation Bible. It seems more helpful to begin with the common ground for the two parts of *1671* and to consider the implications of the volume's sequence as the book presents it. Part of my point is that doing so requires a studious avoidance of Milton's own critical framework whether in the prose (of 1642 and 1654), or the verse (the invocation to Book 9, or the way epic bard and tragic chorus propose to classify types of heroism [*PL* 9:32; *SA* 1287–88]).

15 Carey, similarly, observes (1093) that either the Son's "memory is returning, or that God has granted illumination" (citing 1:293).

16 With its double focus on the root promise of Scripture and an indeterminate moment of "verification" perhaps inclusive of the poet's own prophetic successes, this passage is a convenient point to mark the disappearance of the kind of narrative "presence" which Arnold Stein believes is almost entirely missing from the poem until its conclusion (*The Art of Presence*, p. 160). The finest recent study of the protevangelium in *Paradise Lost* finds in Books 11 and 12 a rendition of the "experience that compromises 'explicit faith'" (*Science* 178). As I read *1671*, the same could be said for both *Paradise Regained* and *Samson Agonistes*, whose respective territories seem virtually mapped out in *PL* 9:31–32.

17 "Directive," l. 37.

18 On the Son's "difficulties": As in Samson's opening soliloquy and the grand original itself in the fourth book of *Paradise Lost*, these are disorderly thoughts, "swarming" like those bees so energetically conferring "their state affairs" at the end of Book 1. And Milton presents them in a deliberately disorienting fashion. At 1:227, we may notice the peculiar placement of "These growing thoughts" in the sentence well ahead of the governing verb that might orient us historically. As it turns out, the verb ["perceiving"] dehistorifies the moment. And we are further disoriented temporally by the repeated "at times."

19 In an apt passage of the *Advancement*, Bacon specifies that "the unlearned man knows not what it is to descend into himself or to call himself to account" (p. 67). The ritual of a literary or cognitive "perfection" helps to account for the coldness or appetitive empti-

ness on the part of Jesus, a common complaint in studies of the brief epic. See, e.g., Elizabeth M. Pope, *Paradise Regained: The Tradition and the Poem* (Baltimore: Johns Hopkins University Press, 1947), p. 40, and Christopher (*Science* 206). And it clarifies the likely impression that the work itself is abstract or doctrine ridden, as in Anthony Low's opinion that *Paradise Regained* appears "schematic, and too purely theological" (*The Blaze of Noon: A Reading of Samson Agonistes* [New York: Columbia University Press, 1974], p. 116). In light of Milton's idiom in *Of Education*, it is interesting that the Son remembers the Law specifically as a "delightful" text.

20 See Martz 1964, p. 199, and Woodhouse 1972, p. 294. Like the Son, Samson is capable of such deliberate imitative flights, once answering the Chorus's evasive reminder that he could at least resist "the dancing Ruby" (*SA* 543), and later in his elaborate challenge to Harapha of Gath. If in these works Milton practices a late plain style, he does so partly by localizing and heightening its opposite within the idiom of his flexible, virtuoso protagonists. In the case of Samson, at least, the "opposite" style may also be Samson's own former one, from his effeminate days of riddles and garrulity.

21 Carey cites Matt 3:2 in glossing 1:20, but the related 1 Pet 3:18–20 takes us back to Noah (see *PL* 11:723–25) while at the same time glancing ahead to the Resurrection.

22 A Sermon Preached Before the King's Majesty, at Whitehall, on Wednesday, the Twenty-Fifth of December, A.D. MDCXX., Being Christmas-Day, *Ninety-Six Sermons by . . . Lancelot Andrewes* (Oxford: John Henry Parker, 1856), 1:235.

23 The lines, 416–20, are almost lifted from *PL* 1:53ff., and there are also echoes of Gabriel at the end of Book 4.

CHAPTER EIGHT: "WITH CURIOUS EYE"

1 It is interesting, in this context, that Mary appears twice, but only the second time in propria persona, to voice "motherly cares and fear" (64). We first encounter her in the Son's memory of a past conversation with him "apart" (1:229–58); it is here that we hear the poem's first extended use of Scripture. Somewhat like the Son in the third book of *Paradise Lost*, she speaks naively and sometimes as though by rote; here the text may strike us as a rush of undigested "thoughts," not at all the powerful encapsulations of the later books. Her Gospel, so to speak, adds the wise men's interpretations to Luke; enveloped as it is within the Son's report of a past conversation, this bit of "Scripture" becomes "secondary," in the sense of yielding to the Son's own vocal performance during the balance of *PR*. Like the "new baptized," the fishermen are attached to the personal experience of this preministerial moment: it matters too much that they have "heard / His words," hardly the true locus, at this point in the Son's career, of a true "wisdom full of grace and truth" (2:33–34). Though not as impressed as the new baptized with the notion of divine rapture, they are more self- than history-minded. Hughes's note on p. 495 points to their mistake here, though we should note that line 37 makes it a past position. For all the severity of 59, however, some of their lines (2:53–57) are impressive. And it is important, in light of my comments above on the poem's sense of its era, that Milton's use of Acts 1:6 antedates the disciples' question and attributes it to the "plain fishermen."

2 *The Sacred Complex*, p. 90.

3 In the invocation to Book 7, Milton had spoken of silence as one of the likely obstacles

to successful epic, wishing for a voice "unchanged to hoarse of mute" (7:25). The various "stops" on music's quill, he seems to have believed, were "tender" in the sense of a liability to modulation; a special problem with the "higher moods" of epic and tragedy was their proximity to satiric "hoarseness" and outright silence. (The *Reason* had included an interesting fantasy on the notion of enforced muteness as a punishment for political hesitancy.)

4 As discussed earlier (chap. 6, n. 1), Milton's most notorious lapse as a literary scholar, in the very document which recommends "our sage and serious Spenser," concerns just this question of Guyon's company in the Bower of Bliss.

5 Editors have frequently commented upon the relative scarcity of allusions and echoes in *Paradise Regained*; Newton thought it "composed from memory and with no other help from books" (H. J. Todd, ed., *The Poetical Works of John Milton, with Notes of Various Authors*, 5th ed. [London, 1852], 3:202). Several parallels have been cited, however, for Milton's account of the Son's descent, including Apuleius' description of Psyche (IV), Ovid's *Metamorphoses* (IV–V), and Giles Fletcher's *Christ's Triumph on Earth*. See Todd, 3:195, and the notes of John Carey in *The Poems of John Milton*, ed. John Carey and Alastair Fowler (London: Longmans, 1968), pp. 1076–77, 1163–64. On Milton's treatment, Thyer comments acutely: "There is a peculiar softness and delicacy in this description," a quality he finds appropriate, given the dangers from which the Son has just been removed. Also interesting is his general point that Milton has "throughout the work thrown the ornaments of poetry on the side of errour, whether it was that he thought great truths best expressed in a grave unaffected style, or intended to suggest this fine moral to the reader, that simple naked truth will always be an overmatch for falsehood, though recommended by the gayest rhetoric, and adorned with the most bewiching colours" (Todd, 3:195, 168–69).

6 Howard Schultz, *Milton and Forbidden Knowledge* (New York: Modern Language Association, 1955), p. 92.

7 "His element was sublimity,—but he possessed . . . the opposite qualities of tenderness and grace. He who, with the power of heroic song, could stir the soul, as with the sound of a trumpet, knew also the "tender stops" of the pastoral flute; and the same hand that armed the rebellious legions, and built up the radiant domes of Pandemonium, mingled also the cup of enchantment in *Comus*, and strewed the flowers on the hearse of Lycidas": from the *Conversations* of June 1833, reprinted in J. A. Wittreich, Jr., ed., *The Romantics on Milton: Formal Essays and Critical Asides* (Cleveland: Case Western Reserve University Press, 1970), p. 275; see also Harold Bloom, *The Anxiety of Influence* (New York: Oxford, 1973), pp. 11, 19–20, 26.

In describing the error of mistaking the "furthest end of knowledge," Bacon offers a precise gloss on the problem raised by the treatment of landscape in the brief epic:

> For men have entered into a desire of learning and knowledge, sometimes upon a natural curiosity . . . sometimes to entertain their minds with variety and delight; sometimes for ornament and reputation; and sometimes to enable them to victory of wit and contradiction; and most times for lucre and profession; and seldom sincerely to give a true account of their gift of reason to the benefit and use of men; as if there were sought in knowledge a couch, whereupon to rest a searching and restless spirit; or a terrace, for a wandering and variable mind to walk up and down with a fair

prospect; or a tower of state, for a proud mind to raise itself upon; or a fort or commanding ground, for strife and contention; or a shop, for profit or sale; and not a rich storehouse, for the glory of the Creator and the relief of man's estate (*Advancement*, pp. 41–42).

CHAPTER NINE: SAMSON'S JURISDICTION

1 For a valuable discussion of the controversial term "forerunner," see Heiko Oberman, *Forerunners of the Reformation: The Shape of Late Medieval Thought* (rpt. Philadelphia: Fortress Press, 1981), pp. 3–43.

2 Henry Parker provides an example of this kind of word play in the well-known *Observations*: "We see, not that Prince which is the most potent over his subjects, but that Prince which is most Potent in his subjects, is indeed most truly potent" (*Observations Upon Some of His Majesties Late Answers and Expresses*, in *Revolutionary Prose* p. 36).

3 Despite the considerable common ground, few writers on *Samson Agonistes* find the kind of problems so widely discovered in the final two books of *Paradise Lost*, including the sense of tyranny by doctrinal abstractions or a vaguely defined weakness in the verse (see, e.g., Stein [1977], p. 159). Louis Martz's observation, that the final historical books of Ovid's *Metamorphoses* have provoked similar discussion, can be extended to *Samson Agonistes*. And certainly, the tragedy involves the predicament of keeping Samson (or the reader) "from being 'a heretick in the truth'—that is, one who had knowledge of words only or who believes 'by a deputy.'" This is Georgia Christopher's description of what the final two books of *Paradise Lost* are meant to accomplish for Adam, at "considerable esthetic risk" (*Science* 178).

4 See chap. 3, n. 5, and chap. 7, n. 14.

5 For the fullest discussion of Samson as a "type," see the studies by Lynne V. Sadler: "Typological Imagery in *SA*: Noon and the Dragon," *ELH* 37 (1970), 195–210, and *Consolation in "SA": Regeneration and Typology*, Elizabethan and Renaissance Studies No. 82 (University of Salzburg, 1979).

CHAPTER TEN: THE SENSE OF HEAVEN'S DESERTION

1 In Milton's expatiation upon Judges 15:11, Samson had retired "Safe to the rock of Etham, / . . . Not flying, but forecasting in what place / To set upon them, what advantag'd best" (252–55).

2 This passage, with what appears to be a clear reference to the very "warrant" Milton had singled out in the *Apology*, does not appear in the manuscript version; its modern editor finds it unusual, for 1681, in its authenticity.

CHAPTER ELEVEN: *SAMSON AGONISTES* AS LAMENT

1 The sense of timelessness here can be usefully compared to the poise of the Nativity's final movement beyond history, announced by "And then at last our bliss / Full and perfect is, / But now begins" (165–67). "Begin" is a prominent word in both works of 1671, but most readers have found a very different outlook from Milton's early millennialism, something like what Georgia Christopher has called a final "downward

spiral of history" (see *Science* 192, 189, 251). Northrop Frye has recently offered an interesting corrective to the common view of a "disillusioned" Ecclesiastes (*The Great Code*, pp. 123–25).

2 *Lives of the English Poets*, ed. L. Archer Hind (London and New York: J. M. Dent and E. P. Dutton, 1925), 1:111. The better-known objection to the deficient "middle" of the tragedy occurs in *Rambler* 139.

3 On "toward the 'rousing motions'"—not necessarily back to some past condition; it is interesting to notice how persistently Milton disallows our distinction between Samson's recovery of a lost psychological integrity and the establishment, perhaps for the first time, of the conditions for this very "special" event.

4 The issue of penitence in *Samson Agonistes* is a useful test case for the common scholarly practice of privileging the *Christian Doctrine* as a reference point for difficulties in the poetry. Even in *Paradise Lost*, where Milton appears to stage a neatly phased penitential process, there are interesting problems: contrition and confession are conflated following the great monologue which seals Adam's "own conviction" (10:831). We might say—Milton does not—that the final stage in the process, the departure from evil and conversion to good, is a central purpose informing the entirety of Books 11 and 12; Adam is meant to be morally, not just "vicariously," involved in the spectacle of human history from the death of Abel to the trials of our own time. Milton calls our parents "penitent" though, at the end of Book 10. As presented in *Samson Agonistes*, penitential theory provides an important link between Christian regeneration and the complexities of tragic catharsis. Milton is by no means obliged to complete the process in *Samson Agonistes*, even if his protagonist is conceived along the traditional New Testament lines, typological or otherwise. See the salutary comments of Georgia Christopher (*Science* 16, 78) and Joseph Wittreich's insistence upon a nonregenerate Samson.

5 Compare the Chorus's punctuation of Dalila's exit: "She's gone, a manifest Serpent by her sting / Discover'd in the end; till not conceal'd" (997–98).

6 But see John Huntley, "A Revaluation of the Chorus' Role in Milton's *Samson Agonistes*," *MP* 64 (1966), 135; Edward Tayler, "Milton's *Samson*: The Form of Christian Tragedy," *ELR* 3 (1973), 312; and Bouchard, pp. 140–41. In *Interpreting Samson Agonistes* (Princeton: Princeton University Press, 1986), Joseph Wittreich takes the narrative's silence as one indication that Samson ultimately acts as a "private," his own agent (p. 142).

7 "Of Darkness from Vain Philosophy," *Leviathan* pt. 3, chap. 46.

8 Compare Harapha's greeting: "I come not, Samson, to condole thy chance, / As these perhaps, yet wish it had not been, / Though for no friendly intent. I am of Gath" (1076–79).

CHAPTER TWELVE: UNAPOCRYPHAL VISITORS

1 Milton records the common metaphors for renovation (hearing, or hearkening, and tasting) in *De Doctrina Christiana*, 1:17, in CE 15:355. Dalila calls Samson "more deaf / To prayers, than winds and seas" (960–61); Samson remarks to Harapha, "The way to know were not to see but taste" (1091). For a full study of the parallels between *Samson Agonistes* and the regenerative process, see John M. Steadman, "'Faithful Champion': The Theological Basis of Milton's Hero of Faith," *Anglia*, 77 (1959), 12–28,

and French Fogle, "The Action of *Samson Agonistes*," in *Essays in American and English Literature*, ed. Max F. Schulz (Athens: Ohio University Press, 1967), pp. 177–96.

2 The nearest thing to a precedent would be the banter of Belial and Moloch on the verge of igniting the gunpowder during the War in Heaven.

3 Oberman (p. 14) quotes Augustine: "Peace is where there is obedience to Christ." The view that Samson's final words constitute "a thinly veiled threat," of course, involves the assumption that Samson knows what will happen next. (See Wittreich, pp. 74, 112.) For a discussion of Marvell's use of metaphysical wit in this sense, see Leo Spitzer, "Marvell's 'Nymph Complaining for the Death of Her Fawn': Sources Versus Meaning," *MLQ* 19 (1958), 231–43.

4 This is Adam's term for his own monologue at 10:829. For two recent arguments that Dalila is an agent of Samson's recovery, see Heather Asals, "In Defense of Dalila: *Samson Agonistes* and the Reformation Theology of the Word," *JEGP* 74 (1975), 183–94, and Joyce Colony, "An Argument for Milton's Dalila," *Yale Review* 66 (1977), 562–75.

5 *SA* 1074, "Or peace or not, alike to me he comes," is one of several close approximations to the construction.

6 On the point of a discourse based on "If" (in *As You Like It*, Jacques "only peacemaker") see *PL* 8, where Raphael pointedly disclaims affirmation of his hypothesis, intending rather "To show / Invalid that which thee to doubt it mov'd" (116). It is interesting that Dalila describes doubt, an essential attitude and art in the fallen world, as "timorous." See *Paradise Lost* 12:473.

7 As in the early books of *Paradise Lost* (and perhaps in a different way throughout the brief epic), we have contention for narrative, something like the "contrarious" mind of Satan writ large, its various voices distributed among the whole dramatis personae. Even in *Paradise Lost*, as Arnold Stein views it, we do not have a naive narrator, or even a single, isolable one (*The Art of Presence*, p. 156; see Bouchard's similar point, p. 92). A prime function of the invocations is to keep before us this narrative susceptibility, which Milton had earlier called the "tender stops" of his elegy's "various quills." See pp. 162–63 and 188–93, for a discussion of the messenger (Samson's successor-in-narration) and his reception.

8 In this context, it is interesting to recall that, like Milton's typically isolated hero, readers of this work have no way of knowing what Dalila looks like, or even (at first) who she is. As she winds her way into our consciousness with the assistance of the Chorus, her name is the last thing revealed: "Dalila, thy wife." Like their thought, their naming seems a function of hindsight, their Dalila "a manifest serpent by her sting / Discovered in the end, till now concealed" (997–98). This is worth remembering later, when we assess those impressively swaying rhythms of the work's conclusion, where they reflect on how it is that divine intentions are "best discovered." The entire work can be read as a meditation on the need for warning Uriel himself about hypocrisy, that evil which walks invisible save to God alone.

9 In effect, *Samson Agonistes* presents the situation of the Psalms which Milton versified early in the 1650s: the banding together of "the Nations" to resist God's "uncontrollable intent," as perceived (and acted upon) by certain "just men." (As we have seen, this is the situation recalled in 1654.) The obligatory victory of Samson over the Philistines has been displaced in Milton's tragedy and is rendered as a victory over himself

and his own nation. While a choric part within Samson is extinguished and its place taken by a freer, dramatically more flexible Samson, the Danite chorus remains sage, aloof, unremov'd. Bouchard makes a similar point in discussing Manoa's proposal to erect a shrine (pp. 153–54; see also p. 142).

10 An interesting feature of this passage—it disappears from Samson's speeches—is the way in which the early abuse involves the demeaning of mere words. As the locus of value shifts during the work, the passionate interruptions seem more artfully managed at least on Milton's part, as when Samson says that he "lov'd (Dalila) as too well thou knew'st, / Too well" (878–79; here Milton transfers to Dalila's knowledge a telling phrase applied by Othello to the quality of his own love for Desdemona).

11 See chap. 3, n. 3.

12 For the view that Samson's decision to accompany the Officer is a sharp reversal of earlier decisions, see G. A. Wilkes, "The Interpretation of *Samson Agonistes*," *Huntington Library Quarterly*, 26 (1963), 377–78, and the response of Edward Tayler, "Milton's Samson," p. 307.

13 It helps to think of this as the hermeneutic device which had retrieved Milton from the difficulties in his argument for divorce. See Sirluck's fine discussion in *CPW* 2:150–58.

14 In his recent rebuttal of the long-standing view that Samson is a regenerate or Christianized hero, Joseph Wittreich has argued for a Miltonic distance on the flawed hero that I do not believe the work provides. Wittreich is right, in my view, to emphasize that there is more to a New Testament-style Samson than the too narrowly conceived tradition explored by Krouse, Woodhouse, and others. (See Woodhouse 1972, pp. 295–96, and Low's discussion of "the Christian solution," pp. 8–9.) For Wittreich, the poem's innovations (and even its silences) serve the poem's—and also the poet's— "humanitarian impulses" (p. 78). *Samson Agonistes* "is both an index to the current historical reality and an indictment of it" (131); further—and this is an altogether different matter—it is "an undoing with the hope of transforming that reality" (131). As with the earlier scholars, Wittreich seeks a humanist (or "visionary" Milton; he has not quite escaped the kind of criticism which in his own words "confuses its own ideology with Milton's" (p. 221). For Wittreich, as a result, Samson has accepted a mistaken theological model as a justification for his behavior" (p. 232)—mistaken, perhaps, because it does not correlate with the ethical imperatives of the *Doctrine* or its literary surrogate, *Paradise Regained*. Among other things, Wittreich asserts that those imperatives "never . . . compel a man to violence" (p. 361); hence, Samson is "unregenerate" and subject to our (and Milton's own) critique. Wittreich's reading seems to me overly generous to his author (more so, finally, than William Kerrigan's wider ranging *The Sacred Complex*), less suspicious than Milton of things "visionary," of "profound interiority" (p. 351). The essence of Samson's heroic deed, of course, is the resolve to do nothing upon compulsion; the narrative norms which should apply, I believe, are not the *Doctrine* or *Paradise Regained* (which perhaps do not provide them) but those provided by the Messenger and Samson himself, and by the failure of "answerability" which cuts off this reporter from his potential successors in the Danite community. One might say that this failure makes the "Messenger" a bard-like epic historian-in-the-making, the fallible, passionate kind we meet in the third book of *Paradise Lost*. In *1671*, Milton constructs a sequence that confronts us inescapably with an Old Testa-

ment world as an aftermath to the Son's last hours as a private "citizen"; that is, he creates a world reverting to the way things were "in the beginning" of the postlapsarian world. As we have seen, Milton's eschatology found connections between the most ancient ("Ethnick") divinity and the projected realities of the last days.

CHAPTER THIRTEEN: TASTING THE GREAT EVENT

1 For the Nativity Ode, see the illuminating discussion of Lowry Nelson, Jr., in *Baroque Lyric Poetry* (New Haven: Yale University Press, 1962); in addition to the work of Georgia Christopher, see also Boyd M. Berry, *Process of Speech* (Baltimore: Johns Hopkins University Press, 1974), and Barbara K. Lewalski, *Paradise Lost and the Rhetoric of Literary Forms* (Princeton: Princeton University Press, 1986).

2 Arnold Stein, *Heroic Knowledge* (Minneapolis: University of Minnesota Press, 1957), p. 193.

3 "Moabites or Phineas," *Trinity* 39.

4 *CPW* 1:326; see pp. 36–38.

5 Shakespeare, Sonnet 18. For two quite different claims regarding the Chorus, see Joan S. Bennett, "Liberty Under the Law: The Chorus and the Meaning of *Samson Agonistes*," *Milton Studies* 12 (1978), and Kathleen Swaim, "The Doubling of the Chorus in *Samson Agonistes*," *Milton Studies* 20 (1984), 225–45.

6 Joseph H. Summers, *George Herbert: His Religion and Art* (London: Chatto & Windus, 1954), chap. 6.

7 Donne, "Satyre III," l. 77. With Dalila's complaint, compare the narrator's "Event perverse" (*PL* 9:405); for a discussion of Paul's advice, see pp. 88–94.

8 See Cleanth Brooks, *The Well-Wrought Urn*, and for the notion of religion-by-deputy, the *Areopagitica*, esp. Milton's discussion of a "heretick in the truth" (*CPW* 2:543–45).

9 Joseph Brodsky, "The Condition We Call Exile" [written for a conference on exiles held by the Wheatland Foundation in Vienna, December 1987], *New York Review of Books*, 34, no. 22 (1988), 18.

Index

Index

Index